Konrad Dietzfelbinger

The Spiritual School of the Golden Rosycross

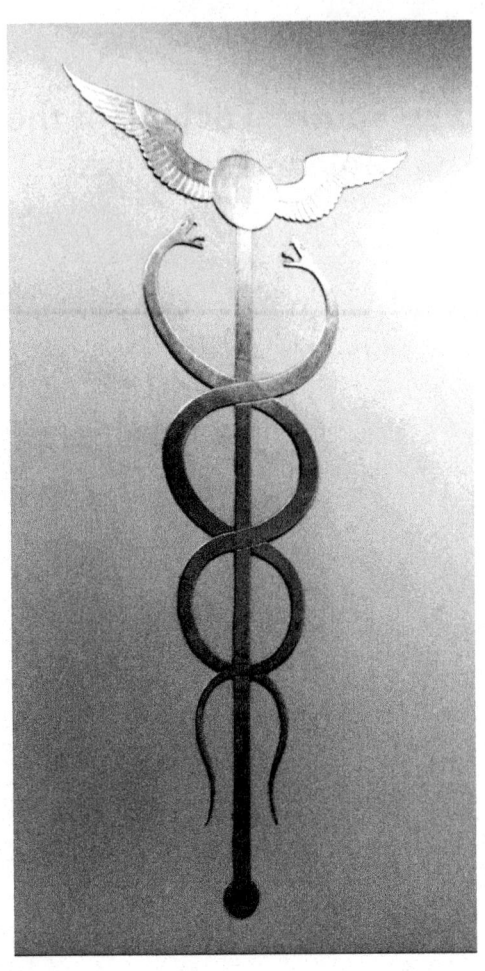

The staff of Hermes (Mercury). This very expressive symbol with several levels of meaning represents, for example, the movement of the human being and of all of humanity through the various world periods from the origin in the divine world up to the nadir in the material world and back to the origin. It also represents the spiritual path, and thus this symbol also brings to expression the development of the transfigured human being.

Konrad Dietzfelbinger

The Spiritual School of the Golden Rosycross

LECTORIUM ROSICRUCIANUM

A Spiritual Community of the Present

Translated from German
Original title:
Die Geistesschule des Goldenen Rosenkreuzes: Lectorium Rosicrucianum
Eine spirituelle Gemeinschaft der Gegenwart
© Konrad Dietzfelbinger, München

English translation:
© 2010 Nova Natural, Inc, 478 Rigor Hill Road, Ghent, NY 12075, USA
Translated by Herbert Horn
1st edition, 2010

ISBN: 1-4392-6898-3
ISBN-13: 978-1-4392-6898-8

Table of Contents

Declaration of Principles of the
Lectorium Rosicrucianum ... 10

Introduction ... 11
  Longing ... 11
  Tranquility ... 14
  Community ... 17

Principles of the Universal Doctrine ... 20
  External Assessment ... 20
  Basic Experiences of a Spiritual Student ... 22
  Divine World ... 23
  Non-Divine World ... 24
  The Beyond – the "Reflection" Sphere" ... 27
  Microcosm ... 29
  Abolition of a Disturbance ... 30
  Justification for a Spiritual School ... 32
  Development of Humanity ... 34

Origin of the Spiritual School ... 37
  Preconditions ... 37
  Turn of a Century ... 39
  Psychoanalysis ... 42
    Sigmund Freud ... 42
    C. G. Jung ... 43
  Artists ... 44
  H. P. Blavatsky ... 45
  Rudolf Steiner ... 48
  Max Heindel ... 50
  Jan van Rijckenborgh ... 52
  The Beginnings ... 59

Jan Leene and Zwier Willem Leene	59
True Christianity?	61
A.H. de Hartog	62
The "Rosicrucian Cosmo-Conception"	64
The "Nederlandse Rozekruisers Genootschap"	65
Independence	67
Spiritual Work	70
Henny Stok-Huizer	73
Further Clarifications	74
Transfiguration	75
Jan Leene as Writer	79
Expressionism	79
Technology	82
The "Living Body"	83
Spiritual Roots of the Lectorium Rosicrucianum	88
Christian Rosycross	88
"Christian Rosycross" as Spiritual Principle	88
Awareness	88
Universality	90
"Christian Rosycross" as Formula	92
The Historical Rosicrucians	94
The Writings of the Classical Rosicrucians	95
The Historical Reality of Christian Rosycross?	95
A Classical Order of the Rosycross?	97
The Cathars	100
Teaching and Way of the Cathars	101
End of the Cathars	104
Antonin Gadal	104
Freemasonry and Alchemy	107
Freemasonry	107
Alchemy	109
Relationship of the Sexes	111
The Gnosis	113

"Son of God"	115
Salvation	116
Two Worlds	116
The Universal Doctrine	117
Syncretism or Universal Doctrine?	117
The "Universal Spiritual School"	120
Developments during and after the Second World War	121

The Path of the Spiritual School

The Goal	127
The Spiritual Path	129
Longing for the Spirit	129
Obstacles	130
Inherent Aim of the Human Being	131
The Path as Subjective Experience of the Pupil	132
"Insight"	133
"Longing for Salvation"	136
"Self-Surrender"	137
"New Attitude of Life"	140
"Becoming Conscious"	141
Special Characteristics of the Path	143
Faith, Knowledge, and Deed	143
Realization	145
Objective Changes on the Spiritual Path	146
Inner Structure of the Spiritual School of the Rosycross	152
Relationship of the Stages to each Other	153

The Work of the Spiritual School of the Golden Rosycross

	155
Three Helping Factors	155
The Founders of the Spiritual School	156
The Teaching	159

Connection to the Spiritual World	160
Experience of the Spiritual World	161
Realization of the Spiritual World	162
Outer Rules of Conduct	164
The Teaching as Power	166
Sacraments	167
The Group	167
Temple Services	168
Themes	168
Symbols	169
Conferences	172
Secrecy?	172
No Exercises	173
Prayer	176
The Structure of the Spiritual School	179
Entry into the Lectorium Rosicrucianum	180
Pupilship	180
Withdrawal	182
Membership	182
The Youth Work	183
Aspects of the outer Organization	186
Directed in Freedom	187
Installation of Co-workers	187
Purity of the Doctrine	189
Freedom of the Pupil	190
Diversity in Unity	191
Owned in Love	192
Material Property	192
Immaterial Property	194
Spontaneity and Crystallization	195
Doctrine	196
The Individual and the Spiritual Community	196
First: Community in Spirit	197

Second: Enhanced Exchange of Forces	198
Third: Growth of Responsibility	198
Fourth: Self-Realization	199
Relationship of the Sexes	200
Working together with Equal Rights	201

The Spiritual School of the Golden Rosycross in Society — 203

Declaration of the Brotherhood of the Rosycross	203
Developments in recent Decades	205
The Spiritual School of the Rosycross in its Environment	209
Political Neutrality of the Spiritual School of the Rosycross	210
The Lectorium Rosicrucianum and the Sciences	213
A New Picture of the World	213
Natural Sciences	214
A New Medicine	215
A New Psychology	216
Social Sciences	217
The Lectorium Rosicrucianum and the Arts	219
The Lectorium Rosicrucianum and Religion	221
The Universal Church	222
The Sacred Scriptures	224
The Lectorium Rosicrucianum and the Churches	226
The Lectorium Rosicrucianum and Esoteric Movements	229

The Revelation of Christ — 235

Notes — 238

About the author — 245

Declaration of Principles
of the Lectorium Rosicrucianum

The Lectorium Rosicrucianum has taken its name from the classical definition of "Rosycross" or "Christian Rosycross." The Lectorium Rosicrucianum takes the point of view that this name did not belong as a family name to any person having actually existed, but that it relates to a certain spiritual directedness.

We call ourselves Rosicrucians to indicate that Jesus Christ is a living factor in our lives and that we want to go his path in practice. For that reason the name Christian is used.

The Path of Christ is a way, a method, an attitude of life, a religious conviction directed at "working on the rose". The rose is a latent principle that rests in every person and on which basis the childship of God can be realized. One can find this principle in every human being.

"Working on the rose" in the power and the grace of Christ and according to the indications of the classical wisdom, the Universal Doctrine, gives everyone who wants the opportunity to attain the great purpose for which every human being is born. As the prologue of the Gospel according to John says: "To all who received him, he gave power to become children of God." This whole aim can be understood by the name "Christian Rosycross."

Introduction

> *All falsehood is condemned to die; all that is born of the eternal sun heart of the father is called to life.* (Jan van Rijckenborgh, *The Call of the Brotherhood of the Rosycross*)

Longing

The most important question a human being can ask himself is: How do I live in accordance with my true essence? How do I live in accordance with my actual identity? This true identity is something eternal in the human being of which he is generally unconscious but which still urges him to become conscious and realized: the still undeveloped "image of God"[1] as the Bible expresses it.

The human being also has a false identity consisting of his egocentric desires, interests, and adaptations. The question of the life in accordance with one's essence does not seek to investigate how this false identity is to be realized, how the egocentric needs and interests of the human being are best satisfied, or how to respond in the most conventional manner.

On the contrary, the question of the life in accordance with one's essence puts into question a life that only consists of the satisfaction of needs and interests and the adaptation to convention. It demands an answer as to whether such a life really corresponds to the essence of the human being, to his actual possibilities, to his true self.

The human being can answer this penetrating question, this deepest urge to realize his true identity, in a thousand different ways. In general he projects his longing onto things that cannot possibly still this longing and goes from disappointment to disappointment. Some put their hopes on career, power, riches, and success: on aspects of their false identity. But the call from the innermost essence cannot be answered through even the greatest power, riches, security, and success.

Many hope for the fulfillment of their deepest longing through interpersonal relationships. But feelings of harmony, love, trust, and recognition, as beautiful as they may be, do not quiet the urge of the human being for the realization of his true self. The longing for the life in accordance with one's essence is also projected onto scientific knowledge, technological progress, the establishment of appropriate social systems, or humanitarian activity in service of the sick, poor, and weak. Here also the realization will fail in the long run, for even the greatest scientific knowledge, the most refined technology, the best political system, and the most self-sacrificial humanitarian help cannot enable the true self to come to life.

Furthermore, the efforts to answer the innermost urge for the life in accordance with one's essence through religious beliefs are countless. Yet even though many religious people believe they are saved in principle, they notice that in spite of their faith and the religious rituals, the experience of a life in harmony with eternity fails to appear. Therefore, they project this life to the "time" after death. They hope that what has been denied them in this life will appear after death: the realization of the image of God, which the human being essentially is.

But why should the image of God (the divine in the human being with the qualities of infinite love, wisdom, and freedom) suddenly unfold after death if it was not unfolded during life? The projection and shifting of this condition to a life after death even prevents its unfolding during the present life—and thereby also after death.

Ever greater numbers of religious people come to this insight and therefore plunge into esoteric methods to realize the true self in the present. For example, some suppose to be able to gain entry into the essential life through the awakening and schooling of supersensible organs so that the true self would come to the fore and be active.

One can investigate the countless paths that are taken in this regard. Then one discovers that many paths already by their presuppositions alone cannot possibly lead to the goal aimed for. For example, exercises that refine the mind, feeling, and will of the egocentric human being are not suitable to the unfolding of the innermost essence.

For in this way, only qualities that are not of this innermost essence are developed further. Even though the consciousness may then also expand and new dimensions may open to the human being, with those presuppositions, however, only the old can be expanded. The longed for new true life will not come to the fore.

Other paths to consciousness expansion act in just the opposite way. They do not intend to refine and develop the faculties of the egocentric human being further, but, on the contrary, to consciously let go of them so that other powers can come to the fore that had been inactive before then. What is decisive here, however, is for which plane and which powers the egocentric qualities are let go of. In many cases they are not let go for the innermost essence of the human being but for contacts to spheres that do not belong to this innermost essence. If the human being opens himself to the world of the dead and hopes for demonstrations from it, if he opens himself to so-called "higher regions" and expects prophetic inspiration, if he makes himself a channel for influences from these "higher regions" and channels messages, then certainly in many cases, results, insights, and new sensations will appear. Thereby, however, the innermost essence of the human being is just as little unfolded as before.

Tranquility

Now if all these efforts and ways do not lead to the life in accordance with one's essence inwardly foreseen—then how should it be recognized and realized?

It is done by recognizing that all those efforts and ways are insufficient and by no longer practicing them. For only then does the true self hidden in the human being receive a chance to become ever more conscious and then also to live. After many fruitless material, religious, and esoteric attempts, countless seekers for the life in accordance with their essence have penetrated to this insight or are close to it.

They have a presentiment of their actual identity and have recognized through experience that it is realized neither through material nor conceptual and interpersonal happiness nor through a connection with the beyond, the so-called "higher regions." Therefore they stop striving for these goals, ideals, and improvements and try to come to rest within themselves. For they sense that this tranquility is the prerequisite to the stirring and unfolding of the true self.

Here it is not a question of a pronounced quietism, a withdrawal into inwardness that leaves the world to itself, but of a quiet contemplation of the world without becoming party to one goal or another. Human beings who have come to this attitude on the basis of their life experience are not just resigned, but now invest all their energy—as paradoxical as this may sound—in an "attentive waiting": an awake state in which, on the one hand, they observe and recognize the connections in everything that happens in life and, on the other hand, give more and more space to the inwardly arising impulses of the life in accordance with their essence.

Such a condition of intense, conscious wakefulness and waiting has been described in world history ever and again. The "not-doing" of the sage is spoken of in Lao Tse's *Tao Te Ching*[2]: not to be idle but to abandon all activity that seeks for the life in accordance with one's essence in the wrong direction. Only thereby does Tao receive the chance to unfold in the human being.

With Buddha, there is the dissolution of the human being's identification with the world on this side and with the beyond. He experiences that the life in accordance with one's essence is not to be found in the activities on the five planes of the ordinary life of the false identity: not on the plane of the body, not on the plane of perceptions, not on the plane of feelings, not on the plane of thoughts, and not on the plane of the ego-consciousness—be it in the coarser or in the finer regions of the world.[3] Thereupon, the human being suspends all activities on these planes with which he hoped to find the life in accordance with his essence.

In the Kabbalah, this suspension of all egocentric efforts for redemption or enlightenment is called "tikkun." It is the "doing for nothing," a life that never expects a reward.[4]

In the "Phaedo," Socrates spoke of the philosopher who out of love for wisdom, for the life in accordance with his essence, gives up all expectations from the transitory life and all fears arising from it and quietly opens himself for the eternal. The philosopher "dies" to these expectations and fears and comes to an eternal life.

Jesus—who is to be seen as the prototype of the human being who realizes the true self—explained that the human being had to lose his life "for my sake," then he would keep it. Whoever loses his false identity for the sake of the true self will keep his actual identity, the true self.[5]

The Cathars of the Middle Ages designated this condition as the "endura"—which is not suicide (as this process has been misunderstood) but the attitude, born of experience, to give no more energy to activities that seek for the eternal life in the transitory world and to "wait" for the life in accordance with one's essence to unfold.

In all these traditions, the human being withdraws from the agitation of this world and the beyond, which he had maintained through his own striving, and lets the life of his essence ripen within him. This life is another power and dimension of existence. If it ripens, then the transitory life in this world and the beyond will also change. The pupil of the modern Spiritual School of the Rosycross behaves accordingly. For example, in the book *Dei Gloria Intacta* is written: "It is suggested that, for once, he shall not associate that longing with any particular tenet, with any special trend of thought....Any desire (must be) neutralized, not by suppressing it, but in such a way that there is neither approval nor disapproval, but only vigilant, objective observation."[6]

Community

Human beings who have come to such an attitude on the basis of their life experiences have always come together in communities. On the one hand, because people with similar experiences and understanding attract each other. On the other hand, because they also want to gradually experience and realize the life in accordance with their essence from this common point of departure. They feel they are standing on a new path, which is to be explored and walked.

The Lectorium Rosicrucianum is such a community in the present. Its members want to explore and walk a path together that leads to the realization of the life in accordance with their essence. The Lectorium Rosicrucianum is called a "spiritual school," because this life in accordance with one's essence is a life in a spiritual dimension and one that works out of this spiritual dimension into the dimension of the transitory world.[7] The path into this spiritual dimension is comparable to a school: although not a school in which knowledge and abilities are learned and examinations taken but a school of experience. Through experiences with influences from the world of the eternal spirit and experiences in the transitory world of appearances, the pupil of this school learns to give his true essence space to unfold: "The School of the Rosycross appeals to three faculties which slumber in the mysterious microcosmic system of man as if in a sleep of death:
    the faculty of the new will;

    the faculty of the new wisdom;
    the faculty of the new activity."[8]
This book seeks to explain in detail the beginning, the goal, the path, the organization, and the appearance of this spiritual school and its members.

Among other meanings, the Rosycross is the symbol of the human being on the spiritual path. On the "cross" of the natural personality—at the intersection of the vertical with the horizontal—is found the "rose of the heart," the germ of the spirit-soul human being. At present it is undeveloped in most human beings. On the spiritual path, it unfolds and blooms: A new consciousness and being develop, and the cross of the old, mortal personality is transfigured into the new, golden cross of the immortal personality.

Principles of the Universal Doctrine

External Assessment

Looking at the Lectorium Rosicrucianum superficially from the outside, it can appear strange and incomprehensible, and misunderstandings can occur. This is understandable, if one considers the basic principles of the members of this school compared to the goals of outsiders who look at and judge such a school.

A human being who is perhaps entirely caught in the conventions of society and believes he can find his happiness in riches, success, power, and security will necessarily regard to regard the member of a spiritual school who consciously separates from such striving as, at least, not being entirely "up to date."

Mainstream psychology, which does not think beyond birth and death and reduces the human being to a bundle of biological suppositions, drives, desires, and thoughts, between which certain mechanisms are active, also sees him within this perspective. From this standpoint, a human being who searches for the life in accordance with his essence and sees it in a greater context than in the span between birth and death appears as someone who has been disappointed by life—someone who has been shortchanged, who cannot accept reality, and who has to compensate for his deficiencies. Indeed, such a psychic disposition is also very often really the starting point for a turning to religion and esotericism, and this turning may be nothing but a flight from insurmountable daily problems. Yet in general, living in accordance with one's essence cannot be explained from such a deficiency, but rather from the deficiency of "normal" life as opposed to the spiritual life that is latent in the human being. That both deficits—the one of the person disappointed by life and the one of the person who does not realize a life in accordance with his deepest essence—often coincide and strengthen each other is something else again.

The difference between a person who is bound to a religious system of belief and a member of a spiritual school is essentially more complicated. For the question of the life lived in accordance with the essence, worked into consciousness from the true self, may yet be still or again alive in the believer, yet his faith claims he is already saved or eventually will be saved in the beyond.

The religious person senses intuitively that the pupil of the Spiritual School starts out from the same basic question as he does but comes to other answers. Thus, the religious person has to take the pupil of the Spiritual School seriously as a brother in the spirit, because the inner point of departure is the same. But as a rule, the religious person does not understand the goal of the other, because he himself projects the image of God on the transitory human being and hopes he will someday live eternally in the beyond. He also does not understand the path that the other goes because it differs from his own convictions. Any understanding would already mean a certain loosening of the certainty of faith that is decisive in his life.

In earlier times the classification of the other as a "heretic" who strayed from the "only true doctrine" and the emotional charge of this verdict sprang from such considerations.

Someone striving in an occult or esoteric manner will also recognize the spiritual student as related in spirit, as one who starts off from the same question of the life in accordance with one's essence. But because he follows with energy and enthusiasm his own method to find this life, he will not be able to understand the attitude of patient waiting and discernment that the spiritual student has adopted after following many wrong tracks. To him also, such a spiritual student is a poor fool because he seems to pass by the great possibilities of consciousness expansion, mysticism, or magic.

Basic Experiences of a Spiritual Student

It is hard to do justice to a spiritual school like the one of the Rosycross. For the experiences of its members and therewith their views of the world and their standards do not coincide with the views of the world and standards of the majority of human beings. But despite this, all human beings can at least have a presentiment of these experiences, because they originate from the innermost essence common to everyone. They are only mostly covered over or not admitted because other experiences or goals in life are still more important for now, or because unsuitable ways to the life in accordance with one's essence are taken. But because the experiences of a spiritual student exist as possibilities in every human being—even will inescapably be had by everyone one day as they correspond to the inherent aim of the human being—everyone can also understand them in principle. He only has to be prepared to distance himself from his own view of the world and his own ideals at least on a trial basis in order to admit the possibility of such experiences.

Divine World

The basic experience of a spiritual student is: There is a life in accordance with the essence of the human being, a life that consists of the unfolding of his innermost, deepest talents. These talents are of a spiritual kind.

The concept "spiritual" needs to be explained. What is meant here are not intellectual faculties or mental images and thought forms but indestructible creative "lines of force" that in their totality form the eternal, divine world. They are structures, "information," that at the same time delineate unfolding energies and that are continually active, similar to an electromagnetic field. They are simultaneously the first causes, information, power, and consciousness at the basis of all being, or also, to speak with the words of the prologue of the Gospel of John—Word, Life, and Light. These creative, indestructible lines of force are what are called "spiritual" here, and it is clear that they differ from the usual thought forms of the human being, although he can grasp them mentally under certain conditions.

But human thought forms and these spiritual lines of force are analogous in so far as both are creative, living, and conscious structures. It is possible to designate these structures with "Word" (Logos), "Life," and "Light," because the common human words also represent information, forces, and aspects of consciousness. But common human words are only an analogy to the divine word and something much weaker. The divine "Word," "Life," and "Light" represent the totality of the spiritual force lines of the world that created the world and still continue to create the world, to develop it, to maintain it, and to urge it to consciousness.

The innermost essence of the human being is also such a "creative line of force"; only this true spiritual essence of the human being is presently latent. He is inwardly connected thereby with similar structures in other human beings, with the divine world, and with the countless beings and hierarchies therein. In the Spiritual School of the Rosycross, this original spiritual world is also called the "divine nature order" or "super-nature." In this context, the Bible speaks of the "Kingdom of God"; Lao Tse of "Tao"; the Buddhists of "nirvana"; the Cabbalists of "en soph"; and Plato of the world of "ideas."

The spirit as Word, Life, and Light expresses itself in and through the so-called "primal substance"—matter-energy in various gradations of density. In this manner, energetic-material worlds that are pure reflections of the divine "Word" arose before the world of appearances known to us with a total harmony between "spirit" and "matter" as well as between being and appearance. The primal substance in comparison to the creative spirit is like a shell in comparison to the nucleus, the outer in comparison to the inner, shadow in comparison to light. Although the primal substance, energy-matter, is eternal like the spirit and necessary to the self-expression of the spirit, it is nevertheless created by and dependent on the spirit, not the other way around.

Non-divine World

But there are worlds that are not exact expressions of the spiritual lines of force, the "world Word." The material world in which we live is an example of such a world that does not purely reflect the unfolding process of the "Word," indeed, it even forms an antithesis to it.

How is this possible? Because the creative spiritual lines of force always create new lines of force out of themselves. Divine spirit itself is untouchable and only follows its own being. It generates "creatures," "life waves" as they are called in esotericism, just as a stone thrown into water generates waves in concentric circles that distance themselves ever further from their origin. The creatures are also creative. But they can "detach" themselves from their origin because of their creative freedom and go their own ways oriented to themselves. One of these life waves is the human life wave. A part of it is developing in harmony with the world of the original spirit. Another part has separated from its origin. This is our humanity.

Although the human beings of our world are spiritual beings in principle and live out of the spiritual world—for they arose out of it as "creatures"—they always bend the impulses of the spiritual world and falsify them. They have made themselves increasingly independent in face of the laws of the spiritual world and because they are no longer in harmony with them, have lost their consciousness of them. From this arose an energetic-subtle-material world—the beyond—and a gross-material world—the world on this side. These are not pure expressions of the laws of the spiritual world, but mirror the egocentricity of the human life wave and the resulting distortion of the original spiritual world.

A creative spiritual line of force lies at the basis of every human being, also at the basis of every species of animal and plant. The so-called laws of nature are also such structures that regulate the unfolding of nature and its creatures and drive it forward. But because they mirror the spiritual world not in a pure but in a "broken" way through the principle of self-maintenance, the forms of expression created by them are mortal. If they would purely mirror the process of unfolding of the divine "Word," then an uninterrupted stream of becoming would appear. The primal substance would never condense too much; a being would never harden and rigidify too much, and it would never come to an abrupt dissolution of the rigidified, to "death."

But the processes of unfolding of the creative spiritual beings are slowed down through their egocentricity. Thereby the energy substance in which they express themselves becomes ever denser, and also their forms of appearance become ever denser and more rigid. The original spirit cannot use them any longer and withdraws from them. This is death. All forms of the beyond and the world on this side are mortal: minerals, plants, animals, human beings, planets, and suns.

So that the human spiritual beings can unfold further and gather experiences, new forms have to be made for them ever again. In the world on this side, such forms originate from procreation and conception. In the beyond, forms of subtle matter are built up for the spiritual beings corresponding to the experiences they had in former lives. These forms of subtle matter step into the forms on this side, into the bodies originating from procreation, as into vessels fitting them and enliven them. This happens before and at birth. At death, the dissolution of the form of gross matter, they again step out of this "vessel" to die themselves in the beyond. Thus arises the constant change between birth and death, death and birth, a wandering of the human spiritual being through the world on this side and the beyond, which results in the chain of embodiments, reincarnation.

Furthermore, the self-maintenance of the beings in the beyond and on this side creates opposition between them. For the interest of one being is not that of another. If they would live without self-maintenance purely according to the divine laws, an unbreakable harmony would reign among these beings. But as one interest is opposed to another, constant conflicts are the result.

The world on this side and the beyond thus together form the non-divine world, which stands in self-maintenance in opposition to the divine world. It is a "dialectical" world filled with antitheses in constant conflict with each other and thereby held in constant movement. Its characteristics are change, opposition, and the law of the alternation between birth and death, death and birth. "Mankind manifests itself in a dialectic field of life, both on this side and on yonder side of the veil of death. The dialectic sphere of life involves a constant interchange between the two poles of life; it involves the fact that *all things, all values, all situations, turn into their opposites!* Day becomes night—light becomes darkness—good becomes evil, etc., and vice versa! There are no static values in our field of life."[9]

The Beyond—the "Reflection Sphere"

To the beyond belong, firstly, the invisible, subtle-material forms in which the structures of spiritual force lines broken by egocentricity express themselves. The subtle-material forms are the causes of the visible, gross-material forms.

To the beyond belongs, secondly, "karma" or destiny. The spiritual laws ever again correct the human spiritual beings deviating from the original spiritual laws in egocentricity, be it through "strokes of fate," be it through death. The entirety of these corrections is called karma, destiny, or fate. It is nothing other than the reaction of the original spiritual world to the human spiritual beings' deviations from the laws of the supernature.

Karma is active so that in the long run, the human being learns through experience where he deviates from the spiritual law and what the consequences are. So ultimately he will also learn to unfold in harmony with the original spirit after all. Then he will again become conscious of the spirit and no longer be subject to the law of reincarnation.

All gross-material expressions of the beings in the world on this side also have a subtle-material aspect and are mirrored in the subtle-material realms. For this reason, the Spiritual School of the Rosycross also designates the beyond as the "reflection sphere." The thoughts, feelings, will impulses, and actions of the human being have a subtle-material component and thereby belong to the reflection sphere. Moreover, they do not exhaust themselves the moment of their execution but continue to be active in a transformed way as elements in the reflection sphere. All the thoughts that were thought, the feelings that were felt, the will impulses that were lived, and the activities that were executed in the millennia of human history continue to be active as components of the beyond.

Since death is only the separation of the more subtle aspects of the human being—thoughts, feelings, and energies—from his gross-material body, the dead, as the thoughts, feelings and energies of the human being separated from the material body, also belong to the reflection sphere until they have dissolved there as forms.

The fact that the subtle-material forms of the beyond are invisible, "supersensible," has led to the reflection sphere often being and having been referred to as "higher worlds," even as "spiritual worlds," in esoteric literature. As will be clear from the foregoing, however, these "higher" worlds are in no way identical with the original world of the imperishable spirit.

Microcosm

The human being is designated as a "microcosm" in the Spiritual School of the Rosycross. This is a concept and a truth with a long tradition. The macrocosm as the totality of the two nature orders, the original divine nature and the non-divine nature with the beyond and the world on this side, is expressed in the human being as a microcosm. As a creation of God, the highest spiritual plane, the human being is in principle a creative line of force, a thought of the divine mind, an "image" of God.

As a biological being having come forth in the course of evolution from the world of self-maintaining matter, he is a body with feelings, aspirations of the will, and thoughts—an egocentric personality of the world on this side. And as the location of the working of karma and the subtle-material mental and emotional collective creations of humanity, he is a focal point of the beyond, just as he in turn maintains and enlarges the "reflection sphere" through his behavior.

A perfect human microcosm is a spiritual being who lives in harmony with the realm of its origin, the world of the spirit, who is conscious of its lines of force and unfolds them without egocentric distortion. Its body or personality as well as its subtle-material life essence or soul are pure expressions of the spirit. A perfect human microcosm does not have any karma; it is not subject to death. But present-day human beings are microcosms who arose from a disturbed relation between spirit and matter and who even continually contribute to maintaining this disturbance. The spirits of this humanity have made themselves independent in the face of the world of the spirit. Their forms of appearance—soul and body—express this independence.

Thereby they deactivate the creative forces of the spirit in the microcosm. The non-divine nature order of the beyond and the world on this side, active in the microcosm as egocentric soul and personality, dominates over the divine nature order. The latter is now only still present as a latent, unconscious formula in the microcosm, which can no longer realize itself or only in a very distorted way, because it is covered over by the egocentric soul and personality. It is as if the seed of a plant, which contains the creative information of the whole plant, was hindered in its growth and only brought forth a caricature of this plant.

Abolition of a Disturbance

Nevertheless the original spiritual world is working towards an abolition of this disturbance in the world on this side and in the beyond. In the microcosm, this tendency is seen in the longing of the soul to again live out of the spirit, to relinquish its egocentricity, and to let the personality become a pure instrument for the spirit. For all power in the universe ultimately comes from the original spirit and its creative structures. Egocentric beings also are maintained by this spirit and thereby continually experience a tendency towards the removal of egocentricity. As great as the egocentricity, the resulting inertia of matter, and the distortion of the image of the spirit may be—in the end, the spiritual lines of force must and will unfold. The Divine Word, Life, and Light will be experienced and become fully effective in the human being.

Furthermore, over time the egocentric soul experiences ever again the karmic consequences of its egocentricity: death and suffering. It will gradually learn from this, voluntarily or under compulsion, that its egocentricity is the great obstacle to the unfolding of the spirit and the cause for death and suffering. It will then gradually relinquish this egocentricity, voluntarily or under compulsion.

This tendency is strengthened in the universe by all the beings who still or again live with spirit, soul, and body in their right relationships—in other words, beings who either unfolded from the beginning without egocentricity in harmonic unity with their basic structures of spiritual force lines, or beings who corrected the disturbed relationship of the two nature orders in their microcosm on a long road back. In the Spiritual School of the Rosycross, the totality of these beings is called among other names the "Brotherhood of Life" or also "the Hierophantic Spiritual School, the Mystery School of the Christ-Hierophants, the Inner Church, the Order of Melchizedek, the Order of the Rosycross."[10]

The principal task of humanity and the human being is to bring the disturbed relationship of the two nature orders in the microcosm back into order. For the tendency of development in the cosmos, in humanity, and in the human being lies in this direction. In the microcosms of our humanity, the egocentric soul and personality dominate. The human being regards both of these as his identity. But in reality his identity lies in the spiritual lines of force that are waiting to potentially unfold in him, like a seed. They are only hindered from this by the egocentric soul and personality.

The relationship has to be reversed now: The spiritual nucleus in the human being has to unfold, cleanse the soul from its egocentricity, and thereby build up a personality that gives unobstructed expression to the spiritual lines of force. Then the real order of the microcosm would be restored. Then the human being would feel to be in harmony with himself and his deepest essence. Then he would again be connected to his inherent aim—to consciously receive the universal spirit through a soul free of egocentricity, and to consciously express it through a body free of inertia.

This condition is the result of "transfiguration": "Transfiguration is a gnostic method of accomplishing the endura, which is the process of completely replacing the mortal, separative, earth-born human being with the original, immortal, divine being, the true Spirit-Human-Being intended by the divine plan of creation."[11] This spiritual human being with soul and body is immortal and free from the law of reincarnation.

Justification for a Spiritual School

In this necessity to restore order in the human microcosm lies the justification of all spiritual schools in human history including the modern Spiritual School of the Rosycross. Spiritual schools are an expression of the universal spirit's tendency to overcome the egocentricity of the soul and the inertia of the body. They reinforce this tendency and are active among humanity for this purpose. They attract all human beings who want to take this tendency into account in their own microcosms. The structure of spiritual force lines at the basis of the microcosm of such human beings no longer wants to wait to unfold, urges mightily to become active, and storms against the egocentricity of the soul and the inertia of the body, like a seed that finally wants to break through the hard crust of the soil. This urging of the spiritual nucleus is expressed consciously in the human being as a longing for the realization of his actual identity. Such a human being has learned through many lives that suffering and death are the consequences of egocentricity—the obstacle preventing the unfolding of his true identity.

Since spiritual schools are an expression of the tendency of the universal spirit to overcome the egocentricity of the soul and the inertia of the body, they are in harmony with the structures of spiritual force lines, "spiritual law," and receive their power from them. "The new will is developed in the pupil by the Spiritual School by means of the spiritual law; the new wisdom by the philosophy of the spiritual law; the new activity by the application of the spiritual law….The spiritual law can also be indicated as God, from whom we have been severed; the philosophy of the spiritual law can be indicated as Christ who in infinite love emanates from God to save us, who bends down to what is fallen; the application of the spiritual law can be indicated as the Holy Spirit which applies, executes and proceeds with the entire process of rebirth."[12]

Spiritual schools can therefore also count on the forces of all those beings who are in harmony with these structures of spiritual force lines and who work towards an abolition of the disturbance in the universe: the "Brotherhood of Life." Also those who found and maintain such schools can also only be human beings that move in conscious harmony with these force structures.

Development of Humanity

The Spiritual School of the Rosycross sees the development of all of humanity with this perspective: Human beings as "images" of God originate from the original spiritual world. Now, however, due to the misbehavior of many images of God, humanity lives in the "dialectical" world ruled by opposites, which is no longer in harmony with the divine world of the spirit. In this humanity, the cosmic relationship between the divine world on the one hand and the world on this side and the beyond on the other hand is disturbed.

But because the spiritual lines of force want to remove this disturbance, one day this will happen in all of humanity and harmony will be reestablished. "Our very enlightened and godly Father Brother Christian Rosycross has labored hard and long in order to bring about a general reformation, and in his service the brothers have gone forth in all times for the same purpose, that of establishing a world order which is 'not of this world', the world order of which Jesus Christ spoke. 'Verily, verily, I say unto thee, except a man be born again, he cannot see the Kingdom of Heaven.'"[13]

Spiritual schools are representatives of this tendency on the plane of matter. They help human beings to carry out the process of the removal of the disturbance and the reestablishment of harmony. All members of present-day humanity live in egocentricity of soul and inertia of body. They experience the results of this disharmony with universal law in the form of suffering and death. Many still do not see the consequences of their experiences and will have to continue to suffer from them. Some wake up, perceive the tendency of the spiritual nucleus in their own being, and try to react to it. Numerous reactions that do not lead to the goal appear. Some individuals recognize that only one reaction leads to the experience of harmony with the spirit: the relinquishing of egocentricity and inertia in favor of the tendency in the spiritual nucleus of the microcosm. Eventually, all human beings will take the right steps to the realization of their actual task in life.

Eagle in the garden of the Dutch Conference Center "Renova." The eagle is the symbol of the masculine aspect of the spirit: creative force, which sees through everything and renews it.

Origin of the Spiritual School

> *Those who are guided by the light know the Christ. They can no longer lose their way, for eternity lives in them.* (Z. W. Leene)

Preconditions

As it is the task of spiritual schools to give new accents and impulses to the development of humanity, their origin can only be explained in connection with this development. On the one hand, spiritual schools are instruments of the tendency of the universal spirit to unfold the spirit within all human beings who are trapped in the world on this side and in the beyond. All beings of the original spiritual world that live out of spiritual laws and forces are actively participating with this tendency in one way or another, thus contributing to the birth of spiritual schools. On the other hand, the longing in humanity for the unfolding of the spirit, the true essence of the human being, has to have reached a certain magnitude, before an impulse from the spiritual world can ensue.

It is like in a thunderstorm: Electricity accumulates in the atmosphere—this would be comparable to the urging tendency from the spiritual world—while the earth, as the polar opposite, is simultaneously expecting this electricity—such is the longing of human beings for the unfolding of their true essence.

The buildup of such a field of tension does not occur haphazardly but rhythmically in definite time cycles. Just as the biological development of a human being follows a certain lawfulness, so the cosmos and the spiritual field in the cosmos also follow certain patterns of unfolding. The unfolding of the spirit of humanity has to orient itself to the unfolding of the cosmic spirit field and react to it because humanity is connected to the cosmic spirit field.

This can happen harmoniously and voluntarily on the part of humanity but can also happen chaotically. It is as in school: One class follows another. A certain "curriculum" is followed, and the students are inevitably confronted with it. They can learn and understand and thereby progress in harmony with the curriculum. But they can also misunderstand or even oppose it, whereby what is heard can only create chaos in them.

The "curriculum" of the cosmic spirit is its own structure. It can be indicated with the symbols of the signs of the zodiac. The signs of the zodiac, such as Taurus, Aries, Pisces, Aquarius, designate certain aspects of the original spiritual world that become active in sequence.

But these aspects also project into the beyond, and there they become "secondary" structures of force lines. In esotericism, they are what are generally referred to as the zodiac. Thus, there is a zodiac of the primary spiritual world and a secondary projected zodiac of the subtle-material worlds. The latter represents a distortion of the original qualities of the spiritual zodiac.

When we speak here of the influences of the "curriculum" of the spiritual world, what is meant are the influences of the primary zodiac, which influence the latent spiritual nuclei of human beings in order to bring about a reaction. Whenever one aspect of the original spiritual world withdraws and makes room for the next one, a certain tension always develops, a "thunderstorm situation" between the spiritual world "above" and humanity "below." A new spiritual impulse urges to realization, while the true spiritual essence in the human being is touched by this urge and wants to answer it.

Turn of a Century

A very incisive "thunderstorm situation" of this nature developed in the decades around the turn of the 19th to the 20th century. Materialism had reached its peak in the 19th century. As a reaction against this, a longing for the spiritual world, whether conscious or unconscious, had grown in many human beings. This created the receptivity on the earth for impulses from the divine nature order. On the other side, a new aspect of the divine nature order stepped into the foreground: the "Aquarius" aspect. The atmosphere was loaded with this "curriculum." The structure of the world of the spirit, its laws, qualities, and forces wanted to become conscious in the human being. This becoming conscious is the characteristic of the Aquarius aspect of the spiritual zodiac.

The term "morphogenetic field"[14] coined by Rupert Sheldrake can clarify these circumstances. A morphogenetic field is a structured field composed of mental, emotional, or energetic elements that acts on all those receptive to it, so that these contents become conscious or at least active in them. Sheldrake's morphogenetic fields are nothing other than structures of the subtle-material world. But one can also use this concept analogously on the structures of spiritual force lines. Then such a morphogenetic field of the spirit was active in the atmosphere in the decades around the turn of the 19th to the 20th century—"Aquarius" impulses from the original spiritual world were waiting to be transposed and to become conscious in humanity.

Like bolts of lighting in a thunderstorm, impulses from this field now struck and were processed by human beings receptive to them: processed in varying degrees of purity and with different stamps depending on the clarity of consciousness and the preconditions of soul and body of the recipients. One knows of similar phenomena also elsewhere in the realm of thoughts and feelings, such as when several human beings simultaneously come up with the same invention independently of each other. It "is in the air." Everywhere the soil is prepared when receptivity is present, and the "morphogenetic field" of this invention discharges in the form of various flashes in different places that have the right polarity. C. G. Jung spoke in this context of "synchronicity."

The stirring time around the turn of the 19th to the 20th century bears witness to this spiritual thunderstorm situation and its discharge. On the one side, below, there was the feeling that everything old had lived itself out and become rigid. A "new human being" and a new society had to come. A mood of departing to new horizons was everywhere. On the other side, above, there was the "morphogenetic field" of the spirit with contents that could nourish the longing below. An aspect of the spiritual world was becoming newly active: Aquarius demanded a related reaction from the spiritual structure within the human being.

When a flash from the spiritual atmosphere strikes a human being receptive to it, then first the rigid shell of the soul (which habits of thinking, feeling, and acting have erected around the spiritual nucleus of the human being) begins to weaken. The personal ego, the egocentric consciousness, that is, the soul trapped in the beyond and the world on this side, is broken up. Now, not only do the spiritual impulses stream into the consciousness of this human being but also impulses from the beyond that are their distorted reflections. Perhaps he projects these impulses to the outside and expects the fulfillment of his longings from changes in the social, economic, and political situation. Many ideologies in society, politics, and economics arise in this way. But if these impulses are really evaluated as a summons to change within, then there are still many possibilities to mistake the impulses from the beyond with those from the original spiritual world. It may come to a long inner struggle until an unequivocal clarity has been achieved.

All persons who react to the "thunderstorm situation" are at first wrestling consciously or unconsciously for clarity. The impulses from the world of the spirit, which lead past the world on this side and the beyond, want to be realized in a pure way. But influences from the beyond that want to put human beings under their spell are always pushing to the fore perhaps under the pretence that they are spiritual influences.

What reactions are possible and what a process of clarifycation (at the end of which the impulses from the spiritual world become manifested in a pure way) looks like are here represented by way of a series of reactions that have shaped the modern world and still shape it.

Psychoanalysis

A very strong reaction to the spiritual "thunderstorm situation" was psychoanalysis. In evaluating this phenomenon, one can well recognize that the condition of the human being who receives such spiritual "flashes" decides how they are transposed. An adequate transposition can only occur if the human being develops a consciousness with the spiritual "organs" that are adequate to perceive the field of the spirit. He will then be able to form a "world picture" that corresponds to this field of the spirit.

Sigmund Freud

A human being can also be receptive to the impulses of the spiritual world and the beyond, however, and nevertheless maintain his old materialistic picture of the world. Then he will seek to describe the spiritual impulses, if he does not altogether shut them out or repress them, and the structures of the beyond in the framework of his materialistic picture of the world. Sigmund Freud is an example of someone who did this.

As clearly and correctly as he may have described some psychological mechanisms—their interpretation, their classification in the whole psychic picture, and the resulting therapeutic aims remain nevertheless unsatisfactory if the larger frame of the beyond working into the soul with its own laws and especially the all-encompassing world of the spirit are not taken into consideration. With the patients treated according to the Freudian method, a process of becoming conscious arises that is a caricature of a path to spiritual realization: Besides psychological mechanisms purely belonging to the world on this side, influences from the beyond come to consciousness in the soul but are not recognized as such and therefore cannot be adequately processed.

Above all, the impulses from the world of the spirit that influence the soul are then not admitted or are explained away as reactions of the human being to disappointments in the world on this side. But in reality, the decisive soul conflicts arise due to the soul not answering or not being able to answer to its inherent aim, which is to live in harmony with the spiritual world. It would depend on the soul developing a consciousness that perceives and transforms the spiritual forces active in it. Then it would gradually fulfill its inherent aim and be whole and free. Whoever denies the innermost longing of the soul for a life in the spirit and does not show it a way to fulfill this longing—even limits the soul life expressly to the world on this side—destroys instead of healing.

C. G. Jung

In contrast to this, C. G. Jung tried to include layers of soul lying deeper than the material-biological into his theories and therapies and to take into account the influences in the soul from the realities of the beyond and the spirit. He investigated old traditions and contemporary dream contents for symbols of such influences and hoped to solve spiritual crises through the interpretation of these symbols. Thereby, however, he could merely determine the psychic precipitates of the spiritual experiences of the individual and of humanity and lift them into the light of a limited rational consciousness. But becoming conscious of these precipitates without a new intuitive consciousness open to the spirit world means only a connection of the soul with its own world of images and with the past of humanity.

The appropriate answer to the world of the spirit would be that the human being develop an intuitive organ of perception that corresponds to the world of the spirit and that can perceive it purely and directly in order to recognize and dissolve in the spiritual forces the entrapment of the soul in the world on this side and in the beyond.

But Jung believed he owed it to the rational empirical science of his time to renounce statements about direct spiritual experiences and their special laws that could only be grasped intuitively, even though he himself and his patients often had such experiences. It is also indisputable that he turned to his patients with an unprejudiced love of humanity and prepared to make sacrifices and opened doors to the beyond and the spiritual world in them and with them.

But his absolute clinging to the empirical method of science hindered him to freely acknowledge that objectively there is a beyond and a spiritual world and that they work with their own laws. (It is only a matter of learning to distinguish between objective manifestations of these worlds and subjective projections of the soul.) The spirit world is also objectively perceptible—only with an organ of perception different than the mind bound to the senses.

Artists

Some authors and artists of this time were sensitive to influences of the light of the spiritual world and influences of the shadows in the beyond related to it and fought for a distinction. They include: Friedrich Nietzsche, Gustav Meyrink, Alfred Kubin, and numerous composers like Scriabin, Satie, Debussy, as well as symbolist painters, etc. Partly spiritual impulses, partly impulses from the beyond shine through everywhere in their works. For example, Count Hermann Keyserling founded his "School of Wisdom" as a reaction to a touch through the field of the spirit without, however, in his own words, being able to gain direct access to it. We are also here reminded of the unjustly forgotten Eugen Heinrich Schmitt of Berlin in whose consciousness this field was clearly reflected.[15]

H. P. Blavatsky

Helena Petrovna Blavatsky (1831–1891) can be seen as the first great purveyor of the Aquarian impulse who recognized that it had as its goal a complete reorientation of the consciousness of humanity: a conscious directedness to the original world of the spirit as the actual home of the human being and a conquest and dissolution of the materialistic and dogmatic orientation of the egocentric soul that knows only the sense world and—after death—the transitory world of subtle matter. The actual task of the human being in the cosmic development was to become clear to humanity and to the human being who in modern times had matured principally to an individual, responsible consciousness and could consciously recognize his place in this development and cooperate in it.

This impulse was felt worldwide, in the West as well as in the East. This can be documented already by the fact that the founding of the Theosophical Society in 1875 occurred in New York, that the headquarters of the Society was moved in

1882 to Adyar in India, and that H. P. Blavatsky worked the last years of her life in London.

The spiritual world from which H. P. Blavatsky received her inspirations and that worked through her also let the great traditions of the past come to life again. Madame Blavatsky drew from two great sources: from the spiritual Christianity of the West and the Eastern traditions of Hinduism and Buddhism, whereby the emphasis was placed more and more on Eastern wisdom in the course of time.

The personality of Madame Blavatsky worked like an icebreaker in the frozen sea of dogmatic religions and materialistic science, which increasingly ruled over the thinking and feeling of humanity in the 19th century. Filled with the forces of the spiritual world, she broke through this crust and through all enmity and slander with tremendous energy.

No outer religion or dogma had priority for her. Decisive was only the inner experience with the living truth, which comes to expression in all religions ever again with other symbols and more or less veiled. Thus her motto was: No religion stands higher than truth. Essential for modern times was the formulation of this experienced truth in a living philosophy. All later, modern esoteric movements took up this first wave of the Aquarian impulse.

Isis Unveiled (1877), H. P. Blavatsky's first great book, as well as the following *Secret Doctrine* (1888) showed these components of her work: She took position against religious dogmatism and materialistic science and presented on the other hand the universal wisdom religion of all times and the philosophy of antiquity and the middle ages pertaining to the spiritual world, as they have perpetuated themselves as an underground stream up to the present.

Madame Blavatsky was also the first who began to fight against "lower occultism" in the form of spiritualism and the desires of some human beings to acquire "supersensible" faculties for ego gratification. If the cover of materialism is pulled away, the impulses from the original world of the spirit as well as the influences of the world of the beyond in the form of lower occultism, at first almost indistinguishable to the human being, come to the fore. Madame Blavatsky at first believed that spiritualism was a useful medium to make human beings generally aware of non-material realities—and therewith also of the original spiritual world. She soon recognized, however, that spiritualism, the occupation with the beyond, only distracted from the spiritual world and broke consequently with this movement.

She was furthermore sensitive to parapsychological influences and herself possessed the faculty to generate supersensible "phenomena." In the first years of her activity, she felt such phenomena could serve as a bridge to the spiritual world, but then noticed that the human beings' belief in miracles was a great obstacle to their own experience of the spiritual world, and so she gave up the production of such phenomena. Indeed, very soon she took a very decisive position against spiritualism and supersensible phenomena as supposed means of spiritual development.

Her last book, a translation of old Tibetan precepts for the spiritual path, *The Voice of the Silence*, is an expression of pure influences from the original spiritual world and characterizes the worlds of the beyond and on this side in their limitations from this spiritual perspective.

Rudolf Steiner

After H. P. Blavatsky and her coworkers, Rudolf Steiner (1861–1925), founder of the Anthroposophical movement, was a human being who reacted directly to impulses of the spiritual world but also perceived influences from the beyond and struggled for a clear differentiation.

He first tried to systematically bring order to the contents of the spiritual world and the "supersensible worlds" of the beyond of which he became conscious. He brought the cosmological and anthropological developments that H. P. Blavatsky presented still very unsystematically into a comprehensible order. On this basis, he founded a "path of knowledge" that was to lead human beings into the spiritual worlds.[16]

His striving was in the direction of anchoring the Christ impulse as a pure impulse from the world of the spirit in the consciousness of human beings and to emphasize the esoteric traditions of the West. He did not do this to assert the priority of Christianity over other religions but in order to characterize the new step in development that all of humanity has taken since the Christ became flesh in Jesus.

According to Steiner, the task specific to the present in this connection is that the human being experiences the Christ as the true self within his own being. This experience becomes exemplary and visible precisely in the path of Jesus. The lower self "dies" in favor of the true self, the Christ, and this in the full consciousness and responsibility of the pupil. This is exactly the intention of the Aquarius impulse that began to unfold in the whole world in the last decades of the 19th century.

In spite of this, there is in Steiner's work an obscurity that can lead to misunderstandings. He did not always differentiate clearly between the immortal, eternal world of the spirit in which there is no self-maintenance and the supersensible or "higher" worlds of subtle matter saturated with self-maintenance, which stand behind the appearances of the visible world as forces and causes from the beyond.

Therefore, a reader of his writings can easily confuse the supersensible, "higher" worlds of the beyond, which are not permeated with the Christ forces, indeed, are often their adversary, with the eternal world of the spirit and believe that there is a continuous transition from the beyond to the world of the spirit.

Correspondingly, Steiner did not differentiate clearly or not clearly enough between the true self of the human being which belongs to the eternal world of the spirit, and the personal ego as a part of this world or, as the case may be, the "higher" self as a part of the beyond. The self-maintaining higher self of the human being is not an expression of the eternal and not identical with the true self, the Christ self of the human being. Therefore, there is the danger that the exercises and developments that Steiner described, for example, in *How to Know Higher Worlds* are taken up by the personal ego of this side or by the higher self of the beyond. A path of knowledge would emerge from this that would make the self-maintaining ego—Steiner himself would speak of an ego permeated by "Lucifer" or "Ahriman"—conscious in the supersensible worlds of the beyond and produce "clairvoyance" in these regions. The goal of the Christ impulse, however, is to dissolve the self-maintenance of the lower as well as of the higher self so that the true self, the inner Christ in the human being, can come to the fore.

Who knows what clarifications in this regard would still have come if Steiner could have built up the planned "three classes" of his esoteric school. Even though in his writings and lectures, the decisive characteristics of the modern path of initiation—self-responsibility and self-knowledge—are again and again addressed, not clearly presented is that the surrender of the self-maintenance of the lower as well as the higher "supersensible" ego is the prerequisite of the unfolding of the Christ ego. The ego cannot develop itself into the Christ ego. Rather, its self-maintenance has to disappear. Then the eternal world of the spirit will appear in the human being.

Max Heindel

Max Heindel (1865–1919) (actually Carl Louis Frederik Grashoff) emigrated in 1896 from Denmark to the USA where he stayed in Los Angeles from 1903 to 1906.[17] In his own words, these years were characterized by an insatiable hunger for spiritual realization. He joined the Theosophical Society in 1904 and soon became Vice-President of the society for California. In 1905, driven by his great desire to communicate to others what he knew, he started giving public lectures in the northwestern USA—especially on astrology—with such an engagement that he developed heart trouble.

His longing for spiritual knowledge led him in 1907 to Rudolf Steiner in Germany via the mediation of Alma von Brandis. In Berlin he attended Steiner's lectures and introductory courses but was still not satisfied yet in the core of his being, although he accepted portions of Steiner's discourses. He was only really satisfied when later in the year of

1907 he met the "Elder Brothers" of the Rosycross, as he recounts it. He received instruction from them near Berlin. He received the mission to record the teachings received and to publish them before the end of the year 1909. He made a first draft still in Germany but completely rewrote it after returning to America. In 1909 the book *The Rosicrucian Cosmo-Conception* was published in Chicago.

Until then Heindel had given further lectures and courses in Columbus, Seattle, and other cities, which led to the founding of the first Rosicrucian Fellowship Center in Columbus, Ohio. He placed special value on distributing articles containing his teaching via the press.

During 1909–1910 Max Heindel was again active in Los Angeles. He received a further assignment from the "Elder Brothers" of the Rosycross, that is, to build up the Rosicrucian Fellowship and to build a temple in which the students of the Rosycross were to gather regularly and send out spiritual healing power. This Ecclesia Temple on Mt. Ecclesia in Oceanside, California, was completed on December 25, 1920, well over a year after Heindel's death.

Max Heindel also was a person who drew from the field of the spirit and at the same time was confronted with impulses from the beyond. To be sure, in his cosmology influenced by Rudolf Steiner and developed in the book *The Rosicrucian Cosmo-Conception*, he differentiates between the "Absolute," an eternal spiritual world, and the world of invisible forces that directly rule the world on this side of the veil. But it is not yet sufficiently clear that the invisible and visible worlds are no longer in accordance with their original purpose.

Max Heindel emphasized that presently the intellect of the human being has become the slave of desire and no longer listens to the influences of the eternal spirit. He also valued the statement that the power of Christ has to be active in the heart and to change the entire human organism. The exercises he describes, however, are tied to the attributes of the human being on this side. They would therefore not be oriented to the world of the Absolute, but to the realms of subtle matter of the beyond.

Jan van Rijckenborgh

In the course of time, Jan van Rijckenborgh (1896–1968), founder of the Spiritual School of the Rosycross, brought the process of clarification that was still in full swing with Steiner and Heindel to its end. He took over the cosmologies of both, but he evaluated them totally differently. According to his insight, there exists an absolute, eternal world, origin of all, including the world on this side and the beyond. But this world and the beyond in their present constitution, as well as in their development through the different periods of creation, are no longer a pure expression of the eternal spiritual world, the "Word," but a "fallen world" cut off from the original spiritual world. Indeed, they are in opposition to that world although always surrounded and carried by it.

"The original world of mankind is of everlasting glory. There, mankind fulfils the divine plan underlying world and mankind in perfect obedience." This obedience is "voluntary, conscious cooperation in a free binding of love with God." But "one should become used to the idea that involution might well be a fall as a consequence of a catastrophe....All world religions mention this."[18]

Therefore Jan van Rijckenborgh explained the concept of the "two nature-orders": the eternal, divine nature-order unfolding its inherent spiritual laws in eternal becoming and a "dialectical" nature-order with its movement of opposites, in disharmony with the divine laws and determined by self-maintaining rebellion against these laws. This "dialectical" nature-order also develops in periods of creation but separate from the divine order. It is, as Jan van Rijckenborgh says basing himself on Jakob Böhme, the "house of death" with the characteristics of transience and futility.

This dialectical order is at the same time an "emergency-order": It is not only the result of a "fall" but also has its purpose. It is the realm of existence of the fallen spirit beings who precisely by the characteristics of this order can recognize their condition and find a way back to the divine nature-order. "God does not let go the works of his hands."[19]

Within the human being who lives in this fallen nature-order, there exist correspondences to both nature-orders. On the one hand, the ego permeated by self-maintenance belongs to the fallen nature-order and like it has two aspects: To this visible world belongs the conscious personality ego; to the invisible beyond belongs a "higher self" also permeated by self-maintenance, the concentration of all self-maintenance beyond the personality. On the other hand, the eternal, true self, the "spirit spark" as Jan van Rijckenborgh terms it, that belongs to the divine nature-order is also active in the human being; although it is mostly a latent principle in present-day humanity.

The great Aquarius impulse of the Brotherhood of Life has the aim to make the human being conscious of his home in the imperishable spiritual world and to lead him back to it. Thus it speaks to the true self, the spirit-soul of the human being, which is connected to the original world and wants to return to it.

This is something different than a path by which the personal ego penetrates the supersensible realms of the beyond and acquires the faculty of clairvoyance. It is also something different than a path by which the human being becomes conscious of the concentration of all self-maintenance beyond the personality, the "higher self," and unites it with his personal ego.

On the contrary: The awakening of the true self requires that the personality ego and the higher self "go under" and dissolve in the true self and become its servants. "The idea is not that the 'I', now bound to the lower human being, must, at a given moment, find its true self and be united with it. No, the true 'I', the true divine spark, lies in the true self, and this true divine spark of the Heavenly Self must be liberated from the 'I' of earthly man. So, we reverse the matter: the earthly man who wants to be liberated must perish! The Other One, the divine son of God, must increase and the earthly man must *decrease*."[20]

The point of departure on the path intended for us by the great Aquarius impulse of the Brotherhood of Life is the spirit spark, the true self, which has been connected to the spiritual world since the beginning. The personal ego is addressed on this path only to have it cooperate with the removal of the obstacles that stand in the way of this development. It should recognize its own self-maintenance, surrender, and serve the eternal. Then the rays of the spirit of Christ penetrate with mighty power the spirit spark, the individual representation of the Christ forces in the human being, bring it to growth, and demand the endura—the surrender of all self-maintenance on this side and in the beyond.

The clarity that results from this explicit distinction, can well be seen if one reads, for example, in Rudolf Steiner's *Rosicrucian Wisdom—An Introduction* (also entitled *Theosophy of the Rosicrucian*) or in Max Heindel's *Rosicrucian Cosmo-Conception* about the stages of the Rosicrucian path and then studies the description of these stages in Jan van Rijckenborgh's *The Coming New Man*. In Steiner and Heindel, the main concern is the unfolding of the supersensible perception of the "higher self" in the supersensible spheres of the beyond, thus in the etheric or astral realms. A connection to the world of the eternal is thereby silently implied or regarded as the last stage in a continuous development. On the path shown by van Rijckenborgh, on the other hand, primarily the spirit spark develops, and at the same time, the egocentricity of the lower and higher personality diminishes. A new personality free of egocentricity is built up from the spirit spark. The higher self cannot pass from the supersensible realms into the eternal spiritual world.

Subjectively these two possibilities correspond to two different motives in the human being. Driven by the desire for a higher development of his personality, the human being can certainly also want to gain insight into the supersensible worlds of the beyond with the goal of better serving humanity in this way. If he enters an esoteric path on this basis, he will develop the capacities of his higher ego and let his lower ego awaken therein, or he will altogether only develop the lower personality.

But the human being can also realize, when he has reached a boundary in his strivings in this world and the beyond, that only an awakening in the eternal corresponds to his innermost desire and actual inherent aim and that he has to become free of all striving for development in this world or the beyond.

The reason that Jan van Rijckenborgh gave for the liberating path he described also corresponded to this clear distinction and was different from the reasons that Rudolf Steiner and Max Heindel gave for the paths shown by them. Steiner and Heindel say that the human being can and should develop the higher capacities latent within and thereby serve humanity better.

According to Jan van Rijckenborgh on the other hand, the path that unfolds the eternal in the human being and subordinates the transitory is a necessity. A mistake, a fall, has to be reversed. The human being has deviated from his destiny to live in harmony with the divine laws, by which he brought forth the chaotic world on this side and in the beyond with their many evils and death as the greatest evil.

If he wants to satisfy his inherent aim again, then he has to correct this deviation and the evils that have resulted from this. But if he furthers this development on this side and in the beyond, then he strengthens this deviation even more and maintains this world and the beyond, the nature-order that is not divine. So he has to come to "neutrality" in face of the self-maintaining influences from this world and the beyond in order to give to the spirit spark and the divine order the space to unfold.

Only then and only in this way can the human being serve humanity so that it eventually becomes aware of its catastrophic situation, recognizes its deviation from the divine, and recognizes and finally also fulfills its inherent aim.

H. P. Blavatsky, Rudolf Steiner, and Max Heindel founded not only societies in which their doctrines and corresponding paths of development were delineated and could be studied but also special groups within these societies for all who wanted to consciously go the path. Such "esoteric schools," as it was known for example with Madame Blavatsky, represent force fields in which the spiritual forces of the founders and all members of the school become active in a structured way and help the members on their path. Esoteric schools that have the goal of the development of the lower or higher personality have to feed on forces that originate in this world or the beyond. Such forces are not inexhaustible and the effort that is necessary to invoke and transform them will certainly eventually lead to a backlash.

Only if spiritual schools connect with the eternal in the human being, unfold it, and therewith liberate the Christ forces from the divine world, do they have an inexhaustible reserve of forces at their disposal. And these Christ forces must not be forcibly invoked and strengthened through concentration and meditation to build up a strong personality that has to die eventually anyway. The Christ forces are the basis of the world, the divine as well as the undivine—although continuously falsified by the latter—and are always available to the human being. He does not need to force them. He only has to agree to let them work in him and permit that they dissolve the self-maintenance that stands in their way.

Another result of the process of clarification brought about by Jan van Rijckenborgh was that he built up a spiritual school corresponding purely to the Christ forces and the path that is their consequence according to the purpose of the great Aquarius impulse. A "living body" arose, an organism that represents the structure of the spiritual world and the way leading to it. The Christ forces are transformed for all stages of the spiritual path and become available to the benefit of all members of the living body. These members find themselves within the living body in an environment that promotes the growth of the spirit spark and lends them all the forces to consciously dissolve their respective obstacles. Vice versa, the pupils strengthen the living body in the measure that the Christ forces are liberated in their own spirit spark, their true self.

Seen outwardly, the living body consists of the organization of the Lectorium Rosicrucianum, the rituals, symbols, conferences, meetings, and the universal doctrine. The "power field" of the Rosycross, the inner aspect of the living body, is active in these forms. It represents for all pupils the Christ, the true self, surrounds them like a great true self, and every individual self can gradually grow into this Christ self. Jan van Rijckenborgh thereby anchored the spiritual impulse of Aquarius from the divine world firmly in the undivine world. This impulse can and will continue to work in the world as long as there are pupils who react positively to it with their spirit spark and liberate the Christ forces in their own being.

The Beginnings

It is surely not a coincidence that the Spiritual School of the Rosycross began in Holland. The Netherlands were ever and again an asylum for free-thinking human beings who were persecuted elsewhere. The impulses from the spiritual world could flow in and be anchored in the best way in such an atmosphere, so it is no wonder that the founders of the Spiritual School of the Rosycross were born there.

Also, with regards to an international activity, this country offered especially favorable conditions. Imagine that the Lectorium Rosicrucianum had begun in Germany in the 1920's: From 1933 on it would no longer have been able to work openly, and after the war its international activities would have been strongly hindered by the reservations about Germany.

Jan Leene and Zwier Willem Leene

Jan Leene, later to be known as Jan van Rijckenborgh, was born on the 16th of October 1896 to a family belonging to the Dutch Reformed Church (Hervormde Kerk). He died on the 17th of July 1968. His elder brother, Zwier Willem (Wim) Leene, came into the world on the 7th of May 1892 and died on the 9th of March 1938. Their father, Hendrik Leene, was a wholesale merchant of textiles in Haarlem. Together with Zwier Willem Leene, Jan Leene later took over this wholesale business. The first outer spiritual, religious influences on Jan Leene were those of a Christianity with a Calvinistic stamp. As he tells it, there were already very early inner spiritual influences. At six years old, a vague consciousness awakened in him that there had to be something like "the Rosycross."[21]

Zwier Willem (Wim) Leene (1892–1938), brother of Jan Leene, one of the founders of the Spiritual School

True Christianity?

From their youth on, the Leene brothers recognized that there was truth and a mighty power in Christianity but that the forms that Christianity had taken in the churches were rather a hindrance to this truth and power. Where were the fundamental change and inner rebirth of the human being for which the gospels called? Christian faith as the conviction of the human being as already saved, or as only a moral varnish over a practice of life essentially no different than that of all "decent" human beings, frankly cut off the living, revolutionary experience of the powers of the spirit that wanted to become active in true Christianity.

An intellectual theology was just as unsuitable to favor a living experience of the Christ forces. And was "conversion," in the sense of a contrite submission to "God's commandments" or a hasty flight into the loving arms of a savior, the "rebirth from water and spirit" that Jesus had spoken of and lived?

In these questions and this longing for true life-renewal, the spiritual kernel of the human being came to expression in the Leene brothers. This kernel, unknown to most human beings, strives to unfold yet usually finds no adequate means of expression in the forms offered for its unfolding. This spiritual kernel must have been already very awake and active in the two brothers, and certainly it must also have been inwardly connected to the cosmic structures of spiritual force lines. Otherwise, the young men would not have longed for truth with such a radical impetuosity and could not have recognized so clearly that the given religious forms of life offered no home to the spirit. The urge for truth and an independent experience and realization of that truth were the first expressions of the spiritual kernel that longed for the "rebirth from water and spirit."

The Leene brothers sought for a form of true Christian life on this basis. Although very different in character and talents, they complemented each other splendidly in their need for a way of life corresponding to true Christianity resting on a conscious recognition of spiritual laws. So began a close cooperation between them that formed the basis for the later Spiritual School of the Rosycross.

A. H. de Hartog

The theologian and preacher Professor A. H. de Hartog (1869–1938),[22] who was well-known at the time in Holland, provided a good example for the Leene brothers. He professed a "realistic theology" and demanded a life of realized Christianity in the sense of Romans 12:1: "The new life is the true sacrifice." With this intention, de Hartog carried on a dialog with the worker's party of his day and was a founding member of an institute for comparative religious science in Amersfoort. But his Christian realism and his practical Christianity were by no means exhausted in social engagement and ecumenical strivings. De Hartog was much more concerned with a renewal of Christianity from a spiritual dimension and experience lying deep in the human being. In the writings of Jakob Böhme he found hints to this dimension—the "un-ground" as Jakob Böhme called it. According to de Hartog, the Word manifested from this un-ground in three forms: as creative Word, by which is meant the creative structures of the spiritual force lines that are at the basis of all development of world and humanity; as Word that has become human: these structures of force lines manifest in human beings such as Jesus, for example; and as Word that has become scripture: from such human beings, the spirit emanates as power in the form of actions and words. In them, the spirit is revealed in the "flesh"—eternity in time.

All this seemed to the brothers as spoken from their soul and gave nourishment to their inner need for renewal from Boehme's "un-ground." The belief in a dogma or the saving power of ritual was not decisive. An expression of de Hartog held great meaning for them: "The essential truth is not presented to us through the letter but has to be conquered and realized through the human consciousness." Along with Angelus Silesius, whom de Hartog liked to quote, Wim and Jan Leene also said: "Though Christ a thousand times in Bethlehem were born, and not in you, you would still be eternally forlorn."

Nevertheless, the spiritual hunger of the Leene brothers was not yet satisfied by de Hartog's theology and practice. To be sure, de Hartog pointed to the spiritual world in the cosmos and in the human being and demanded that the human being make room for this spiritual world in spite of convention, self-interest, and habit. But he did not yet show a way to the direct experience and unfolding of this spiritual world in the human being. However, they felt the need to consciously experience the Christ in their own being and liberate it from all coverings in a process; yes, they knew: Only when Christ roots out the ego being of the passions and the mind, which the human being takes for his true self, can his true essence, the Christ, come to the fore. They wanted to be able to testify like Paul: "I live, yet not I, but Christ lives in me."[23]

The "Rosicrucian Cosmo-Conception"

After they left the church, the search for this way led Wim and Jan Leene to Max Heindel's Rosicrucian Fellowship.[24] In 1917 Mrs. van Warendorp had become the first Dutch member of the American Rosicrucian Fellowship of Max Heindel. At the beginning of the 1920's, a small study group of members of the Rosicrucian Fellowship had already formed in Amsterdam for which Mrs. van Warendorp functioned as the leader. In the month of April or May of 1924, the Leene brothers encountered this group. In the *Rosicrucian Cosmo-Conception* by Max Heindel, they found a cosmology that nourished the spiritual consciousness seeking to unfold. Leaning on the works of Rudolf Steiner, the creation and evolution of the world and of humanity out of lawful impulses of the spiritual structures of force lines is presented in this book. In this development, the spirit in the human being could find its own past. The *Cosmo-Conception* also describes the efforts of the spiritual world to again reverse the wrong relationship between spirit, the beyond, and this world, which culminated in Christ's becoming human in Jesus. Finally, Max Heindel also seemed to give a path of exercises by which the human being could grow again into the spiritual world. All these elements gave to the spiritual seed in Wim and Jan Leene the nourishment and opportunity to finally consciously unfold and become active.

What especially attracted the Leene brothers to the path shown by Max Heindel was that it was formulated in the form of a "philosophy" that, although stemming from spiritual experiences, could also be understood by those who were not yet able to have independent spiritual experiences. This path also simultaneously spoke to the three main human qualities—thinking, feeling, and doing—and demanded their equal, harmonious development. Thus, it included the whole human being.

The "Nederlandse Rozekruisers Genootschap"

On the 9th of September 1924, the Amsterdam study group was constituted under the name "Nederlandse Rozekruisers Genootschap" as a branch of the "Amerikaanse Rozekruisers Genootschap"—the Rosicrucian Fellowship.

In the 1980's Mrs. Catharose de Petri gave the 24th of August 1924 as the founding date of the later Lectorium Rosicrucianum. What is expressed thereby is on the one hand that the root of the organization of the later Lectorium Rosicrucianum actually was the Rosicrucian Fellowship of Max Heindel. On the other hand, however, from the beginning an impulse worked in Z. W. Leene and Jan Leene that, although it developed originally within the Rosicrucian Fellowship, had an independent connection to the spiritual world as would be seen later. In the following years, it slowly separated itself from the Max Heindel movement as an independent organization and spiritual path.

By then the Leene brothers already must have been conscious that they had a special spiritual task. Madame Blavatsky, Steiner, and Heindel had made preparations for this task, for they had broken through the hard crust of materialism and re-enlivened traditional spiritual paths. Even though they may have placed in the foreground the occult faculties of the human being, his becoming conscious in the "higher worlds" of the beyond, and his coming into contact with the masters from the beyond, they had also opened perspectives to the Absolute, the original world of the spirit.

On the basis of these preparations, the special spiritual task of the Leene brothers was to directly connect with the super-nature through the unfolding of the spirit spark, to found a spiritual path that had transfiguration as the goal, and to go this path themselves. Personal contact with masters from the beyond was not sought, but a conscious binding of the spiritual principle in the human being with the Brotherhood of Life. This bond exists in a completely different manner in the super-nature and is totally inaccessible to the personal consciousness of the human being of this side and the beyond.

If the spiritual kernel of the human being is to unfold, the personality on this side and its possibilities of contact with the beyond may not be developed further; so the personality on this side has to be "broken up" in so far as it is an obstacle to the spiritual personality.

Something new can only arise if the old, in so far as it hinders the new, is broken up and, in so far as it can serve the new, is transmuted so that it corresponds to the new. The whole human being must be partly "broken up" from within, from the spiritual kernel, through the forces of the spirit with the conscious cooperation of the human being, and it must be partly transformed until it has become an organ that can perceive and enliven the structures of spiritual force lines that surround and penetrate it. Of what use would it be to the human being if his old personality were conscious in this world and the beyond but gave no opportunity to the super-nature to build up a new personality that would be a conscious instrument of the spirit? Although John the Baptist, the highest developed earthly human being, was the greatest among mortals, the smallest in the Kingdom of Heaven was greater than he.[25] The human being had to really enter the

Kingdom of Heaven, that is, to become a conscious carrier of the Christ.

This was the vision of the Leene brothers, and therein also lay the basic principle of a future spiritual school. The basic principle was a pure realization of the Christ in the human being through the liberation from all influences from the beyond as well this side.

The 24th of August 1924, 14 days before the constitution of the Dutch branch of the Rosicrucian Fellowship, must have been the date when this vision of the Leene brothers was expressed at a meeting of the members of the Dutch Max Heindel movement to become the basis for further developments.

Independence

From 1925 on the Nederlandse Rozekruisers Genootschap operated a small publishing house with a mail order book business in Amsterdam. This operation was dissolved on the 15th of February 1928 and replaced by a "Publicatie-Bureau van het Rozekruisers Genootschap" in Haarlem, at the center (smaller organizational entity) to which Z. W. and Jan Leene belonged. This office had three departments: a book business, the editorial office of the monthly periodical "Het Rozekruis" (first issued December 1927), and the subscription and advertising department. By then the Rozekruisers Genootschap had built up four centers in Holland. The Leene brothers were the leaders of the Haarlem center.

In December 1929 Mrs. van Warendorp became ill and was hospitalized for some time. From then on the Leene brothers also took on the leadership of the Amsterdam center.

In 1933 the Max Heindel Foundation was established as a legal entity of the Nederlandse Rozekruisers Genootschap. All property of the Genootschap became the possession of this foundation. Its task was to manage this property and to work for the inner development of the society. For this purpose, the property De Haere was purchased in 1935, where from then on instruction and continuing education courses in the Rosicrucian philosophy were given in the so-called Rozekruiskamp (Rosicrucian camp).

After Max Heindel's death in 1919, quarrels ensued in the American Rosicrucian Fellowship. Two parties had formed. The leaders of the Dutch group kept out of this quarrel and steered an independent course. Moreover, Z. W. and Jan Leene had led the group ever more on a spiritual path free of occult tendencies in accordance with their vision and also had drawn the corresponding consequences in a personal regard. "When we began our work in 1925, we were confronted with a Rosicrucian movement whose name was the only thing it had in common with the Rosycross.... This movement was teeming with negative occultists, who would never be able to make any progress and who were very ill. Besides, there [were] a large number of 'black' intentioned people who had penetrated everywhere. Finally there were a certain number of serious people who, having been led astray, had sold their true birth-right for imagined happiness.... It was in this situation that the foundations for the new work had to be laid."[26]

In 1934 the parties of the conflict in America decided to make peace with each other. This led to a compromise that also gave room to the occult tendencies. This compromise was supposed to be simultaneously valid for the Dutch section. But the leaders of the Nederlandse Rozekruisers Genootschap, who in years past had made such efforts to bring about a process of clarification, could not agree to this. Should one allow the occult tendencies and the personalities that represent them to muddy the laboriously achieved spiritual purity? "For we were now to be forced to fraternally shake hands with the black magic elements, which we had been able to remove from our organization with much effort, and to let them destroy through their 'cooperation' the work purified over the years."[27]

This was the situation that led to the Dutch section making itself independent with the decisive participation of the Leene brothers. After a failed attempt to found an "International Federation of Rosicrucian Societies" (in which the American Rosicrucian Fellowship was to be a member with equal rights), the Leene brothers and the third leading personality of the Haarlem center, Lor Damme, declared the independence of the Nederlandse Rozekruisers Genootschap on Christmas 1934. The name Rozekruisers Genootschap was kept, and most of the members at that time joined the new organization.

As a reason for this step, the Leene brothers and Lor Damme referred to a "mandate of the Order of the Rosy-cross," that is a spiritual instance, according to which the leadership of the esoteric work of the Rosicrucian Fellowship was to be temporarily centralized in the Netherlands (letter from the 27th of March 1935).[28] On the 25th of September 1935, the new organization became a legal entity.

In 1936 the name was changed to "Orde der Manicheen" (Order of Manichaeans), in 1941 to "Jacob-Boehme-

Genootschap" (Jacob Boehme Society). One sees thereby towards what goals the developing group was striving at that time and in what spirit it sought to come closer to these goals. Only in 1946 did it take the name Lectorium Rosicrucianum, which it has carried up to the present.

Spiritual Work

The years between 1925 and 1940 were characterized by an intensive lecturing activity by the Leene brothers, self-study, internal schooling, and Jan Leene's activity as an author. He later told of the difficulties he had to struggle with in the beginning: how he often stood in front of rows of empty chairs after intensive preparations for a lecture; how first individuals, then groups of interested people came together whom he confronted with the Rosicrucian path; how some of these only followed their own interests and did not strive for serious spiritual development; and how therefore at first a highly unstable group with high fluctuations developed. Then slowly a core group took shape, which truly had spiritual development in their heart, and then did all in their power to understand what was at stake and to convert this into life practice.

"With about fifteen sympathizers we rented...part of the house at Bakenessergracht 13 in Haarlem... Here it was possible to furnish a little Temple and in the back of the house a meeting room. All this on a very modest scale... Here...the work could develop its own necessary rhythm, despite all the disappointments that were so often met, especially in the beginning. Disappointment when, for instance, nobody came when the hall was ready and the meeting had been announced."[29]

There also ensued an intense examination of the theosophical literature of H. P. Blavatsky, her coworkers and successors, as well as literature in a similar direction. In later books, van Rijckenborgh mentions, for example, R. Bucke's *Cosmic Consciousness*, Baird Spalding's *Life and Teachings of the Masters of the Far East*, and Krishnamurti's works; indeed, he tells how he "devoured" the philosophical-religious literature of all times to find points of contact and aids to formulate his inner experiences. Under the pseudonym John Twine, he wrote articles for pertinent periodicals, his first books (*Het mysterie van de bijbel*—The Mystery of the Bible, *De blijmare van de Gave Gods*—The Glad Tidings of God's Gift, 1931 and *In het land aan gene zijde*—In the Land on Yonder Side, 1933) and was active as publisher. For example, he published a Dutch translation of Jakob Böhme's first work *Aurora oder Die Morgenröte im Aufgang* (*Aurora: The Dayspring or Dawning of the Day in the Orient*) with a foreword. And in the periodical "Nieuw Religieuze Orientering" (New Religious Orientation), he published in installments the Dutch translation of *Die geheimen Figuren der Rosenkreuzer* (The Secret Symbols of the Rosicrucians).

Of special significance for his own inner development and that of the group, which he led with others, was a trip to the British Museum in London. There he discovered the Rosicrucian writings from the beginning of the 17th century and could take home a copy of an English edition of Johann Valentin Andreae's *Christianopolis*. He published this book in a Dutch translation and with detailed commentaries. The most extensive book that he published under the pseudonym John Twine, in 1938, was a grandly laid-out interpretation of the *Fama Fraternitatis* by Johann Valentin Andreae.

Henny Stok-Huizer (1902–1990), founder of the Spiritual School with the Leene brothers

Henny Stok-Huizer

Mrs. Henny Stok-Huizer encountered Jan and Z. W. Leene's Rosicrucian group on the 24th of December 1930, whereby her husband who belonged to this group himself acted as the connecting link. The brothers Jan and Z. W. Leene and Mrs. Stok-Huizer recognized each other directly as of like mind and coming from the same inner understanding. From this meeting developed a life-long cooperation, exemplary for the insight of Jan van Rijckenborgh (also emphasized repeatedly later) that in a group on a spiritual path to the conscious experience of the spiritual world, both human expressions, the feminine and the masculine, have to work together and are entitled to equal rights. Without such cooperation and the resulting bundling of all human spiritual forces, such a path is condemned to fail.

Mrs. Henny Stok-Huizer, who later took on the spiritual name Catharose de Petri, was born on the 5th of February 1902 and told that already as an eight-year-old girl, she was concerned with the decisive question of the meaning of human life.[30] Already very early in life, she became conscious of her inner connection to the medieval Brotherhood of the Cathars: "Even in our early childhood we wandered very consciously in our ether-vehicles packed with karmic experience through the caves, the mountains and the valleys of the land of Sabarthez."[31]

Because Mrs. Stok-Huizer, coming from a family belonging to the Reformed Church, was not satisfied with the answers that the church gave to the great questions of life, she unceasingly searched for the truth in other groups and streams. Her meeting with Jan van Rijckenborgh made it clear to her that she had sought the truth in the same direction as he. When Z. W. Leene died in 1938, Henny Stok-Huizer together with Jan Leene took on the leadership of the group.

Their spiritual names tell something of their spiritual identity in contrast to their common status and of their function as spiritual leaders. Jan van Rijckenborgh: John, the rich guarantor. He sees himself like John the Baptist as a forerunner of Christ and clears the way in himself for the Christ. Thereby, he creates the possibility to help others with the same task. Rich in spiritual forces, he testifies in this world of the world of the spirit and represents it or steps forward in the spiritual world as guarantor for the pupils entrusted to him. Catharose de Petri: Continuing the tradition of the Cathars, she unfolds the "rose of the heart," the seed of the spirit, in herself and gives others support and power as a strong spiritual rock (petra).[32]

Further Clarifications

Through the work with interested people and with his group that gradually became larger, it became more and more clear to Jan Leene what the actual goal of being human is and what the path thereto would have to look like. In the measure that this clarification occurred within him, he could also contribute to the clarification of the consciousness of his group and develop the power of discrimination. One is thereby reminded again how different reactions arose in the whole world and especially in Europe to the Aquarius impulse that became active around the turn of the 19th to the 20th century.

Jan Leene saw himself facing an immense ocean of competing or quarreling esoteric streams. Besides groups occupied with magic, clairvoyance, astrology, spiritual healing, tarot, palmistry, spiritualism, etc. for entertainment purposes or for egocentric goals, there were other groups that were seriously striving for the spiritual development of the human being: theosophy, anthroposophy, Rosicrucians, freemasons, mazdaism, Sufis, and many others, partly based on past teachings and traditions and re-enlivening them, partly attempting to experience the spiritual world in the present. Some were connected to western, Christian traditions; some took up eastern teachings and techniques.

Besides these there were also the psychological methods and the faith traditions of the great churches that also claimed to connect human beings with the spiritual world. In whoever wanted to find the goal of human existence and the path to its realization in this chaos of conflicting streams, spiritual truth would have to act very strongly, like a compass that shows the helmsman the direction in a rough sea. He would also have to have clear instruments of feeling and understanding in order to formulate the intuitively-grasped truth for himself and others and thereby also make it accessible to the ordinary consciousness.

Transfiguration

Jan Leene's departure point for the clarification of this chaos was transfigurism: The spirit exists as a seed in the human being. But his soul, the composite of his finer forces, is presently more or less a victim of the reflection sphere and of matter. His personality, the active ego that he is conscious of at this moment, is more or less its willing instrument. The goal now consists first of the reawakening of the spirit in the human being, and then of this spirit also becoming active and expressing itself through the soul and the personality. But as long as the soul and the personality are exclusively servants of the beyond and of this world, the spirit cannot express itself through them. On the contrary, it is hindered in its unfolding. Thus it is necessary to cut the ties of the soul and personality to the beyond and this world. Then new impulses can go out from the spiritual nucleus in the human being to the liberated soul and personality. These impulses "break up" the old soul and personality, as far as they are egocentric, that is, steered from this world or the beyond, and make everything in them that can serve the spirit into a suitable means of its expression. Practically, a new soul and personality, which no longer live out of the substances and forces of the transitory world, are built up in this manner. A type of "personality exchange" has to occur if the human being wants to fulfill his destiny.

This is by no means a new esoteric goal and process. It is rather becoming serious with a goal and process that are at the basis of the original Christianity. They were only less and less understood over the centuries and were finally forgotten. "Whoever wants to lose his life for my sake and for the sake of the gospel, will save it," Jesus says. This formula contains the goal and path of "personality exchange," "transfiguretion." "For my sake" means for the sake of the prototype of the true human being, the spiritual human being, which Jesus represents and which is waiting in every human being to be unfolded as the true spiritual self. Whoever wants to lose the life of the self-maintaining soul and personality, which are imprisoned in the transitory world, for the sake of the spiritual human being will find the life in the spirit. The latent spirit nucleus awakens in him. This spirit then builds a new soul and a new personality for itself that live out of and express the spirit. "The method of initiation of the new era aims at [the exchange] of the personality, the secret of the evangelical rebirth...which means to build up, in and through the Power of Christ and His Hierarchy, a completely new personality."[33]

But most esoteric streams of the east and the west, at least in their present forms, fail to recognize this goal and this path. Certain directions, especially those traditionally active in the west, want to reach the goal of spiritual consciousness through refinement and development of the soul and personality, through "culture of the personality" as Jan van Rijckenborgh calls it: "the uplift of the anthropos, of man, from the bottom up. Thus, systems of racial and blood purification were instituted, according to magic norms.... Thus too, consciousness in higher regions and a splendid extension of the sense faculty came about, but this was rooted in matter."[34] For a personality system built up entirely of the elements of the non-spiritual world will not be able to go beyond the non-spiritual worlds, no matter how much it is refined, indeed, this would even bind it still tighter to them. Thus what is necessary is a loosening of the ties to this world and the beyond, to benefit a surrender to the spiritual world, instead of a refinement of these ties. The hope to bring the present personality into a condition in which it becomes conscious of the spirit by means of exercises and techniques is deceptive. If it becomes conscious of new realms through such methods, then it is those of the beyond, the reflection sphere. On the contrary, this hope is just the expression of the personality's and soul's egocentricity, which with all its effects hinders the unfolding of the spirit.

Other esoteric directions, more likely eastern-influenced, attempt not so much to develop and to refine the personality through exercises and techniques, as to split it into its material and finer components. The efforts are in the direction of, for example, stepping out of the material body or "body-free" experiences of the soul. But as long as the soul and the personality are imprisoned in the reflection sphere, such experiences will in general be caused by the reflection sphere and do not originate from the spiritual nucleus of the human being. Jan van Rijckenborgh called these esoteric methods "splitting of the personality." "By dietetic methods, breath control and asceticism, concentration and contemplation, and by control of the powers of speech the candidate had to learn how to bring about splitting of his fourfold personality. By means of such splitting...the pupil was able at will to effect a separation between his physical body, with its etheric counterpart, and his two more subtle vehicles, so that he could travel in full consciousness in the so-called Higher Regions."[35]

With the concepts personality exchange, personality culture, and splitting of the personality, Jan van Rijckenborgh had worked out classifications by which he could analyze the different esoteric directions. But of course this was not possible from the outside, but only from within; only thereby could a human being experience the spiritual world, the beyond, and this world within himself and thus experience which powers were active in a given group.

According to Jan van Rijckenborgh, both systems, personality culture and splitting of the personality, had their justification in earlier times and even still had a function at the beginning of the Aquarius era. For "the two old systems have seized hold of Occidentals rushing to their doom and linked them for a time with the past, so that they would not become crystallized beyond remedy."[36] But this function consisted only of a preservation of the western human being from a complete sinking into materialism and a preparation for a new, truly liberating spiritual impulse. "If, in the dim past, it was possible for the esoteric candidate to be liberated in the described ways and to celebrate this glorious return; if, in the first part of this century, it was necessary to fix the mind of the seeking Occidental idealistically upon the past, mankind has now entered an era in which the future alone must be considered."[37]

Jan van Rijckenborgh and Mrs. Catharose de Petri could continue working uninterruptedly with their group until 1940. But when the Germans occupied Holland, the Nederlandse Rozekruisers Genootschap [Orde de Manicheen] was prohibited and had to act illegally. During the war, Jan van Rijckenborgh continued to be absorbed in the spiritual literature of the past, for example, the texts of the Corpus Hermeticum, of the Manicheans, and of the Gnostics and occupied himself with the history of the Cathars in southern France. This served to bring more depth and clarity to his own spiritual experiences, which precipitated a series of pioneering works after the war.

Jan Leene as Writer

Expressionism

The first works of Jan van Rijckenborgh that appeared in the 1920's and 1930's are stylistically very much defined by expressionism. In those times there was a desperate quest for renewal. When this longing came to expression, it also did not shy away from a certain, at times excessive, pathos. But where such pathos appears in Jan van Rijckenborgh's early works, it is always an outlet for the power of his spiritual experiences. It shows his struggle for clarity amidst countless ideological streams and his insight of how urgently necessary it was and is to show humanity a clear, comprehensible, and practicable path to the spiritual world in order to tear it from its inertia and illusions, and thereby spur it on to actually go this path. When the spiritual world opens a path in a human being through all inner and outer conventions, then this is like a volcanic eruption. The power of this eruption also colored Jan van Rijckenborgh's language in his books of that time. Ever again he made it clear that a spiritual path is a decision of life and death, in two regards: Firstly, the times and the individual had reached a point where faith in matter and influences from the beyond in the form of megalomania and exaltation were driving humanity to the most dangerous experiments and ways of behavior in the scientific, social, political, and economic realms, all of which threatened existence. Only a spiritual path through which the human being again connected to his origin in the spiritual world could give a direction to the unbound psychic and physical forces so they could work constructively, not destructively.

Secondly, the spiritual path requires being radically uncompromising. Whoever directs himself to the spiritual world and wants to make it a priority in his life may in no wise still look to success, power, and fortune in the transitory world. All such looking is a chain that binds one to the transitory world and that collides with the forces of the spiritual world in a most sensitive way in as far as a human being has already made space in himself for the spiritual world. Therefore, van Rijckenborgh made the motto from Henrik Ibsen's *Brand* his own: "Everything or nothing!" If the human being directs himself without compromise to the spiritual world, then the concerns of the transitory world also receive their place and are integrated in the order of the spirit: Perhaps not like he had imagined it—but he can shape his life

FAMA FRATERNITA-
TIS R. C.

Das ist/

Gerücht der Brü-
derschafft des Hochlöblichen
Ordens R. C.

An alle Gelehrte vnd Heupter Europæ
Beneben deroselben Lateinischen

CONFESSION,

Welche vorhin in Druck noch nie auß-
gangen/ nuhnmehr aber auff vielfältiges nach-
fragen/ zusampt deren beygefügten Teutschen Version
zu freundtlichen gefallen/ allen Sittsamen guther-
zigen Gemühtern wolgemeint in Druck
gegeben vnd communiciret.

Von einem des Lichts/ Warheit/ vnd Friedens
Liebhabenden vnd begierigen
Philomago.

Gedruckt zu Cassel/ durch Wilhelm Wessel
ANNO M.DC.XV.

Original German edition of the "Fama Fraternitatis," which Jan Leene (Jan van Rijckenborgh) interpreted under the pseudonym John Twine in such a way that the concerns of the transitory world are also taken into consideration. Here the words of the Sermon on the Mount apply: Seek first the Kingdom of God and its righteousness, then all this—the necessary requirements of existence in the transitory world—will be added unto you.[38] True, this does not happen without the cooperation of the person concerned. But such an arrangement of life will always succeed.

Technology

As a visionary, van Rijckenborgh foresaw that science and technology would play an ever greater role in the coming decades. He vehemently characterized not only the insanity of the atomic bomb but also recognized that the peaceful use of nuclear energy touched the basic building blocks of nature and thereby endangered the balance of the human life field to the utmost. He knew that the influence of the mass media on human beings would increase tremendously and that even occult powers would misuse the mass media in order to greatly strengthen the illusions in humanity.

On the other hand, he also liked to use scientific and technological concepts in formulating the universal philosophy. After all, the symbols of the doctrine were to be appropriate to the consciousness of the modern human being and to open doors for him. Therefore, for the spiritual nucleus in the human being, which Meister Eckhart still called the "little soul spark," which the Buddhists referred to as the "jewel in the lotus," which Jesus compared with a "seed of grain" that grows in the field of the personality, which the Rosicrucians of the 17th century symbolized with the rose bud, he chose the symbol of the "spirit spark atom," to express that this nucleus contains a whole world within itself like an atom and has potentially tremendous forces at its disposal. For this reason, he also spoke of a "power field" when speaking of the field of the spirit as well as of the unfolding spiritual potential of a group like the gradually developing Spiritual School. He used the terminology of nuclear fission for certain developments in such a group. These are all symbols that by analogy can bring particular spiritual facts and processes closer to the scientifically-oriented modern human being.

The "Living Body"

The inner development of the Rozekruisers Genootschap occurred parallel to the inner development of Jan van Rijckenborgh and his coworkers: For in the measure that the recipients of the spiritual impulses reacted to them and admitted them as experiences in themselves, they could and had to pass them on to those receptive to them. After all, this was the inner task of the founders of the Spiritual School: as human beings especially intimately connected with the world of the spirit, to free the path of the spirit in themselves in order to gradually create the possibility for an independent reaction in other human beings who could not directly react to the world of the spirit. Their own experiences and realizations became the catalyst for similar experiences and realizations in other human beings. Conversely, the experiences induced in others had an influence on the originators and caused increasing awareness and clarity. Thus, the basic principle of the doctrine and the path unfolded gradually in the founders of the group, as they became conscious of it in their direct connection to the world of the spirit. This basic principle then also unfolded always a little later in the group that was inwardly connected to them.

The members of the group tried to reach a clear understanding of the world's and their own condition, always stimulated and supported by the philosophy conveyed to them by Jan van Rijckenborgh and Catharose de Petri. They also tried to draw the consequences in their life. Through these efforts born of the longing for life renewal in the spirit, the forces of the spirit came into circulation in every individual and in the group. Gradually a "living body" arose: an organism in which every individual pupil formed a cell into which the forces from the spiritual world streamed and whose structure and life principle were the result of the structure of the spiritual world. "A Spiritual School…has a sevenfold Living Body. It is built up of living stones. That is to say: it is built up of some thousands of souls who expect their entire salvation from the living Christ."[39] This principle and the manner and way it had to unfold became ever clearer to all participants.

In 1936 a building in Haarlem was acquired in which a temple as a special place for spiritual work was set up for the approximately 200 pupils of that time.

The inner condition of the group after the phase of "contact" could now be called the phase of "working with the powers of the spirit." A preliminary result of this work was a condition that one could call the "phase of neutrality." The group of pupils gained a certain inner freedom from the egocentric tendencies of the personality on the basis of the powers of the spirit. They became neutral and tranquil, without agitation, and calm in the face of inner and outer influences from the world on this side and from the beyond.

When this phase was maintained for long enough, at a given time, the pupils had to become conscious of the forces from the true self to which they had only reacted intuitively until then. Jan van Rijckenborgh describes this situation in his book *The Gnosis in Present-Day Manifestation*. He compares the "living body" of the group in the condition of neutrality with a sphere, a three-dimensional power field in which forces circulate. But these forces are not yet ignited, have not yet become light. Further inner work of the pupils, further addition of energy is necessary until one day the sphere of forces becomes a sphere of light, in other words, until the forces of the spirit that circulate in the group break through into the consciousness of the pupils and can be experienced as light. "Suddenly we see how light breaks through like the dawning of daybreak, like the rising aurora at the top of the magnetic body, at the north pole of the magnetic sphere of the Spiritual School."[40] And quoting the Gospel of John, Jan van Rijckenborgh continues: "'In the Word lies life, and life is the light of men.' In other words: the manifestation of the light-field follows the manifestation of the force-field. The most characteristic feature of that light-field is that it is also a life-field." And further: "'Christ is the light of the world; this light is the first-born of the Father.' What else does that signify but his prophesied return....Christ's return is a fact, becomes a fact in every magnetic body in which it is becoming light, in which the force-field develops and becomes a light-field. Then Christ has returned....Christ has not only risen, according to his promise, but he has returned, the light has been born."[41]

It would still take years, until long past the war, before at least the beginnings of this new condition could be realized. Until then it was important to maintain the level that had been reached, to continue the necessary processes of purification, and to gain the power of discernment to recognize which influences from the transitory world of this side and from the beyond and which influences from the world of the spirit were active within the pupil.

Cathar cross

Spiritual Roots of the Lectorium Rosicrucianum

Christian Rosycross

Why does the Spiritual School founded by Jan Leene, Z. W. Leene, and Henny Stok-Huizer carry the name "Rosycross"? Is the School referring to a historical movement of the Rosicrucians, taking up their traditions, and continuing them? Or does it live out of a spiritual principle to which the name Christian Rosycross applies? Both are the case.

"Christian Rosycross" as Spiritual Principle

The aim, path, and working method of the Spiritual School of the Rosycross are contained in the principle "Christian Rosycross." It documents the direct connection of the Spiritual School and its founders with the world of the spirit.

Awareness

The actual task that the original spiritual world has set humanity since the impulse of Christ is the realization of this Christ impulse. The human being is to go under as to his egocentricity so that the Christ latent in him, the true self, can resurrect in order to totally transfigure his nature. Out of the Christ impulse becoming conscious and active in the human being, gradually a new personality is to arise in place of the old one. This new, transfigured personality is again in harmony with the laws of the spiritual world, recognizes and realizes them.

But today the Christ impulse has to be realized under other conditions than those at the time of Jesus on earth. Humanity has continued to develop. At least Western humanity has trained a sharp intellect over the course of centuries. This development of the mind went hand in hand with a greater consciousness in the world of the senses, greater independence, and greater individuality. Today the human being wants to understand what he is doing; he wants to act from insight and can thereby also act responsibly. He no longer wants to simply accept the doctrines of others and live by them but wants to understand them in order to live out of his own insights. This is one result of the Aquarius aspect of the spiritual world stepping into the foreground.

Christian Rosycross stands as a symbol for the necessity and need of the modern human being to understand the Christ impulse and the consequent spiritual path in order to finally consciously experience the Christ forces in his own being. This does not exclude that the spiritual student of modern times allows others to teach him. He even has to do this on the spiritual path, because as a rule he cannot yet directly experience the impulses from the spiritual world. He is dependent on human beings who experience the spiritual world first-hand and report to him about it. But he will then examine these reports and doctrines very closely and will make them his own only when he has understood them and if they seem plausible to him.

Therefore the master has a different function for a spiritual student of modern times than before. Formerly the student bound himself with absolute faith to the master and allowed himself to be led like a child. True, today he receives teachings and forces from the master, and also a faith in the trustworthiness of the master is necessary. But the guidance has now transferred to the student's own inner being. The real master is the true self of the student. For this reason, in the Spiritual School of the Rosycross there is a spiritual path and a comprehensible, conceptual philosophy about the goal of this path, which the student does not develop out of himself but that he can examine, that he can understand, and that can serve as a foundation to his behavior until he experiences the spiritual world firsthand in his own being. The philosophy serves him as a guide until the faculty to directly receive the impulses from the spiritual world has arisen in him.

Today's human being and spiritual student then wants to and must independently and individually apply and verify his insights in his life. He will want to be active as a responsible member of society who at the same time has his own sphere of activity in the world. Today's spiritual student no longer withdraws from the life of the world in a cloistered community but lives responsibly in his occupation, family, and society and realizes his path individually and responsibly in this regard.

Universality

Christian Rosycross is a symbolic figure for still another principle. The Christ impulse is a deepening and extension of all former revelations of the divine world to humanity. Although all human religions before the Christ impulse also stemmed from the divine world and therewith go back to Christ, each only brought aspects of this world to humanity in

"So, Brother Rosycross, you are also here?" Christian Rosycross enters the reception room of the castle of the alchemical wedding and is mocked by the charlatans. Illustration by "Johfra" from the "Alchemical Wedding of Christian Rosycross."

order to gradually prepare it for the reception of the entire Christ impulse.

In the centuries after the comprehensive Christ impulse that became manifest in Jesus, people, especially also in the Eastern Mediterranean realm, tried to permeate, change, and extend the traditional philosophies, religions, and mysteries with the Christ forces. Greek, Indian, Egyptian, Persian, Jewish, etc. traditions were touched, transformed, and made to serve the decisive, central task of humanity: the conscious transfiguration of the human being. Christian Rosycross is the symbol for these processes. The comprehensive Christ impulse is alive in him. He received within himself the contents and forces of all former great religions that streamed to him, permeated them with the Christ forces, thereby lifted them to a higher stage, and joined them in a new unity as different aspects of a great endeavor by the Brotherhood of Life that climaxed in the Christ impulse.[42]

"Christian Rosycross" as Formula

The spiritual kernel of all religions, philosophies, and mystery traditions stemming from the spiritual world is contained like a formula in the name Christian Rosycross. The first name, Christian, indicates that Christ is this kernel and that a human being who wants to fulfill the present task of humanity has to be a Christianus, a human being filled with Christ. The last name, Rosycross, indicates the present condition of the human being, also the way to fulfill the task of humanity, and the goal of this way, the new condition of the human being. For now the spiritual principle, the Christ self or true self in man, is still latent, like a closed rose bud, and fastened to the cross of matter and the personality on this side. At present the personality consists of a self-maintaining ego—the vertical of the cross—and egocentric interests—the horizontal of the cross. These two main streams of his life on this side directed to matter cross in the heart of the human being.

But if the cosmic Christ forces enter the heart where the individual Christ principle, the spirit spark, is found, then this human being begins a path of inner change leading to transfiguration: The rosebud unfolds into bloom. The spiritual principle is awake, active and finally conscious. The vertical beam of the cross of the personality is opened to the vertical influx of the cosmic Christ spirit. This gradually replaces the old, self-maintaining ego and thwarts the ego-serving "horizontal" interests directed to this world and the beyond.

This process continues until the "cross" is completely changed and the personality is transfigured. The rose is then in full bloom and the "dead" Christ, the true self, "buried" in the human being is resurrected. Man then possesses an immortal, transfigured, resurrected personality as an instrument that consciously receives the spiritual—"vertical"—forces and "horizontally" distributes them lovingly, without self-interest, in the service of humanity. The pupil goes this path from beginning to end in and with the help of the Christ forces but with independent insight that he puts into action in practical life.

Thus the formula "Christian Rosycross" contains the core of all religions. But this core is carried to the full ripeness of esoteric Christianity: The task of humanity can now be carried out in all aspects and completely. Not only the subtle-material worlds and the subtle-material bodies of the human being, that is, thinking, feeling, and willing, can be grasped and changed by the Christ impulse, but this change extends into matter and the gross-material body. A new heaven—a new subtle-material world—as well as a new earth—a new material world—arise.[43] And this all becomes possible in the special life circumstances of today's human being who possesses a self-responsible individuality conscious in the material world.

The Historical Rosicrucians

The principle "Christian Rosycross" describes the present condition of the "atmospheric spiritual field," which has directly connected itself to humanity since about the middle of the 19th century. It contains within itself the sum and concentration of all former developments of this spiritual field. If one opens himself from below, from the humanity developing in the sense world, to this principle and unfolds in his own being the spiritual aptitude corresponding to it, then he becomes ever more conscious of it and can finally also act out of it. Jan Leene, Z. W. Leene, and Henny Stok-Huizer were three persons in whom this process occurred.

But a person in whom such a spiritual impulse manifests will always also seek to trace earlier manifestations of this impulse in human history and try to establish a connection to them. On the one hand, he draws directly from the impulse of the spiritual field, but on the other, he also seeks an outer confirmation of this impulse in connecting to its traces in the material world.

The Writings of the Classical Rosicrucians

For Jan van Rijckenborgh, these traditions became outwardly concretely palpable in the Rosicrucian writings from the beginning of the 17th century[44] among others. In the *Fama Fraternitatis*, he discovered the program for the realization of the spiritual principle—the formula "Christian Rosycross"—in life and society and the goal derivable from it. In the *Confessio Fraternitatis*, he recognized the theoretical formulation of this principle. And in the *Alchemical Wedding of Christian Rosycross*, he found the description of the way to this goal: the reception, transformation, and realization of the spiritual impulse leading to the unification of spirit with the renewed consciousness—the "alchemical wedding"—and finally to transfiguration, the resulting construction of a new personality.

The Historical Reality of Christian Rosycross?

Since this spiritual impulse took concrete historical forms in the Rosicrucian writings, it has often been asked if the principle itself, "Christian Rosycross," was embodied in a concrete historical personality. For example, Rudolf Steiner answered this question in the affirmative and presented to his audience a concrete human being with a concrete lifespan (the Rosicrucian writings give the time of 1378–1484) but whose civil name may not have been Christian Rosenkreuz (Rosycross). As a result of his spiritual-scientific investigations, Rudolf Steiner also presented a series of historical personalities who were to have been earlier and later incarnations of Christian Rosycross. He was to have been a human being who experienced the life of Jesus as one of the closest participants. On the other hand, Carlos Gilly, doubtless the best expert on the historical Rosicrucian writings and the problems connected with them, comes to the conclusion: "There was not a Christian Rosenkreuz of the $14^{th}/15^{th}$ century,"[45] which however only means that according to present knowledge, there was not a human being with the civil name Christian Rosenkreuz.

But such attempts, whether they employ spiritual-scientific/esoteric methods or scientific/historical research, are always subjective, dependent on some imponderables and therefore lack ultimate certainty. The deductive way, on the other hand, is much more certain. If whatever kind of spiritual impulse is to be active in historical humanity, there have to be human beings who can concretely transform and anchor it in humanity, not only in that they represent it philosophically but also in that they embody it. So there must have been beings who embodied the principle "Christian Rosycross."

And why should there not have been such an embodiment in the group in which the Rosicrucian writings arose in the 17th century? This group is called the "Tübinger Circle." The doctor and lawyer Tobias Hess (1558–1614) was the spiritual head and inspiring force of this circle. So he was at least a representative of the principle "Christian Rosycross" in that time. In this sense, Joost R. Ritman asks: "Are not Tobias Hess and Father Brother Christian Rosycross here in line as the prototype of the true imitation of Christ?"[46] Hess's closest coworkers were Christoph Besold (1577–1638) and Johann Valentin Andreae (1586–1654). The latter is regarded as the real author of the Rosicrucian writings named. This does not mean, however, that he had the experiences described therein firsthand. The inspiring source was Tobias Hess. The group around him was either to a certain degree independently capable of such experiences or had access to his experiences and understanding. Andreae, who perhaps had the greatest gift with language in this group, was then chosen to articulate the common understanding and experiences. In this connection, his young age at the time he composed the manuscripts speaks in no way against his authorship.

According to Rudolf Steiner, Christian Rosycross incarnated in every century from the 14th century up to the present. And Jan van Rijckenborgh writes: "We will not follow this method (of historical investigation), even though we have to tell you that C. R. C. did exist; that we know people who were his contemporaries, who saw him and lived quite close to him. There are people who are closely connected with him."[47]

A Classical Order of the Rosycross?

Did a secret Order of the Rosycross exist at the beginning of the 17th century?

Many traces have been followed and no such Order could be discovered. In spite of this, it is justified to speak of a Rosicrucian Order even then, and when the authors of the writings appeared in the name of this Order, then this was not arrogance or an attempt to lead others astray. For all who at that time "synchronously" drew from the spiritual source Christian Rosycross were connected with each other on a spiritual plane. John Dee and Robert Fludd in England, Jakob Böhme, Adam Haslmayr, Michael Maier in Germany, later Amos Comenius in Bohemia and Holland—they were all representatives of this great impulse in the sign of Christian Rosycross. All also knew of the great doctor and philosopher

Paracelsus (1493–1541) and referred to him as their predecessor. The *Fama Fraternitatis* dedicates a whole chapter to Paracelsus and shows how he can be regarded as a Rosicrucian according to his experiences and his thoughts. He also may be grouped with those who drew from the spiritual source "Christian Rosycross" even though he lived a hundred years before the "Order of the Rosycross" was made public.

The circle around Tobias Hess surely planned to have this spiritual connection in the sign of Christian Rosycross become even more effective through a concrete organization. But the publication of the Rosicrucian manifestos aroused a mighty "chaos of opinions regarding the existence, meaning, and purpose" of the supposed Brotherhood of the Rosycross. Between 1614 and 1623 alone, 330 texts about the Rosycross appeared. Charlatans and braggarts also designated themselves as Brothers of the Rosycross and so brought the Order and its goals into disrepute. Beside the serious truth seekers who longingly sought connection to the league announced in the *Fama*, there were too many people who looked for personal advantages and the development of occult faculties from such a path. If these people, "shameless comedians" who had betrayed and corrupted the *Fama* (Andreae), had become determinative in an organization to be built, then the goal and way of the Rosycross would have quickly turned into its opposite.

This may have induced Johann Valentin Andreae (who was widely identified as the author of the manifestos after the death of Tobias Hess in 1614) to more or less unequivocally distance himself from these writings. But he never gave up the program contained in them. In 1620 he tried to call to life a real brotherhood under the name "Societas Christiana." Thus, he clothed "his old program in a new form ... for rea-

Johann Valentin Andreae (1586–1654), coauthor of the three Rosicrucian manifestos: "Fama Fraternitatis" (1614), "Confessio Fraternitatis" (1615), and "Chemical Wedding of Christian Rosycross" (1616)

sons of safety"[48] as Carlos Gilly says. "So I let this Brotherhood go, but never the true Christian Brotherhood fragrant of roses under the cross", Andreae wrote in *Turris Babel* (1619). It was alone the disorder of the Thirty Years' War that made such an attempt practically without prospect. And after the outbreak of the war, circumstances demanded a concentration of energies on mitigating the misery of the war. It would have been wrong to close one's eyes to the distress of those times. Thus we see Andreae's admirable spirit of sacrifice when, for example, as superintendent of Calw, he actively helped to remove the devastations of the war and to rebuild.

The "Societas Christiana" as an outer organization was to comprehensively influence science, culture and religion and by means of these also society and politics; such was the plan. This was wholly in the intentions of the *Fama Fraternitatis*, which had spoken of a great world reformation in the sign of the principle "Christian Rosycross." Representatives of science, culture, and religion, but also of politics and society would have found their places in such an organization. Nevertheless, that the group around Tobias Hess in this regard had set their hopes on the "winter king" Frederic V of the Palatinate and that even John Dee and England had played a major role in the development of the Rosicrucian movement are fictions according to the present state of research.[49]

The Cathars

A further root of the new Rosicrucian movement called to life by Jan Leene, Z. W. Leene, and Henny Stok-Huizer was Catharism. The spiritual legacies of all the brotherhoods that ever were active in humanity are contained in the field of the spirit like the links of a chain. It is essential in the construction of a new community of this type that it always consciously connects to the last link of this chain, inwardly-spiritually as well as also in outer tradition, in order to be nourished out of the forces of the whole chain on the one hand and to continue its impulses on the other.

Teaching and Way of the Cathars

The Cathars or Albigensians were the latest spiritual community in Europe that had a large international organization. They spread to many regions in Europe from the end of the 11th to the end of the 13th century, especially northern Italy, southern France, and further up north to Holland and northern Germany. Two extant texts of the Cathars of southern France are the *Interrogatio Johannis* (*John's Interrogation* or *The Secret Supper*)[50] and a "ritual."[50] The *Interrogatio Johannis* is very likely of Bogomil origin. The Bogomils were another community that strove on a Christian basis for a spiritual existence free of inner ties to this world and the beyond. They had already been active in the Balkans for centuries and continued Manichean traditions. They greatly influenced Catharism by way of northern Italy, in fact may have given the decisive impetus to its rise and further development.

The *Interrogatio Johannis* is an example and proof of their influence. One can gather from it the worldview and philosophical basis of the Cathars. Like the modern Rosicrucians around Jan van Rijckenborgh, their point of departure was that the origin of all being is a spiritual order and power that manifests in material forms via soul forces. When this process of manifestation occurs harmoniously, then the material forms are pure expressions of the spirit. The outer then corresponds to the inner. But the world harmony was disturbed when self-maintaining forces—called "Lucifer" by the Cathars—made themselves known in the soul realm and separated from the spiritual world. Since then, these forces dominate in the world and humanity and prevent the activity of the spirit in the human being.

But there is a way to reverse this disturbance. This way is expressed in the "ritual" of the Cathars. It is first of all a matter of the latent spirit in the human being, the light spark, making itself noticeable again. It makes itself perceptible in the form of a hunch or cognition that the present state of the world and humanity is one of a disturbance of the original harmony. From this cognition follows a way of life of conscious self-liberation from the entanglements in this world and the beyond. This was the first segment of the path of the Cathars: cleansing and purification on the basis of the spiritual principle in the human being. The second segment began when the connection between the world of the spirit and the spiritual principle in the human being was re-established. The Cathars symbolized this connection by the consolamentum: The student received the Holy Spirit. Now the final farewell to every inner binding to this world and the beyond could and had to follow. And the love, unity, and freedom of the true self, the light principle latent until now, could become active again.

The Cathars used the name "endura" for the conscious dissolution of self-maintenance, the principle of transitory life, in the forces of the true self that came to the fore again and became active through this process. At that time, it was supported by outer patterns of behavior such as sexual abstinence and fasting.

But the church did not understand that the resurrection of the true essence of the human being is only possible if the false essence, the life in self-maintenance, "goes under" in a process. The "endura" was misunderstood as physical suicide through which the Cathars hoped to enter Paradise by the shortest route. Also later it was still believed that this conception could be documented through the records of the inquisition, which reported that Cathars starved themselves after receiving the consolamentum. But the Cathar "ritual" clearly shows that the endura meant the "death" of the human being's false essence of self-maintenance and egocentricity. If individual Cathars really believed that they had to commit suicide through excessive fasting, then this was a misunderstanding on their part.

The path of the Cathars was carried out by first withdrawing totally from the world. This was still sensible at that time. Later on their spiritual path, however, when they had become rooted in the ground of the spirit, they turned back to the world and went through the land teaching and healing. Their farewell to the entanglements in the world was indeed without compromise and radical.

But this does not mean that they thought "dualistically" as has been imputed to them. True, they bluntly set the world of appearances permeated and ruled by self-maintenance opposite the world of the spirit. But the world of matter also once originated in the spirit and would again be permeated by it and express it when the principle of self-maintenance was dissolved.

End of the Cathars

As the church at that time was strongly defined by a striving for power, possessions, and influence, the worldview and path of the Cathars had to appear to it as a challenge from an enemy. The church saw itself threatened in its claim to power, its influence on human beings, and its self-importance, which explains its behavior in regard to the Cathars. It led to persecution, the establishment of courts to try heretics, the first establishment of an inquisition, and finally a crusade against the "heretics," which ended with the cruel destruction of these "pure ones."[51] A decisive point was set by the burning of 205 "parfaits" (perfect ones) after one of their last places of refuge, the castle of Montségur, became untenable. Allied to the church was the French state, which followed its own political interests with this crusade. The French king saw the conflict as a welcome opportunity to extend the rule of the crown over the still relatively independent south of France.[52]

Antonin Gadal

In their search for traces left by Catharism, Catharose de Petri and Jan van Rijckenborgh traveled several times to southern France from 1946 on. In 1954 they met Antonin Gadal there, who made himself known as the last patriarch of the Cathars in a chain of transmission going back centuries. Antonin Gadal confirmed what had already become clear to Catharose de Petri and Jan van Rijckenborgh through their own experiences.[53]

Like the Cathars, they had recognized that the original harmony between the world of the spirit and the dialectical world of this side and the beyond had been torn asunder when the soul of the human being rebelled against the spirit. Thus the world of matter had become a hell of opposing interests and conflicts. And all striving for harmony in this world are only insufficient band-aids on the bleeding wounds as long as the basic evil, the self-maintenance in the human being, is not removed.

Efforts to create harmony that are undertaken while retaining self-maintenance or that stem from it cannot possibly lead to the goal. It is impossible to penetrate into the world of the spirit from below upwards through the smoothing of the rough edges and through the further development of the material world. One has to radically carry out the endura, the dissolution of self-maintenance. Only then can the spirit work from above downwards, dissolve conflicts and disharmony, and later enable the human being to construct his personality and world anew.

This realization and experience—that there is no bridge from below upwards, meaning through further development of the earthly human being, that instead the bridge can and must only be built from above downwards—was and remained one of the central declarations of Catharose de Petri and Jan van Rijckenborgh, which decisively determined and determines the life and the path of the School of the Rosycross.

Also, the history of the Cathars burned itself deeply into the consciousness of the leaders of the Lectorium Rosicrucianum. The church showed an uncompromising enmity and will to destroy as regards this movement. Seen externally, Catharism ended in an ocean of blood. Therein a lawfulness came to expression for Jan van Rijckenborgh, which he also explicated again and again. When a human being or a group of human beings remember their original inherent spiritual aim and want to free themselves from their political and religious world determined by self-maintenance, then this world will not voluntarily give up its "possession." It will become violent possibly leading to the destruction of the seeker for truth and freedom. Thus it has been throughout all of world history. One only needs to consider, for example, how Jesus was treated by the political and religious institutions of his time, and how then the young church that was organizing and becoming an instrument of power persecuted the Manicheans and Gnostics.

Occasional sharp comments by Jan van Rijckenborgh about the church in books and lectures relate to these historical facts and this lawfulness. He pillories the institutions in so far as they, as organs of the drive for possessions, influence, and power, persecute human beings who want to dissolve this drive for possessions, influence, and power in the unity, freedom, and love of the spirit. At the same time, however, he always indicates that the same lawfulness is active not only in the outer world, but also in every individual human being and also in every student on the spiritual path. In every individual who wants to go this path, self-maintenance asserts itself even stronger and tries to destroy the impulse of the true self. It would be too comfortable to seek for "evil" only outside of oneself and to self-righteously want to separate from it. First it has to be discovered and overcome in one's own inner being.

Freemasonry and Alchemy

In the Rosicrucian writings, Jan van Rijckenborgh encountered freemasonic symbols and alchemy, further roots of the philosophy of the Rosycross.

Freemasonry

He enlisted freemasonic symbolism repeatedly in describing the spiritual path. The goal of every pupil is to become a "living building stone" in the spiritual temple of the Spiritual School as well as of humanity as a whole. He will smooth all surfaces and edges of the stone, that is, remove all his egocentricity so that the true spiritual self will fit well into the structure of the spiritual world. Also as an individual human being, he wants to become again a complete temple in which the spirit can live. Thus he carries out self-responsible, conscious "freemasonic work" to "freely" build himself: to withdraw the true spiritual self from the entanglements in this world and the beyond and to build up a new personality, a new temple, out of the forces of the spirit.

The temple of the individual human being as well as the temple of humanity can only be erected on the "corner stone" Jesus Christ, on the force and in the force of the spirit and in the light, in the new spiritual consciousness. In this work, the pupil stands "on the fourfold carpet": Mentally, emotionally, volitionally, and actively, he leads a life directed to his task.

The Alchemist. Illustration from Manly Peter Hall's (publisher) "Codex Rosae Crucis," Los Angeles 1938

Alchemy

In the Middle Ages and still into the 18th century, alchemy was the generally widespread symbolic language through which esoteric researchers communicated esoteric truths. Seekers for the truth of the spirit carried out alchemical experiments mainly in order to symbolically represent soul-spiritual processes within the human being through outwardly visible occurrences in the realm of metals and minerals. The striving to make physical gold was a materialistic degeneration, a misunderstanding.

Through the inclusion of the symbols of alchemy, which had especially come to development in the Arabic cultural realm, the developing modern Rosicrucian community connected with another link in the chain of brotherhoods from before the time of the Cathars: the Arabic mystery tradition. In the *Fama Fraternitatis*, Christian Rosycross did not travel in vain in the Arabic world, for example, to Damascus and Fez, meeting the local sages and absorbing their wisdom. This expresses symbolically that the Rosicrucian impulse also lives out of the Arabic mystery tradition of Sufism.

Central themes of alchemy were firstly, to turn lead into gold, and secondly, to celebrate the "alchemical wedding" between bride and groom, between queen and king. Turning lead into gold: The present human being is a personality stamped by self-maintenance and therefore degenerated and sluggish like lead when compared to the original condition. This personality is constructed according to the laws and forces of matter and is no longer a pliable instrument of the spirit; on the contrary, it hinders the spirit. The human personality as it should be, however, is free of self-maintenance and is a pure, clear instrument of the spirit. It is "gold." When the alchemists wanted to turn lead into gold, then this meant that the personality dependent on matter was to be transfigured into a personality permeated by the spirit. This occurred in three phases: "dissolution" of the lead; leading it back into the primal state of the metal as such, the "prima materia"; and construction of the gold from the prima materia. The self-maintenance of the personality is dissolved; the primal state of the soul living out of the spirit is reestablished, and out of this primal state arises the new personality permeated by the spirit.[54]

The second great theme of alchemy that plays a major role in the philosophy of the modern Rosycross is the "alchemical wedding" between the king and queen, between the spirit and the renewed soul in the human being. This wedding is the prerequisite for transfiguration. What is meant is that in a personality cleansed of all self-maintenance, a new soul arises that is not determined by the gross-material and subtle-material world but by the spiritual world. The more the forces and structures of the spirit become active in this soul, the queen, the more it will develop a consciousness that is capable of grasping the forces and structures of the spirit, the king, active in it. Then it is consciously permeated and filled by these forces—this is designated as the "alchemical wedding." According to the words of Paul in the Bible, the soul then recognizes as it is recognized, and sees "face to face."[55] The alchemical wedding is the descent of the Christ, the spirit, into Jesus, the soul prepared for this. From then on, the human being who consciously receives and lives out of the spirit has become a source from which the spirit flows for others. The new, spirit-permeated, transfigured, resurrected personality is built up from his new thoughts, feelings, will impulses, and actions that are directed to the spirit. Jan van Rijckenborgh writes about this in the *Alchemical*

Wedding of Christian Rosycross: "And now, in the story of C. R. C., the spirit-soul has become manifest, transfiguration has been completed, and the new, omnipresent consciousness causes Christian Rosycross to enter the fields of the living soul-state, or in other words, to enter those fields of consciousness that far transcend our three-dimensional consciousness and into which, with this consciousness, we are unable to follow C. R. C."[56]

Relationship of the Sexes

The cooperation between spirit and soul brings up a subject that is of great importance for the life in matter as well as for the spiritual path and the activity of the spiritual human being: the relationship of the sexes. In the material world, the human being appears in two forms: as man and as woman. Both possess a personality determined by self-maintenance, which is differently "polarized" in each, however. Man is biologically-bodily active, woman biologically-bodily passive. In their subtle bodies, these functions are reversed. In summary one could say that woman is more inclined to develop feelings and to stimulate thoughts while man is more inclined to stimulate feelings and to develop thoughts. Heart and head, feeling and thinking, stand in a polar relationship in the human being and in man act like plus to minus, in woman like minus to plus. Because of this different polarization, the sexes attract each other.

Man as well as woman will reach the alchemical wedding on the spiritual path: In both of them, a spirit-permeated soul that will one day consciously experience the spirit is constructed on this path. Spirit and soul[57], "king" and "queen," are also factors of different polarity in the individual human being, whether man or woman. As long as both these factors are latent and only the self-maintaining personality is active, the human being lives solely out of this personality, feels incomplete, and feels attracted to the other pole, the other sex. But if both these factors, spirit and spirit-permeated soul, become active again in a human being, be it a man or a woman, then he is in the state of the image of God awakened from its latency and is autonomous, a whole. He does not need to seek for anything lacking in himself in the other sexual partner. What he was lacking, the spirit and soul that have become alive, is again present in him, and the transfigured personality is an expression of this autonomous dual unity, an expression of "king" and "queen" who have celebrated their "wedding."

But there are also two types of this autonomous human being: the spiritual, autonomous "man" and the spiritual, autonomous "woman." For, so writes Jan van Rijckenborgh in the *Elementary Philosophy of the Modern Rosycross*, "it is a scientific fact that the fundamental organic differences which exist, even in the individual cells of men and women, are also present in their soul figures, in their spirit figures and in their archetypes, and that these differences have therefore been taken into account in the central-spirit principles and in the divine plan. This could not be otherwise, because everything that exists is manifested out of the spirit. So there is a divine creation: man, and a divine creation: woman. These two aspects together form the human life-wave."[58] In the spiritual man, the spirit, the active force, works outwardly and the soul, love and devotion, is within. In the spiritual woman, the spirit as active force is within and the soul, love and devotion, works outwardly. Thus both types are autonomous, as both poles work in them together. Both have a transfigured personality that is an expression of this unified dual polarity.

Nevertheless, they are two different expressions of the human being. As such, they can and will work together with equal rights. "We call this liberating collaboration: to be cosmically 'two-in-one'."[59]

This has consequences for the spiritual path: For already on the path itself, both sexes will work together on the level of spirit and soul with equal rights. Even more, there are consequences for the human beings that have become autonomous again who, since they are present in a twofold expression, work together in the world of the spirit. The working together of Jan van Rijckenborgh and Catharose de Petri is an example of this new cooperation. Jan van Rijckenborgh always emphasized that a spiritual path can only lead to the goal if man as well as woman reach inner autonomy in order to then, having become autonomous, work together at a new level.

The Gnosis

Among the medieval alchemists, the father of alchemy was considered to have been "Hermes Trismegistus" or "Hermes, the thrice great": great according to the spirit, the spirit-soul, and the spirit-permeated personality. Through Hermes Trismegistus, a legendary figure of the Egyptian mysteries, Jan van Rijckenborgh came to the Gnostic Hermetic writings and to the Gnosis in general. From 1961 to 1966, four volumes of his interpretation of the Hermetic writings were published under the title *The Egyptian Arch-Gnosis*. The Gnosis is another decisive root of the Spiritual School of the Rosycross.

One will only be able to adequately understand the historical Gnosis if one understands it as a renewal and deepening of the pre-Christian mystery traditions of the Mediterranean realm under the sign of original Christianity. The historical Gnosis is really the impulse of original Christianity and its continuation with the inclusion of the traditions of the mystery schools of the Mediterranean that were newly enlivened by and taken up in the Christ impulse.[60]

But Gnosis is not only a historical movement. Rather, this movement shows especially clearly a timeless existential knowledge, a path of initiation that can be experienced at all times and in all places. "Gnosis" means knowledge. As such, it is not a system of beliefs and not knowledge that can be learned but insight arising from within the human being: the becoming conscious of his true essence.

The way shown by Jesus is nothing else: becoming conscious of the "image of God" that has become latent in the human being of this world and the activation of this image of God as the "Christ in man." On this path, the self-maintenance of the human being of this world has to "die"; in the words of Paul, the "old self" has to be "crucified".[61] From the image of god that has awakened and become active, a new personality can then be constructed that, like Jesus, is resurrected from the "grave" of nature.

Gnosis is therewith also the process that the School of the Rosycross designates as transfiguration. Jesus himself went this path and lived it as an example. When the Holy Spirit—symbolized by a dove—descended on him after the baptism in the Jordan and he was "anointed" with this spiritual fire, that is, became the "Christ," this was nothing other than his becoming conscious and active of the image of God in him, which then opened itself to the forces of the spiritual world and received them. Thereby, the "Son," the "image of God" created by God, again became one with God. Jesus recognized God as he was recognized by God and could say: "The Father and I are one."[62]

After this becoming conscious—realization, Gnosis—the self-maintenance present in his own subtle-material being, symbolized by Satan, approached him, was recognized, and was overcome in the new spiritual forces. Then the activity of Jesus who had become the Christ began out of the spiritual forces: He lived the thoughts, feelings, energies, and activities springing from the spiritual world in love for others. This was the construction of a new personality that replaced the old one permeated by self-maintenance.

"Son of God"

On the one hand, the "Son of God," the Christ, is really the only Son of God, the light of consciousness that goes out from the force of the "Father" in order to illuminate all human beings. In this sense, Christ spoke through the mouth of Jesus: "I am the light of the world."[63] On the other hand, every human being is in principle a son of God, for the immortal image of God is in him, and he becomes a son of God in reality when this image of God in him again becomes conscious and active. He then belongs again to the "children of light"[64]; as a "righteous one," he is a "son of God." The book "The Wisdom of Solomon" in the Bible describes very accurately the characteristics and inherent aim of such a "son of God."[65]

Salvation

According to the experience of the Gnostics, salvation does not refer to the mortal, gross-material and subtle-material personality. Jesus does not save the personality through an act of grace and awaken it to "eternal life." The image of God in the human being has to be saved, not the egocentric personality. And this salvation consists of the image of God, the true self in the human being, awakening from its latency and inactivity and becoming conscious and active. What was formerly trapped in this world and the beyond becomes liberated and saved. This is an inner path that cannot be taken away from the human being by a savior from without. Nevertheless, the human being cannot go this path out of his own power. He cannot save himself but needs the power from the spiritual world for this, just as Jesus was "anointed" with this power. He needs the aid of helpers who stand in a special connection with the spiritual world and who transmit its forces to him, just as Jesus transmitted them after his connection with the Christ force.

Two Worlds

The Gnostics distinguished between a creator god, the demiurge, the "god of this world" as Paul also called him,[66] and the original "Father," the spirit.

The "god of this world" is the god of the world on this side and the beyond. To him corresponds the mortal, self-maintaining personality built of gross and subtle matter, which imagines this god as a person and anthropomorphic in accordance with its own nature. Therefore, this god possesses the characteristics of mercy and wrath, compassion and justice. But above the god of this world is the original spiritual world, which corresponds to the image of God slumbering in the human being. This image of God, which can become conscious in the human being, is not a limited, mortal personality but an individuality of unlimited consciousness. It does not stand opposite the God of the spiritual world like an I to a you, like a person to a person, but experiences itself consciously embedded in God, permeated and animated by God. In this sense, Jesus is a Gnostic and can say: "The Father and I are one," and: "Be perfect, therefore, as your heavenly Father is perfect."[67]

Jan van Rijckenborgh encountered the historical Gnosis first in the Hermetic writings and the *Pistis Sophia*,[68] later also in the writings found near Nag Hammadi such as the "Gospel of Truth" and the "Letter to Rheginus."[69] In the Hermetic writings,[70] Hermes Trismegistus takes the place of Jesus Christ, the helper from the spiritual world who himself has gone the way of transfiguration and makes it possible for others.

The Universal Doctrine

Syncretism or Universal Doctrine?

A philosophy like that of the School of the Rosycross that receives forces from many roots in the past and uses symbols from the most varied times and cultures is often charged with being "syncretistic": that it is artificially assembled from all possible elements of different origin, that it is lacking in originality, and that it actually only lives from the experiences and accomplishments of others.

But the philosophy of the Rosycross has grown out of the authentic spiritual experiences of the founders of this School. It is not a philosophical system pieced together from concepts and arbitrary symbols, also not a system of beliefs erected from dogmas. The philosophy of the Rosycross is rather the expression and precipitate of direct experiences with the world of the spirit, experiences that, since the world of the spirit is characterized by unity, also represent a unity, a living, original unity.

Whoever can inwardly re-experience the basic experiences with the world of the spirit will recognize this philosophy's unity originating out of the singular root of the spirit disregarding its many different symbols. Someone who only looks at this philosophy from the outside, however, will take the variety of symbols as an indication of syncretism.

When a human being becomes conscious, for example, of the spiritual formula at the basis of the development of humanity and the human being, then he directly receives therewith a share of the world of the spirit in which this formula is anchored. He symbolizes it perhaps with the sentence: "Whoever is willing to lose his life for the sake of Jesus, the prototype of the spiritual human being, will keep it, that is, the true life in the spirit." But he can also represent it with Buddhist symbols, perhaps such that the "thirst for existence" has to be totally "extinguished" before illumination will strike like lightning into the resulting emptiness. Or he describes it with symbols from Platonic philosophy: Someone who strives for and loves wisdom will only experience this wisdom, the world of the spirit, when he has liberated himself from the deception of sense perceptions and the entanglement in the sense world. He will also be able to represent this experience with the formula "Christian

Rosycross," which is again a special expression of this experience. Should he hesitate to use and cite the symbols of all these streams that he perceives as confirmations of his own living experience?

Since all original religions and mystery impulses are revelations from the spiritual world and find their unity therein, Jan van Rijckenborgh can speak of a "universal doctrine" in regard to the philosophy of the Rosycross. All religions—and therewith also their symbols—are branches of a great tree, parts of a great organism, with each having different tasks at specific times and in specific cultures. All originate from the one root of the spirit and represent it.

Someone who looks at religions only from the outside, as dogmatic systems, will only notice the differences between them and will demarcate one from the other. But someone who sees them as expressions of a spiritual world that was experienced differently at various times and by various people will recognize the one spiritual world in these symbols.

It is this way also in ordinary life. The experience of joy, for example, can be expressed differently. One person may symbolize it by a bubbling brook, another by an exulting lark. Someone who only sees the pictures and has no access to the experiences that stand behind them will assume it is a matter of two different statements. Someone is acting similarly when he sees the "Kingdom of God" of the Christians, the "Nirvana" of the Buddhists, the "Tao" of the Taoists, and the "World of Ideas" of Plato as different things. Indeed, in order to demarcate his position from others, he wants to do so. But they are symbols that all point to a singular experience.

In modern times, where the cultures of earth come into relationships with one another, the world religions also come into contact with each other and examine each other. If they do not go back to the experiences standing behind the symbols that originate from the unity of the spirit, then they will never understand each other. Today attempts are being made worldwide to find a common denominator in religions, for example, in the form of a "world ethic," and to make it obligatory for humanity. These are artificial attempts that only originate from the outer systems of beliefs. Instead, it would be essential that human beings become ever more conscious of the spiritual world. Then they are one in this experience, no matter how they symbolize it.

But not only the growing together of peoples and cultures forces a new way of looking at things; the Rosicrucian impulse itself is a stream into which all previous streams from the world of the spirit enter, enhanced and permeated by the Christ impulse. This fact once again justifies the inclusion of the different symbolisms in the philosophy of the Rosycross, even makes it necessary. For all previous symbolisms gain new depth and power through the Christ impulse and so can contribute to the development of the consciousness of humanity in a new way.

The "Universal Spiritual School"

In its teachings and structure, the Spiritual School of the Rosycross is an expression of the universal world of the spirit. Someone who experiences its structure and power from within and becomes part of it experiences the structure and power of the world of the spirit in general, just like the becoming conscious of the true self of a human being lets him experience his identity and unity with the spiritual world.

These circumstances often induced Jan van Rijckenborgh to speak of the Spiritual School of the Rosycross as the spiritual school in general and to say that no one who does not belong to this spiritual school could go a spiritual path. He thereby referred to the congruence of the Spiritual School of the Rosycross with the universal spiritual school, the totality of all impulses from the world of the spirit. In fact, no one who is not touched by the impulses from the world of the spirit, that is, the activity of the universal spiritual school, can go a spiritual path.

Seen outwardly as organizations, however, there are also today various spiritually striving groups in the world. The Spiritual School of the Rosycross is not the only one. Jan van Rijckenborgh also indicates this in various places of his work. For example: "There are religious and occult brotherhoods in the world which claim to possess the only true faith. We do not share this point of view, but only want to make clear that the light has been manifested in the magnetic body of the modern Spiritual School, so that Christ has entered and from this light, life came forth.... We are putting such emphasis on this so that it cannot be said later on: 'The Lectorium Rosicrucianum claims to be the only true church.' We repeat that the magnetic body of the modern Spiritual School has become Christ-centered in a very exact sense; that without this light there cannot be life; that the eternal prince of the Light for that reason said: 'Without me you can do nothing.'"[71]

Developments during and after the Second World War

The bases for the Spiritual School of the Rosycross had been laid by the beginning of World War II. The Leene brothers and Mrs. Stok-Huizer had worked out the philosophy of the Rosicrucian path in connection with the principle "Christian Rosycross." They characterized this path and demarcated it on the basis of the original Christianity from spiritual paths of the past of the West and the East that can no longer lead to the true inherent aim of the human being.

Parallel to the spiritual development of these three human beings, a group had arisen that, touched by the Rosicrucian spiritual impulse, had at first occupied itself with the philosophy of the Rosycross and then, solidifying this impulse in their own being, had gained an ever better power of discrimination for how the modern Christian path of initiation looked in comparison to the old paths. Jan van Rijckenborgh described this path in his book *Dei Gloria Intacta* (1946) that he wanted understood as the "Declaration of the Christian Mystery of Initiation for the Present."

After the war, building on these experiences and realizations, Catharose de Petri and Jan van Rijckenborgh could go on to the construction of an "inner school," the real spiritual or mystery school in which the pupils continued their path on the basis of the now well-understood philosophy of the Rosycross and their newly-won power of discrimination.

Catharose de Petri and Jan van Rijckenborgh developed the first stage of this inner school in southern France in close inner contact with the preceding Brotherhood of the Cathars. It was concerned with the endura, the conscious dissolution

The monument "Galaad" in Ussat-les-Bains, southern France. It commemorates the cooperation of the Cathars, Grail knights, and Rosicrucians: the "Tri-unity of the Light."

of the self-maintenance of the personality in the forces of the spirit.

This was at the same time the legacy of the Cathars to the new spiritual school of the present that was to realize the Rosicrucian impulse. The visible transfer of the heritage of the Cathars to the modern Rosicrucians took shape with the unveiling of a monument in Ussat-les-Bains on May 5th, 1957.

It is built up of large stones of the most varied forms, a symbol for the living "stones" of the pupils of which the school of the Cathars consisted and the modern school of the Rosicrucians consists, also a symbol for the chain of communities and mystery schools that over the centuries anchor and further develop the world of the spirit in humanity.

As a special sign for the contribution of the Cathars to this great work, Antonin Gadal added to the monument an altar stone that had survived the centuries in the cave of initiation of the Cathars. In this cave is still found today a life-size pentagon chiseled into the rock, a symbol for the fivefold new soul that develops when the human being carries out the endura.

On the occasion of the unveiling of the monument "Galaad," a three-day conference of the Rosicrucian pupils from Holland, France, and other countries took place on a piece of property for which a down payment had been made for this purpose. Since then, such conferences have taken place at irregular intervals of up to several years. They served to enliven the spiritual heritage of the Cathars: to re-experience their path, which comprises the first steps of the Christian path of initiation, but then to go further on this basis and realize the Rosicrucian impulse as it comes to expression in the principle of "Christian Rosycross" under the conditions of the modern world.

This work manifested outwardly in various occurrences. At the end of 1946, a piece of property with buildings called "Elckerlyc" near Laage Vuursche (Holland) was bought, which later received the name "Renova" (renewal). In these buildings, the pupils met for "renewal conferences" in order to realize and go the path together. In 1951 a large temple serving this work was erected on this property, the "Renova Temple."

Dove in the garden of the Dutch Conference Center "Renova." The dove is the symbol for the feminine aspect of the spirit: the power of harmony that orders and preserves everything that has become new.

The Path of the Spiritual School

> *The truth, the eternal power of wisdom of the world of the living Soul-state will grow within you, according as you will be ascending the seven steps of Soul-birth.* (Catharose de Petri, *The Seal of Renewal*)

The path, work, and structure of the Spiritual School of the Rosycross are determined by its goal. The goal is determined by the fact that presently the relationship between the divine nature order and the non-divine nature order is disturbed. If the spirit, the root of all things, would be received by the human consciousness and expressed in matter, the harmonic development of the spiritual "lines of force" that belong to the spiritual world would be guaranteed. Instead, the human being has dissociated himself from the spirit in self-willed self-maintenance. Thereby the spiritual world has become latent in him.

The Goal

The goal of the Spiritual School of the Rosycross is the reversal of this wrong relationship, first in the human being but, in the long run, also in the cosmos. The School enables its pupils to go a path and goes with them, which leads, on the one hand, to the dissolution of the dominance and self-lawfulness of soul and body, and on the other, to the resurrection of the spirit latent in the human being. The human being should attain inner freedom from the influences of the sense world and freedom from fate, which is the result of the self-maintaining activities of countless egos that preceded the present ego.

This freedom is only thereby possible, if his true essence, his spiritual nature, unfolds again. For a being is free when it lives in harmony with its inherent law of development. In the measure that the spiritual nature of the human being unfolds, the pupil becomes capable of shaking off the influences of matter and destiny that hinder the development of his true essence.

The structure of the spiritual world along with that of the true self of the human being is the truth. Therefore, Jesus says: "The truth will set you free."[72] If a human being lives out of this truth, which means being in harmony with the world of the spirit, then he is one with it and one with all other human beings in so far as they also live out of the spirit. His life will be a conscious realization of the spiritual world and a conscious activity out of the spiritual world. His soul is permeated by the truth and its power, and his personality expresses this truth and power.

The power of the spiritual world is the love that is active without limits and without self-interest: Like water, which nourishes all creatures without having to want and intend it, so the love of the human being living in the freedom and unity of the spirit contributes to the development of all beings, spontaneously and without intention.

If the goal is rightly recognized and the corresponding way trodden, then at the end of the path will stand a personality liberated from all self-maintenance and inertia—a transfigured personality that consciously and self-responsibly reacts to and realizes the impulses of the spirit.

There is then also a new soul that is liberated from self-maintenance, liberated also from fate and the influences from the reflection sphere. It takes up the impulses of the spirit and passes them on to the transfigured personality. Then the spirit in the human being has become one with the infinite, eternal spiritual world and is united with soul and personality. Through them, the spirit distributes understanding and love, and receives the reactions of the environment to this distribution.

The Spiritual Path

Longing for the Spirit

A certain maturity is the prerequisite for the path and attaining the goal. The human being has to have reached a critical point through many of his own experiences and the experiences of the many egos that have summed up to his fate in his microcosm. At this point, life itself becomes "questionable" to him. For his latent spiritual principle makes itself noticeable, at first still unconsciously, and fills him with the presentiment of a life in limitless freedom, unity, and love.

In contrast to this presentiment, he experiences normal life as limited and meaningless. This has nothing to do with the experience of someone who has come up short, who experiences pain due to his unrealizable wishes. The Buddha said: Even if all my wishes were fulfilled and I led a life like the blessed gods in the beyond, my longing would still not be stilled. The longing is only stilled when the human being has united with the inexhaustible world of the spirit. Jesus characterized this principal insufficiency in the course of the things of this world and the beyond in the first beatitude: "Blessed are the beggars of the spirit."[73] What is meant hereby is not a lack of intelligence but a condition in which the human being experiences that he lacks the unity with the spiritual world, the conscious abundance of the spirit, and that he longs like a beggar for the wealth of the spirit. One could also translate the beatitude as: "Blessed are those that long for the spirit, for the Kingdom of God."

This is the basic prerequisite of the path to the goal of the Spiritual School of the Rosycross: longing for the spirit. The latent, ineffective spirit in the human being longs for the conscious ascent into the spiritual world, for the abundance of the spirit in which it can unfold. The stronger this longing for salvation is, the stronger is the chance that the path will be kept to, that wrong tracks will be recognized as such, and that the goal will be reached. Such a longing for the spirit cannot be generated. It has to be born of the experience of the human being that he lives in this world and the beyond as if in exile and painfully longs for his spiritual home. But once it is born, it can flare up to a mighty longing.

Obstacles

A great if not the greatest difficulty on the path of the student of a spiritual school is that the world in general, society, and therewith his entire outer environment, as a rule, follow other goals and take other paths than he does. The goals of the environment of the student are mostly even contrary to his spiritual goal. Societal forces consciously or unconsciously influence every member of society and therewith also the pupil of a spiritual school. Education, training, conventions, and especially the mass media all enjoin him to behave in conformity with society's values and norms and to support them. He is to also strive for success, prosperity, security, and enjoyment and unconditionally affirm them.

If the pupil would not have had the basic experience that his actual goal in life cannot lie in these interests dominant in society and if the longing for true life fulfillment would not have become overwhelming, he would have no chance to develop the weak, little plant of the true human being in himself against the overwhelming unfavorable outer conditions. Just as little would he have a chance if the three remedies of the Spiritual School were not available to him: the forces from the field of the spirit, the community of the "living body," and the Universal Doctrine.

Inherent Aim of the Human Being

Not only subjectively but also objectively, the path of the Spiritual School of the Rosycross would be impossible, yes, a figment of the imagination, if it did not deal with the inherent aim of the human being. The path is anchored in the formula that is active in the individual human being and in humanity as a law of development, as a divine line of force, and is determined by this formula. For this reason, the path of the Spiritual School of the Rosycross is in principle not new but also the path of all other original religions and mystery schools of the past and present. Every original religion and mystery school did not want anything other than to show human beings who were ripe and receptive the path to their actual inherent aim and to help them to walk this path—always under the special conditions of their time.

This path is not a fixed idea, not a meaning given to human life arbitrarily. If it would be so, then the human being on the way to this goal would eventually be exhausted or would give up when the obstacles became too great. The actual justification for this path lies herein: It is the path of the true human being who wants to liberate himself from the sheaths of falsehood—the human being striving for success, possessions, power, and enjoyment—in order to live out of the world of the spirit. The inner tension that allows the pupil to search for the path and to continue walking on the path—and should this path last many incarnations and run up against seemingly insurmountable obstacles—originates from the objective situation that the present world and the present human being have lost their balance. A disturbance in the household of the world and in the psychological household of the individual wants like a pain to abolish itself. The disturbance itself creates the tension that calls up the forces to its overcoming. They are active in the pupil and flow to him from the Spiritual School from its three "remedies."

The Path as Subjective Experience of the Pupil

Words like "path" and "goal" are images. The idea that the pupil is moving forwards and making progress can lead to misunderstandings. The spiritual path does not consist in that the pupil conquers ever-new realms of consciousness, develops ever greater capabilities, and has ever more beautiful and intense experiences. It is better if one imagines the path as a succession of stages in the pupil approximately like a child ripens into a teenager and a teenager into an adult. It concerns an inner growth on the one hand, a "withering" on the other.

Not the development of the personality to greater power, importance, and enjoyment, not an expansion of consciousness and clairvoyance in subtle realms of the beyond are goal and path, but just the "withering" of the egocentricity of the personality. In the measure that the self-maintenance of the pupil dissolves step-by-step, the characteristics of the true self, up to now unknown to him, can awaken within, grow, and change his personality.

These processes yield a succession of states of an ever-greater tranquility, calm—yes, the "not-being" in relation to transient nature—in the pupil, who is gradually permeated by a new freedom, love, and unity with the spirit. In the measure that the old, apparent identity determined by self-maintenance dwindles, the inner law of the spirit unfolds and becomes the new identity of the pupil, which is also his original identity stemming from the spirit.

In the first approach, one could describe the experiences of the pupil on the path with the help of pairs of opposites: In the place of intention steps the allowing of the unfolding lawfulness of the spirit; in the place of desire, the surrender to the spiritual world; in the place of one's own will impulses, the streaming of new forces.

"Insight"

The first stage on this path—or the first state that the Rosicrucian pupil experiences—is the phase of insight. It is not a matter of intellectual analysis. It is a matter of insight that arises into the consciousness from the heart of the pupil. The Rosicrucians speak here of "pre-remembrance," a re-membrance of the spiritual world deeply hidden and buried in the human being. When this pre-remembrance becomes alive in the pupil, then he foresees that his inherent aim is a life in the world of the spirit. In the light of this presentiment, his opinions and views up to this time appear as limited. And the dissolution of this limitation is experienced as liberation and expansion. The intellect certainly participates in this process in critically testing and formulating the new experiences, but it is not the originator of these experiences.

A beginning pupil gains, for example, the insight that human life—his life—has meaning in the grand picture of the development of world and humanity. At the basis of all development of world and humanity lies the spiritual world as lawfulness and power. He also belongs to this spiritual world; it is active in him as the law according to which he set out on his journey as a spiritual being. He is "born of God"—*Ex deo nascimur*—as the Rosicrucians of the 17th century said, a thought germ gone forth from the thought of God that wants to develop and express itself independently. As a thought of God, the human being has a task and responsibility not only for himself but also for the whole stream of development of world and humanity in which he has been taken up.

Coincident with this "remembrance" of his true being, the pupil also becomes conscious of the condition in which he finds himself presently: He is not working responsibly in the spiritual stream of the development of world and humanity. Like all other human beings, he has taken a path with world and humanity that leads ever more into matter. He recognizes that the world is presently in no way the unfolding of its inherent spirit but the unfolding of its anti-spirit also inherent in it.

The experience of "being born of God" brings further insights with it depending from which worldview, which direction, the pupil comes. If he thought materialistically up to now, for example, then the thought of not only being a speck of dust in the universe and not only a fleeting coincidence will bring real meaning to life. Eternity surrounds and protects the world. The world originated out of divine intelligence, power, and formative force, out of eternity, even though it is distancing itself on its own paths ever further from its origin. The big bang and biological evolution may be correct looked at from the outside, from the side of form; but what is decisive is that seen from within, from the side of the spirit, world and humanity have come forth and develop further out of the eternal spirit.

If the pupil believed up to now in a creation of the world through God, who works on an object like a craftsman from the outside, then this idea will now appear limited. He recognizes that the divine "Word" is the structure of lines of creative forces that are at the basis of all existence and develop it from within, just as the creative information present invisibly in the seed of a plant brings forth the visible plant out of itself.

If the pupil believed in an eternal life for the personality in the beyond after death, then also this idea will no longer seem tenable to him in the light of the new experiences. For a personality that originated from and lives out of the anti-spirit of self-maintenance and is not an adequate expression of the spiritual kernel hidden in it cannot possibly endure eternally. It will be dissolved after death and a period of processing experiences in the beyond. The spiritual kernel that has not yet become conscious and active, however, will continue to live eternally. At a given time, it will connect with a new personality born on this side and thereby tie itself to the experiences of the previous personality that are stored in the totality of the microcosmic system of this human being.

So, the beginning pupil will acquaint himself with the idea of reincarnation—not in the sense that a mortal personality returns repeatedly in an ever improved condition, but that the immortal spiritual kernel ever again connects with a new personality whereby the harvest of experience of the previous personalities determine the structure and life of the newly "adopted" personality. The pupil will realize that this process of reincarnation could in principle continue endlessly as long as the personalities persist in self-maintenance. For then the spiritual kernel would never become conscious and active. Only when a personality gives up its self-maintenance can the spiritual kernel become conscious and active, transfigure the personality, and transform the latter to its means of expression. Then the process of reincarnation is at an end. For then its presupposition and necessity have fallen away. It is only necessary as long as the spiritual kernel is unconscious and latent. The human being then steps out of the "wheel of birth and death."

"Longing for Salvation"

The second state that the Rosicrucian pupil experiences on the path is that he orders his life anew. He draws consequences. The insight ascending from his heart about his place and task in the world leads to new actions. When the pupil recognizes that he is "born of God" and that his life should correspond to this fact, he will begin first to bring order into his life. He gradually becomes conscious of his goal in life, and therefore the obstacles to the goal also show themselves.

The Spiritual School of the Rosycross calls this inner state of the pupil "longing for salvation." If the pupil longs for "salvation," the life in the spirit, and acts in the sense of this longing, then, like the diseased and possessed in the account of the New Testament, he will be gradually healed of the illnesses and "demons" of his entanglements, conflicts, fears, and illusions and their consequences. A new order and freedom arise in him out of his new insights and longing for healing.

This phase of pupilship, this state of inner and outer cleansing, is characterized by "neutrality." The pupil withdraws from being ruled by sympathies and antipathies towards people and things. He recognizes how he is led and entangled by fears and hopes of all sorts—and no longer lets himself be led by them but only by the experience: The true self does not fear or expect anything. It quietly and with understanding withdraws from the entanglements in the world of self-maintenance. Through such a way of life, new forces from the world of the spirit come into circulation in the pupil and a new exchange of forces between him and his environment develops.

"Self-Surrender"

In the second phase of the path, the pupil was occupied with untying himself from the effects of self-maintenance, the entanglements in the world caused by hope and fear. Now, in the third phase, he logically focuses his attention on the cause of these entanglements, the self-maintenance within his own being. His I-centrality is the root of all his conflicts and entanglements. He proceeds to dissolve this root step-by-step. How is he able to do this?

This root comes into his consciousness through the recognition and the feeling that it is not his true being, and it gradually dies off like a root that has been dug out of the ground and is exposed to the light. Nowhere else than in this phase does it become clearer what the spiritual path is not. It is not concerned with the human being analyzing with his mind his "strengths" and "weaknesses" and then trying with his will to remove disagreeable character traits. It is an experience common to all human beings: One can recognize some "negative" character trait with one's mind and gain a certain distance to it. One can then also try to remove this trait and to replace it with a new behavior. But in the long run, this method will always fail. The "negative" trait is not removed thereby; yes, through the fight of the consciousness and will with it, it becomes only still stronger.

The realization of the pupil of a spiritual school is of another kind and another origin. It is in principle such that one state of soul is replaced by another state of soul. If the pupil is, for example, filled with criticism of others—a state born of self-maintenance and weakness—then gradually a state of inner strength of soul and of understanding of others can grow out of the unfolding spirit in him. This state takes the place of and dissolves the previous one, just like a cramp disappears when the energies in the muscle flow freely again.

Two aids stand by the pupil in this. The one is the Spiritual School's force field in which he stays. In this force field, the structures and characteristics of the true self of humanity are present and active like lines of force in a magnetic field that surrounds the pupil. They support the structures and characteristics of the pupil's own true self, and with this backdrop, he becomes conscious of his old self-maintenance.

The second indispensable aid to the pupil in this phase is pain. Once the pupil has experienced the new possibility of tranquility and power and the thereto-related freedom from unrest and weakness, and then when he, for example, once again exercises criticism that wounds, he will experience this state as highly unsatisfactory, yes, as painful. And this pain will weaken the old state, if the pupil quietly endures it. The ancients called this type of pain "repentance." This is not a feeling of guilt due to the violation of a rule. It is instead a deep regret over a situation that does not correspond to the true self of the human being.

All these occurrences can be summarized in the formula: "Those who lose their life for my sake [...] will save it."[74] This formula describes especially the process in the third phase of the path of the pupil. For this third phase is the actual phase of the reversal and the change in which the essence of the path of the pupil comes especially to expression: *their* life, that is, the life of self-maintenance and egocentricity, the common state of the human being. When someone loses this life consciously and voluntarily for the sake of the new state, the state of the soul born of the spirit, then the new state, the life out of the freedom, unity, and love of the spirit, becomes active. "For my sake" also means: in the forces of the spirit and with help of the forces of the spirit. Therefore, the Rosicrucians of the 17th century described this phase of the path with the words: "In Jesus we die"—*In Jesu morimur*. Whoever is born of God and in whom God is again active will "die" as to his old being in the forces of the spirit, which are represented by Jesus. The Spiritual School of the Rosycross calls this state of the third phase of the path "self-surrender."

"New Attitude of Life"

The next, fourth step on the path is the anchoring of the new possibilities of life in one's own being. And how could they be anchored differently and better than by the pupil learning to live ever more and more consciously out of the new forces and structures of the soul? This presupposes that he learns more and more to provide room for the new potentiality in the struggle between two forces and potentialities in his own being and to give less room for the old potentiality, recognizing it ever more, and suffering the pain of remorse. It is a question of endurance and of perseverance, of daily attentiveness and ever new decisions.

To live out of the new soul forces and structures means to act out of them. By so doing, they are recognized and strengthened and given the chance to be active as new thoughts, new feelings, and new will impulses thereby completely replacing the old state of the pupil. But what does it mean to live and act out of the soul forces? It means to work together with the structures and forces of the spirit without any self-maintenance—to live for other human beings! It is the state of "not-doing" as the ancient Chinese sages expressed it.

Five essential soul qualities gradually grow in a pupil of the 4th phase: tranquility arising from the harmony with the true self; compassion that knows at the same time what others have to carry and endure; knowledge of what is striving towards truth and freedom in other human beings and things, and what is working against this striving; constructive love that promotes truth and freedom on the basis of this understanding; and finally, joy that gives the activity of the pupil verve and dynamism.

When the old inhabitant of the "house" of the personality, self-maintenance, has moved out or "died" in the fourth phase of pupilship, a new inhabitant, the true self, moves in. The true self now changes the furnishings of the house and the house itself so that it becomes its expression and instrument. All character traits and abilities of the human being freed from self-maintenance are permeated by new forces. They become expressions of the spiritual formula that lies at the basis of the human being as law of development.

"Becoming Conscious"

In such a human being, the structure of the spiritual lines of force unfolding within him gradually becomes conscious. This is the state and the task of the fifth phase of the path.

The contents of this new consciousness differ radically from those of the old. After all, this consciousness is itself brought forth through the individual structure of spiritual lines of force of the human being, whereby it is capable of recognizing these. The thought of God, the human being that has come forth from God's thinking, becomes conscious of itself and experiences thereby that it is God's thinking that is active in him and that mediated this consciousness. In this sense Paul speaks of this: "... I will know fully, even as I have been fully known."[75]

Thus the pupil becomes conscious that he himself as individual intelligence, force, and love is embedded in and permeated by the divine spirit, God. Whoever wants to find a description of becoming united with the world of the spirit can read, for example, *Aurora* by Jacob Boehme.[76] The pupil will also learn in this phase to consciously transform what is experienced and to work with the new forces according to their inherent lawfulness. He now works with the creative spiritual lines of force that go through him (one of which he is himself) in such a way that he promotes everything in his environment and other human beings that belongs to the spirit. He acts in constructive love, which is nothing other than the activity of the spirit. "Reborn through the holy spirit"—*Per spiritum sanctum reviviscimus*—is what the classical Rosicrucians called this phase of the path.

What is learned and experienced on the fifth step at first in a groping way—independent, conscious experience of one's own spiritual being, profound understanding of the environment on the basis of this experience, and experience of the cosmic spiritual being, as well as acting out of these experiences—becomes deepened and enlarged upon on the sixth and seventh steps of the path. The pupil totally submerges in the streams of the spirit and streams out to the world and human beings, whereby a new personality develops according to thoughts, feelings, will, and even subtle materiality.

This path with its seven phases must not be understood to mean that the transition into the next phase always means the closing of the previous one. Every state is a task that remains until the end of the path. Every state has to be continuously enlivened so that the succeeding ones have a good foundation—as with a house whose stories are placed well on top of each other. The process of the first step, for example, the establishing of insight, continues in all the following steps and deepens ever more. Conversely, all experiences of the following steps can and do appear in the previous ones in a germinal form.

Catharose de Petri and Jan van Rijckenborgh once characterized the seven steps of the spiritual path as follows:
"1. the new knowledge, the birth of the new mind;
2. the conscious communion with the Lord, the development of the new mind by means of a new heart-radiation: thinking with the heart;
3. the budding of the new will-being, genesis of the new desire-body;
4. the new activities of head, heart and will give rise to a new life of action, the birth of the new etheric body;
5. birth of the new physical body;
6. union of the new personality with the Spirit-Soul;
7. union of the new personality with the divine spirit—the victory."[77]

Special Characteristics of the Path

The pupil on the spiritual path becomes aware of certain characteristics of this path.

Faith, Knowledge, and Deed

The pupil begins the path in faith and obtains his energy until the end always also from faith. But his faith is not the believing of a teaching or a dogma that he takes up from an authority. This would be a great leveling of this concept. He experiences faith as a motive power from the spiritual kernel becoming active in him noticeable as a longing for a new reality of life—a longing for salvation. He experiences this simultaneously as an openness to this new reality of life, as an inner certainty that this reality of life is his destiny and that of every human being, and that it will sometime also take shape in him. Faith is the experience of being "born of God."

From this state of openness to the goal of the path and the longing for it gradually arises knowledge. The pupil becomes conscious from within of the goal of the new life and the stages of the path thereto. He becomes conscious that as a spiritual being he is embedded in the world of the spirit. He becomes conscious of what obstacles stand in the way of the realization of the new life. He experiences in every moment of the day which action is necessary so that the life in him urging to come forth can grow. Thus he knows what it means "to die in Jesus."

Religious human beings are often distrustful of "knowledge." They stress faith in the truths of religion. The mind is not in a position to understand the "facts of salvation." But knowledge on the spiritual path is something different than mental deliberation. It is a becoming conscious of the true being and the spiritual world. If faith does not lead to knowledge, then the pupil is stagnating on the path.

From the knowledge of the world of the spirit and its forces follows further the application of these forces according to their inherent laws. From the knowledge of the obstacles that stand in the way of the unfolding of the new life in the pupil follows the dissolution of these obstacles. This means a complete change of the old I-central personality and the build-up of a new one, which acts in new ways: "reborn through the holy spirit." From knowledge follows the deed. And since the latter is nothing else than the turnover of the spiritual forces received, the pupil realizes through his deed the love of God in the world.

Faith lives in the nascent new heart of the pupil, knowledge in the nascent new head, and the deed is fed through the energies newly circulating in him.

Realization

The pupil on the spiritual path experiences that this path means independence. He does not get any further if he does not react independently to the impulses coming out of his own inner being. He will discover and overcome the human tendency to honor and to imitate others who go the path thereby withdrawing from his own task. If he identifies the goal that he has recognized with that of others—with saints, with a savior, with an institution—then he honors this goal in others and puts his forces in their service. He no longer needs to change himself. He identifies with the other who has already reached the goal.

Many who brought the spirit into the world and wanted to enflame others with it had to experience how the need of human beings to worship them as bringers of the spirit again extinguished that flame. People glorified them as human beings in whom the spirit had become alive and awaited deliverance from them. In their honor one celebrated feasts and erected beautiful buildings but did not let the spirit in one's own being come to life.

What is decisive on the spiritual path is that realization takes the place of worship. This does not exclude gratitude and respect towards the bringers of truth. But the pupil testifies of his gratitude in the best way by fulfilling the earnest wish of these truth bringers: that the truth is realized.

Objective Changes on the Spiritual Path

The subjective experiences on the spiritual path—premonitions, insights, longing for salvation, self-surrender, new way of life, new consciousness—are expressed in thoughts, feelings, and decisions, that is, psychic experiences. But every psychic experience also has its physical and physiological side. Perhaps they are altogether the same facts, only once seen from within, once from the outside.

On the spiritual path, the whole human being also changes bodily and physiologically. "The person who contemplates the path seriously and decides really to go it, changes physically, biologically and anatomically from that very moment on."[78] It is known from psychosomatics, for example, that to every emotion corresponds a hormonal state. When a new love of humanity with its corresponding hormonal functions becomes active in the human being, hormones corresponding to self-maintenance or fear cannot simultaneously circulate in the blood and trigger actions. In this respect the blood and its composition, the activity of the glands of internal secretion and of the hormones, as well as the composition of the nerve streams and their directions change on the spiritual path. The nerve streams correspond with the consciousness or with thinking.

Thus one can also describe the spiritual path from the outside, physiologically and anatomically, and the Spiritual School of the Rosycross does this to show that the path is not only a subjective factor without consequences for the material body but also an objective factor that changes all the substance of the body. There are three centers of decision in the human being: the head, above all as the seat of thinking and willing; the heart, above all as the seat of feelings and desires;

and the liver-spleen system—in general, the organs in the abdomen—as the seat of energies and drives and as the gate for karmic influences.

On the spiritual path, the spirit spark stirs in the human being and makes itself noticeable at first in the heart. "Usually some great shock in ordinary life causes the spirit-spark atom in the heart to start vibrating. Until this moment due to conduct and blood quality of the ordinary man, this atom had been so latent and enshrouded that it could not be awakened by the Light of the Divine Sun. When, however, as the result of bitter experience, a temporary collapse in life occurs, affecting even blood, then one of the seven heart ventricles is opened, the fire contained therein is ignited and a blinding light is radiated towards the thymus, a small organ located under the breastbone. If the thymus proves receptive... then the thymus hormone carries this light radiation into the lesser blood circulation. When this work has been completed, the light power will certainly in time touch all brain centres to which it is carried by the blood. Upon its arrival in the head-sanctuary, the person concerned will then, in the first instance, be born a seeker... Irresistibly, a whole series of thoughts are now developed."[79] Thus insight arises as the first phase of the path. Through the influence of the light force of the spirit, which is new consciousness, the pupil becomes conscious of the state of the world, his own state, and the new possibility of life out of the spirit.

Everything now depends on the heart being cleansed of the wishes and desires of self-maintenance. This happens thereby that the forces of the spirit become active as longing in the heart, as a new "desire," as the desire to become "whole." This desire, which gradually permeates the whole blood and changes the internal secretion, step-by-step replaces all other wishes and the hitherto existing activity of the internal secretion. This is the second phase of the path, and when the thinking in the head and the nerve streams of consciousness in the spinal marrow submit to the new forces in the heart, an ever greater freedom of thinking develops. Heart and head are referred to each other; one complements the other in the new efficacy of the spirit.

Once this unity between head and heart, the new hormonal activity in the blood, and the new nerve steams are somewhat stabilized and tranquility has entered in the being, then the process of cleansing and if necessary dissolution of the energies and impulses from the center of energy, the liver-spleen system, can begin where the root of self-maintenance is found. For there lives "the 'I', the blood-I, the earthly soul...This location is to be understood not merely in a figurative, but also in a literal sense. The liver, the spleen, the kidneys and the adrenal glands plus the solar plexus (the pelvic cerebral centre) form the realm of the blood-I, the desire-being."[80] Now "through this new circulation of entirely different ether-powers, of pure Christ ethers, the fortress of the 'I' is attacked; the 'I', the desire-being is driven from the pelvic centre and a new desire being, the embodiment of the great Craving for Salvation, is born."[81] Thus thinking becomes increasingly conscious of the impulses from the energy center. And supported by the longing for salvation of the heart, it learns to withdraw from the grip of these energies. In the measure that these energies are no longer used, they become weaker. The pupil has entered the third phase of the spiritual path. The old will is replaced step-by-step by a new one.

The direction of the physiological processes now reverses: As formerly the I-system had directed and subdued the heart and head in a self-maintaining way, so now the heart and head, embedded in the streams of the spiritual world, dominate and give tasks and direction to the energies of the body.

"Once the Divine light has been ignited in the head-sanctuary, we see a surge of power in the right strand of the sympathicus into the plexus sacralis at the base of the spine.... The stream of grace of the gnosis now fills the entire being and descends the tower of mysteries to the earthly chamber of the plexus sacralis.... There the stimulative field is connected to the revealing, reacting field. Now the steam must ascend to the meeting place in the head-sanctuary via this reactive field, i.e. the left strand of the sympathicus."[82]

When thus the new will impulses, born of the renewed heart and steered by the renewed head, stream through the nervous system next to the spinal column from above downwards and then again from below upwards, the so-called chakras (organs of the subtle bodies of the human being), which formerly were in the service of self-maintenance, gradually become servants of the new nerve streams and newly polarized. A new life of action is the result, mark of the fourth phase of the path.

Finally, there comes the point where the forces of the spirit also stream through and newly polarize the last chakra, connected with the pineal gland. Thereby thinking becomes free to take up the streams and forces from the spiritual world directly, not only via the heart, and to steer the actions of the human being out of the conscious knowledge of the laws of the spiritual world. The spiritual forces coming from the heart then stream through the whole spinal marrow with the seven chakras. In the fifth phase of the path, the human being consciously takes up the spiritual forces and uses them responsibly. His personality with the three centers of the head, heart, and liver-spleen system becomes a conscious, sterling instrument of the spiritual world. "A change of the body literally takes place.... We see, as it were, the miracle of the advent of a new personality within the old personality of nature and yet outside it."[83]

The law according to which the spiritual human being has appeared, the spiritual seed that lay near the heart, has unfolded in the whole personality through the heart and head thus transfiguring it. Its thinking, feeling, willing, and acting stand from now on in the service of the spiritual world, which corresponds to the sixth and seventh phases of the path. The biological functions that must still be simultaneously maintained continue to be monitored by the blood, the hormonal system, and the nerve streams without thereby detracting from the whole systems orientation to the spiritual world.

So, "we assert that the power of brotherly affection, which begins to prove itself in the pupil on the sixth step of the sevenfold path, is not a power that can be explained from this nature.... That which proves itself in the new magnetic cycle is 'God revealed in the flesh'.... This is brotherly affection: a new existential faculty actively radiating in the gnosis. The I does not stand behind all this; it is not the result of the decision: 'Now I must begin to show brotherly affection!'... Whoever possesses this faculty is in the service of man, existentially; he cannot stop for this faculty is; it surrounds him on all sides."[84]

"The brother and sister of the seventh step possess a glorified new total personality including a physical bodily form." They live out of "the love which is called God, Spirit and Light. And now you will understand as Paul understood:

if you had everything and had not that love, that new state of being, you would have and be nothing. For this love which is God, this eagle's flight of the spirit, is the ultimate goal, the great and wonderful goal for all who in this epoch are called to the light."[85]

The outcome of these descriptions is that the way of transfiguration differs in principle from some ancient, especially eastern paths of initiation. First of all, the pupil does not work towards awakening the energies of the abdomen, the so-called "kundalini," drawing them up the spinal marrow and letting them conquer heart and head. For this would mean that he could become the victim of not only the biological energies of this world but also of the karmic energies. Heart and head would then not be oriented to the streams of the spiritual world and therefore also not filled by the forces of the spiritual world, which alone could become master over the biological and karmic forces. The human being would only have the usual forces of feeling and thinking at his disposal, perhaps strengthened by moral barriers. But these would altogether not be equal to the assault of the powers of the kundalini and would uncontrollably be flooded by them. "When the unbridled will has ignited the plexus sacralis with unholy fire, that which is unholy cannot be sanctified or spiritualized. At best it can be subdued for some time, until at a specific moment it bursts out, in one way or another, like a devastating fire."[86]

In the way of transfiguration on the other hand, the pupil always takes the spirit spark, the representative of the true self in the heart, as his starting point and takes up the forces of the spiritual world through this entry gate. They enter over his heart into the system of the personality and renew first the heart and head in order to then also bring energies of the will and karma under their dominion. "Thus, the new will is the fire, the creative power according to the spirit, and that fire can only produce liberating and really creative work providing it conforms to the head and the heart in their new state."[87] Thereby freedom, consciousness, and responsibility are always guaranteed. In the end of this process, the pupil lives with his true self in the streams of the spiritual world, this being the destiny of the human being. An awakening of the kundalini not out of the true self and its forces, on the other hand, even if the human being would be able to dominate the karmic forces, would mean that he would dissolve in the streams of the subtle-material worlds to which karma belongs. And this is not the inherent aim of the human being.

Inner Structure of the Spiritual School of the Rosycross

The path of a pupil of a spiritual school is carried out in a succession of seven "steps" or psychic and physical states that are logically and organically built on each other. But the way each individual pupil goes this path is also the way the Spiritual School of the Rosycross in its totality has gone. For at first it consisted of human beings in whom only a presentiment of a more essential humanity had awakened. These pupils then lived through the phases of the path that follow each other under the instruction of the founders of the School—who in their turn went the transfiguristic path.

One can compare the Spiritual School according to its structure with a step-pyramid: The basis is the membership; the first step the so-called preparatory pupilship; the second the so-called professing pupilship, which is preceded by the so-called probationary pupilship. These first two steps form the "outer school." The "inner school," the actual mystery school, begins with the third step. For with the third step begins the actual change of the old personality and its replacement by a new personality living out of new forces of spirit and soul.

Relationship of the stages to each other

Every step has not only significance for itself but also for all other steps. Every state follows logically the previous one. Thus, no state can and may therefore be skipped. So the lower step always has an important significance for the next-higher one—as its prerequisite and enabler.

But also the reverse is the case: Every higher step has significance for the next-lower one. The powers for the process of change in the pupil stem not only out of his own being—the more or less latent spiritual principle in him—but also out of the field of the spirit itself. The powers from the cosmic spiritual field stream downwards from above, from the seventh step, through all steps, stimulate the individual spiritual forces of the pupil on his respective step, and support him in his development. Thereby they adapt according to intensity and content to the state of the pupil on every step, otherwise he could neither receive them nor get any use out of them. On the next higher step, the spiritual forces stimulate the pupil, pull him upward, and give him the power to climb higher. Thus, the striving of the pupil from below meets the help from above on every step in a characteristic way.

Christian-Rosycross Temple in Calw in the south German working field

The Work of the Spiritual School of the Golden Rosycross

> *The question may be asked: but what then* is *the task and work of the Spiritual School in the new era?...The Brotherhood of the Rosycross will, in the years to come,* demonstrate *a certain truth through itself....All of mankind claiming to be spiritual and intellectual is engaged in arguing about what is 'truth' and what is 'untruth'. Now, if we are correct in our contention that the vast majority of mankind is no longer able to differentiate between truth and untruth, then what would be the use of exerting ourselves to the utmost to confront mankind anew with the Rosycross truth?*
>
> *This is the reason why the Spiritual School has instituted no new truth organization; it will not go in for any debate on the truth, but through the results of its labor, it will demonstrate the Power out of which it exists and works. The Spiritual School of the Rosycross is engaged in calling into being a factual situation.... This will make it possible for everyone to gain a clear insight into the state of world and mankind in our present order of existence and, with the factual existence of the new man in view, to determine whether he will be for or against the Light.*
> (Jan van Rijckenborgh, *Dei Gloria Intacta*)

Three Helping Factors

Through what means or factors does the Spiritual School of the Rosycross contribute concretely to the development of its pupils on the sevenfold spiritual path? For this is after all its actual task and justification for existence: to show human beings the path to the unfolding of the true self and to be helpful to their going of this path. The factors that are active in the Spiritual School to enable this to occur are the forces liberated by the founders, the teaching, and the group.

The Founders of the Spiritual School

Help for a human being who wants to unfold his true self—or better: whose true self wants to unfold—can only be given by a human being whose true self is already more or less active. An unfolded state stimulates a not-yet unfolded state. One could speak of a kind of "infection" or also "induction." State acts on state—as far as receptivity is present.

The founders of a spiritual school provide an environment for the true self in which it can unfold and out of which it can draw forces for its development—a soul-spiritual "power field." It represents the structures of the spiritual world and its forces to which the structure and energy of the true self of the pupils corresponds.

Without such human beings, the pupil would be standing before an insoluble task unless the true self in him had already reached a high step of development. In general, the true self is still in an embryonic state and needs a "mother field" for development until after it has been born and then grown-up, it can independently take up the forces from the cosmic spiritual field.

Catharose de Petri (1902–1990), founder of the Spiritual School with the Leene brothers

Jan van Rijckenborgh (1896–1968), brother of Zwier Willem Leene, one of the founders of the Spiritual School

Regarding the self-maintenance of the personality, which is the decisive obstacle for the unfolding of the true self: It cannot dissolve itself. A block of ice cannot melt itself. It must reach an environment that is warmer than itself: Energy must be supplied to it. If one places it in warm water, then it dissolves its hard structures and takes on again the soft "structures" of the water and its higher state of energy. In this sense, the spiritual state of the founder or founders of a school that manifests in a "power field" is a decisive factor without which every development of a pupil would be impossible.

The Teaching

But how does the state of the developed human being act on the state of the undeveloped human being? Does it happen by suggestion, by intentional "magical" influence of which the pupil is not conscious?

This would be against the principle of freedom, which is a basic principle of every spiritual school. No responsible human being with a true self that has become conscious, with spiritual powers, and with a new personality structure will influence other human beings "magically" in the usual meaning of the word. He works rather via the spoken and written word, via symbols or rituals, that is, via a "teaching" that can be consciously taken up and applied by his pupils.

When a human being who is filled with spiritual forces and living out of spiritual lawfulness speaks, then he expresses thoughts, feelings, and energies that correspond to the level of the spiritual world. With thoughts, feelings, and energies with which his words are "charged," he turns to the conscious personality of his listeners. These have complete freedom to discuss, take up, or reject them. If the pupil takes them up, then they touch the true self latent in him via his consciousness. This self is stimulated and fed by the power and structure contained in the words. Thus, the true self of the pupil gradually steps into his consciousness. He "remembers" again the truth that was hidden and buried in him. By means of the word (or appropriate symbols and rituals) the unfolded spiritual state of the speaker comes to expression and touches via the consciousness of the listener his not unfolded spiritual state, stimulates it, feeds it, and enlivens it.

The "teaching" in the broader sense appears in three forms: first, as spoken, written, and sung word; second, as symbol or ritual; and third, as sacrament. In each of these forms, it can refer to three aspects: the aspect of the connection to the spiritual world, the aspect of the experience of the spiritual world, and the aspect of the realization of the impulses from the spiritual world.

An example from the world of symbols, the "logo" of the Spiritual School of the Rosycross, should clarify this: the circle in which a triangle and a square are inscribed.

Connection to the Spiritual World

The circle, symbol for infinity and eternity, for the supernature, describes the aspect of the connection to the spiritual world. It reminds the pupil that eternity is anchored in his own being as the spirit spark. He is connected with eternity through the spirit spark; he can begin with his spiritual path on the basis of the spirit spark. The principle of eternity in him makes the path possible for him. The circle makes the pupil conscious of the connection to the spiritual world and strengthens him for going the path.

Experience of the Spiritual World

All words, symbols, and sacraments that explain the structure and power of the spiritual world, the present condition of world and humanity, and represent the path that leads to the destiny of the human being refer to the aspect of experience of the spiritual world. When such themes are elucidated in an address or when the pupil sees corresponding symbols, he remembers the formerly buried truths whereby they become active forces in him.

The triangle in the logo of the Spiritual School is the symbol for the three universal powers of the spirit that touch the human being in his three centers of consciousness: head, heart, and energy center. They correspond in Christian terminology to "Father," "Son," and "Holy Spirit." In these three centers of consciousness, the pupil experiences the forces of the spiritual world. In the heart, he experiences the certainty that he is called to eternity and opens himself to these forces. In the head, they are active as inspirations guiding his life, and they gradually permeate his whole life and fashion it anew. When he sees the logo and especially reflects on the triangle, then he becomes conscious of which forces are to be taken up and applied by him in the course of the path.

The triangle moreover corresponds to a formula that is often placed before the consciousness of the pupil in the Spiritual School of the Rosycross: "Unity, freedom, love." In the heart grows the unity with the spirit whereby also arises the unity with all other human beings living out of the spirit. Striving for self-importance, pride, turning away from the spirit, and the resulting separation from other human beings gradually disappear. In the head grows the freedom of an independent thinking drawing out of the spirit. A human being resting in the spirit and its laws will be free of expecting things from other human beings. He can release them out of the prison of his expectations of them and does not need to dominate them. He increasingly loses his striving for power. And in the whole being gradually arises a new activity, a spontaneous streaming of the spiritual forces out to others on the basis of unity with the spirit and knowledge of its laws: This is the new love that replaces every self-centered seeking and possessive longing. As these three principles work in the individual pupil, so they also work in the community of pupils when many pupils realize them. When this formula is pronounced and penetrates via the consciousness of the pupil to the "ear" of his true self, then the latter feels the incentive and the power to realize unity, freedom, and love.

Realization of the Spiritual World

The third aspect of the "teaching," the realization of the impulses from the spiritual world, is likewise enlivened through addresses and symbols, texts, rites, and sacraments. Here the Spiritual School works above all with impressionable, short formulas that repeatedly place the pupil before the steps that are coming up on the path and the problems he must especially watch out for. Thereby it continues in the tradition of all mystery schools and original religions. One can think, for example, of the "Golden Verses" of Pythagoras or also of the Sermon on the Mount in the Gospel of Matthew, which is nothing else than a description of the steps of the spiritual path (the "Beatitudes") and the requirements and rules of life on this path that can be realized on the basis of spiritual forces.

This third aspect of the "teaching," the realization of the impulses of the spirit, is symbolized by the square in the logo of the Spiritual School. When the pupil sees it, then he feels called on the basis of the touch by the spirit and the experience of its forces to work on his fourfold personality. He again becomes a temple through which the spirit can be active. The square refers to the realization of the spiritual path in the four bodies of the personality. It is the freemasonic "square of construction" or "square of the carpet" on which the pupil stands. He firstly directs his mental body, his thinking, unequivocally to the spiritual world and receives his thoughts out of it. Thereby he can secondly be "without conflict." His feelings, his astral body, are no longer determined by likes and dislikes, which always create conflicts, but by compassion, love, and neutrality amidst the opposites. If he becomes free from conflicts in this way, then thirdly his life energies, his etheric body, will newly organize themselves. In a harmonious interchange between receiving and spreading spiritual forces, his energy economy comes into order on a new level, and he can perceive his spiritual and worldly tasks. Thereby he comes to act, fourthly, not for himself but for others, in unity with the spiritual world. With reference to his life in the community of pupils, this means "group unity": responsibility for the others, doing for the others, as the fourth side of the "square of construction"—the material body.

Thus, it is perhaps evident how the "teaching" acts out of the power field on the consciousness of the pupil and via the consciousness on his true self. The power field of the living body contains all the structures of the unfolding true self and the spiritual path. They surround the pupil as lines of force. The collaborators working out of this power field and the symbols consciously experienced by the pupil activate and enliven these structures. The true self of the pupil feels thereby how its own structures are stimulated and fed.

Outer Rules of Conduct

The indications for a new behavior by the pupil toward his fellow human beings in his private and professional life are also part of the realizable aspect of the "teaching." Such behavior occurs spontaneously when the pupil begins to live more and more consciously out of the impulses of the spirit spark. These indications also encompass rules that relate to the body, specifically nutrition. The pupil of the Spiritual School of the Rosycross follows an ovo-lacto-vegetarian diet. Firstly, he does not want to be the cause for which highly organized living beings are killed. For every killing of an animal kills something in the soul of the killer—indirectly also in the souls of those who cause this killing—and binds him to what was killed. Secondly, the pupil knows that his material being, on which his consciousness, his thoughts, and his feelings are to a certain degree dependent, must be nourished in such a way that the spiritual impulses are not unnecessarily obstructed. And certainly the constitution of the material body does not become purer through the ingestion of animal flesh and blood in which are still contained in hormonal form the feelings of the animal while being slaughtered. There is protein-rich vegetarian food that can amply replace the nutrient value of meat.

The pupil likewise abstains from smoking, alcohol, narcotics, and tranquilizers of every form. The stimulants and depressants contained in them change the organs of the brain in which consciousness and perception are localized and partly open these organs to uncontrolled influences from the reflection sphere. These delicate organs of consciousness are to become receptive to the impulses from the world of the spirit. When the pupil directs himself to the impulses of the spiritual nucleus, they create changed organs of consciousness for themselves that can perceive and react to the spirit. But if they are opened from the outside through a forced development, they can be damaged, or intruding influences from the reflection sphere can displace and block the impulses from the spiritual world.

The pupil will also develop a special watchfulness in the face of the influences from the modern mass media and advertising that try to mobilize drives, desires, and illusions via the unconscious. The pupil experiences inwardly that all this increases the egocentricity of which he wants to be freed after all. He will inform himself, but not allow himself to be influenced against his will and the spiritual goals he has set for himself.

Such a way of life becomes binding for the pupil only in the second phase of the path after he has independently gained insight in the first phase of the path into the meaning, yes, the necessity of this behavior on the spiritual path. He then notices on the basis of new experiences or perhaps due to alert inner tranquility and clarity how meat consumption, smoking, alcohol, etc. can again rob him of this awakened state of being.

The Teaching as Power

Through his experiences with the three aspects of the teaching, the pupil will gradually learn what this teaching actually is. As a representation and vivification of the lawfulness of the spiritual world, it is in the first place not a system of concepts that the intellect is to acquire and especially not a system of dogma to which the feelings could faithfully cling. Stimulated by description and vivification, the pupil experiences independently the power and structure of the spiritual world and the corresponding soul world.

With this understanding, there can be no quarrel over the truth of dogmas or hypotheses. There are only more or less comprehensive experiences in the world of the spirit, and as experiences they are true even though those of one pupil may differ from those of another. The pupils only experience different aspects of one and the same reality.

In the same way, in so far as it relates to the realization of the spiritual impulses, the teaching is not primarily a system of moral instruction or ethics. Of course, the pupil will attune his outer behavior as best he can to the given rules. But this practice is only a help, not an end in itself. History has always shown that such a practice that has become an end in itself only leads to self-righteousness, fanaticism, and inflexibility. The pupil gradually recognizes instead that the outer ethical-moral behavior is only a necessary condition for the unfolding of the true self but not a sufficient condition. No matter how hard he strives to meet the outer rules and to be a "good pupil," he cannot force his true self to unfold. Only when he recognizes that the outer rules are only supporting measures and derive their authority from this, only when he is prepared to let go of the hope and the belief that alone by fulfilling these rules his true self will be freed, does he give the true self the chance to unfold spontaneously. It unfolds freely according to its inherent laws and then uses the pupil's outer way of life in order to express itself.

Sacraments

Besides the words and the symbols, the sacraments are one aspect of the teaching in a wider sense. The Spiritual School of the Rosycross has several sacraments, among them baptism and the marriage sacrament. Sacraments are outer, visible actions through which a pupil is linked with certain aspects of the power field of the School, that is, with certain forces from the spiritual world. The soul-spiritual occurrences in the pupil are decisive thereby. The outer ritual is only the visible confirmation and thereby strengthening of these occurrences.

The Group

Beside the power field maintained by the founders of the School and the universal teaching, the third great means of help on the spiritual path is the group. The power of the founders, which is taken up via the power field by the coworkers and pupils, and the teaching, which in its three aspects stimulates the true self of the pupils, is enormously strengthened by the group. The pupils of the Spiritual School of the Rosycross constantly stimulate each other through: conversations about the teaching, the orientation to ideals, the help to pupils wrestling with themselves, the common growing new insights and common growing self-realization, the longing for new experiences, and through the communal organizational work in the service of the Spiritual School. Thereby they will very much value letting every fellow-pupil make his own experiences and exerting no social pressure on him, for this would not be a stimulation of the true self, which cannot live other than freely.

Temple Services

The events in the Spiritual School of the Rosycross in which all three "means of help" of the Spiritual School become active in a special way and strengthen each other are the so-called temple services. A temple service consists of a spoken "ritual," generally given by a woman; of an address, generally given by a man; and of music and songs. The ritual speaks to the heart and feelings of the listener. It mostly contains quotes from the universal doctrine, the holy scriptures of all times, and works above all through pictures, symbols, and poetry. The address deals in a more philosophical-conceptual form with an aspect of the universal doctrine and directs itself primarily to the intellect, the head of the human being. The music is attuned to the ritual and the address and supports both.

Themes

The themes of the temple services are many, as manifold as the universal doctrine itself: the structure of the spiritual world, its forces and its unfolding; humanity and the human being as a spiritual being embedded in this spiritual world and developing with it; the present state of world and humanity, its separation from the spiritual world; the path on which this separation can be removed and on which the true self, which is one with the spiritual world, can become conscious and active again; the efforts on the part of the spiritual world to reach human beings in the world separated from the spiritual world via sent ones, who explain humanity's destiny to human beings and who make the path to fulfill this destiny possible. All these aspects of the universal doctrine can appear in the most varied symbols depending on the religion, culture, and people in which they were once articulated, and thus they are presented in the temple services in ever different facets and pictures: be they symbols of Taoism, of Hinduism and Buddhism, of Greek philosophy, of the Gnostic mystery schools, of the medieval mystics, of the Christian Bible, or of the classical and modern Rosicrucians. But all this is not to cultivate the mind or to convey knowledge, rather because in these symbols from all periods of human history, experiences of the human being with the spiritual world come to expression.

These experiences can be revivified through the word and thereby become the means to remind the true self of the listener of these experiences. The true self of the listener recognizes thereby his connection in the spirit with all human beings and through all time periods and is glad of this universality.

Symbols

In addition to the spoken word and the music, the influence of the state of the speaker on the state of the listener also occurs through visible symbols, be they pictures and signs, be they, to a limited extent, ritual actions. The temple that the pupils occupy during a temple service is in itself such a symbol. It reminds the pupil that his own personality is a "temple" in which the spirit, the true self, cannot really live at the moment. The old "temple" has to be torn down, therefore, and replaced by a new, worthy home for the spirit. Like Jesus, every pupil tears down his old temple "in three days" (they correspond to the three great phases of development on the path: connection with the spiritual world = faith, experience of the spiritual world = knowledge, and realization of the spiritual world = deed) and builds a new one in three days: a transfigured personality, a "spirit body."[88] The Spiritual School of the Rosycross connects thereby to Christian symbolism, but also to the freemasonic symbolism of the legend of Hiram Abiff at the basis of which lies the building of the Temple of Solomon. The pupil builds not only on his own new "temple," but he is a "stone" in the great new temple of humanity, which must be erected on the principles of truth, goodness, and beauty.

In the center of every large temple of the Spiritual School of the Rosycross, there is a fountain with a rose. It symbolizes the living water rising in the heart of the microcosm. Seven steps—a recollection of the seven steps of the path—lead from there to the so-called "place of service," a podium from where the rituals and addresses are given. At some distance from this podium stands a seven-branched candelabrum. It reminds one that a sevenfold new consciousness in which the "seven spirit" expresses itself must light up in every pupil. On the other side of the podium stands an altar table with an open Bible. For the all-creating and sustaining divine "word," the structure of force lines of the spiritual world, is waiting to be "read" and "declaimed," that is, to become active and conscious in the human being. On the front wall behind the place of service above the candelabrum is the staff of Hermes provided with two wings at the top and entwined by two serpents that show, seen cosmologically, the path that the development of humanity has taken and will take in the course of the involution and evolution of the spirit. Seen anthropologically, the staff is a picture for the spinal system of the human being in which the fire of consciousness circulates. It must be renewed in the course of the development of the individual and of humanity. Seen cosmologically, the Rosycross that hangs above the altar on the other side of the front wall refers to the special task and place of the Spiritual School of the Rosycross in this development of humanity. Seen anthropologically, it symbolizes the Christian path of initiation.

Thus the pupil in the temple is surrounded by symbols that mirror the structure of his microcosm, his spiritual path, and the spiritual path of humanity. If he knows the meaning of these symbols, then they make him conscious of his state, his task, and his goal in the framework of the development of humanity.

Every temple service is a truly divine service. It is not concerned with the edification of the personality and mystic emotionalism. It is much more concerned with building, through the transformation of divine forces, the new temple of a transfigured personality in which the true self serves God. It serves God by unfolding as the image of God as which it was created. It serves God by liberating the forces of God for others. For all forces being liberated in a temple service benefit not only the pupils but, because of the unity of all of humanity, all human beings receptive to them.

Conferences

The most intensive form of group experience is the so-called conferences: weekend gatherings of many pupils. In the course of two days, the forces from the new life field are liberated in a series of temple services and strengthened through the communal experience. At such conferences, the pupils as much as possible leave behind all the worries and desires that occupy them at home. The activities beside the temple services: common meals, common periods of rest, conversations, and going for walks, are all directed to the reception, the preparation, and the passing-on of the spiritual forces. No disturbing influence through newspapers, radios, and television interferes. The pupil can come to inner silence, which is the prerequisite for the reception, processing, and passing on of the spiritual forces and will also seek the corresponding outer silence that supports and is the expression of the inner one.

Secrecy?

Every interested person can freely inform himself of the goals and working methods of the Spiritual School of the Rosycross and participate in open events. The whole literature of the Spiritual School is at his disposal. And since according to a motto of the classical Rosicrucians, "one has to start with gold to reach gold," the interested person can be sure that already in the literature and the open presentations of the School, he learns principally everything about the goal, teaching, manner of working, and characteristics of the spiritual path. The nucleus of the spirit and the School is mirrored also in its outermost shells. What can be told and conveyed to an interested person is told and conveyed. What he can only experience himself, he has to experience himself. But everyone who decides on this path after freely informing himself of the requirements and goal is invited to go this way freely and to have the corresponding experiences.

To certain events, however, only pupils are admitted. For the spiritual path brings a change in the nature of the human being. He goes through a succession of special psychic and spiritual states that develop out of each other. Whoever does not go this path does not go through these states. Thus, the power field of the Spiritual School of the Rosycross differs in structure and vibration from the power field of the usual life in society. The pupil gatherings of the Lectorium Rosicrucianum represent a spiritual power field and serve the unfolding of the true self of the pupil. A participant in whom the spiritual forces are not yet stimulated or active would lastingly disturb this process—like a magnet that comes into a field of many otherwise directed magnets.

The Spiritual School of the Rosycross would like nothing better than if its goal would be known to everyone and everyone would decide to go the path that leads to this goal. The School would also like nothing better than if everyone would gain the experiences that its pupils do. For in every human being lies the goal of the unfolding of the true self.

No Exercises

The path of the pupil of the Spiritual School of the Rosycross does not include any exercises and techniques of a mental, psychic, and physical nature. This may surprise the outsider after all that he has perhaps heard about esoteric communities and their methods. But this conscious abstinence from exercises and techniques is explicable, yes, logical and necessary if one considers the presuppositions of the work of the Spiritual School of the Rosycross and the character of the liberating path that it goes.

What happens on the path? On the one hand, a gradual growth and through this a becoming conscious of the true self; on the other, a dismantling of egocentricity and of egocentric ties to the world and human beings. And this growth occurs in a power field nourished from the spiritual world.

It is necessary that the true self is supplied with nourishment and energy on the spiritual path. Many esoteric groups therefore have the view that one would have to obtain these energies, for example, through meditation on specific mantras or breathing techniques. But in the Spiritual School of the Rosycross, these energies are available to every pupil through the continuously present power field that is regularly vivified in the temple services. No special techniques are needed to obtain them. With this, there is also still the question of whether the spirit can really be compelled hither by such methods. The spirit blows where it will, and intentional efforts to "procure" it will shut it out. One will only attract energies and forces from the subtle worlds of the beyond through such efforts.

It is further a question of whether inner growth can be accelerated through methods. The true self has its own rhythm of growth and grows in the forces of the spirit that are placed at its disposal in the power field of the Spiritual School. Every forcing of this process would only hinder it. "Meditation" is for the pupil of the Spiritual School of the Rosycross the spontaneous result of the connection of his true self with the world of the spirit. This connection is always present in principle, if he opens himself to the spirit in "longing" for the spirit and lets the true self grow through his soul work on the spiritual path. The forces of the spirit working in the pupil become more active and conscious when he moves them through thoughts and feelings. They clear and cleanse his thinking and feeling life and show him what is to be done. This "meditation"—a spontaneous but conscious movement in thoughts and feelings of the spiritual forces arising from the heart—can be stimulated by reading sacred scriptures and through the above-mentioned formulas that describe the path and its realization. It is also regularly induced through the temple services.

On the other hand, how does the pupil on the spiritual path become conscious of his egocentricity and the corresponding ties to human beings and situations and how does he overcome them? The decisive prerequisite is that the true self in the pupil makes itself noticeable in the form of the longing for the spirit. With this background he can recognize his egocentricity and then also dissolve it actively—or by conscious forbearance—in the forces of the spirit.

The Spiritual School of the Rosycross also has the view that outer silence can promote this becoming conscious. Inner silence, however, is the necessary prerequisite for this. But an inner silence produced through meditative exercises will not be a spontaneously grown silence. In the pupil of the Spiritual School of the Rosycross, the inner silence arises again and again spontaneously through the activity of the spiritual forces in him that are strengthened by the power field of the School. This can occur in meditative seclusion but also in violent outer unrest. Thus the pupil can always become conscious of his egocentricity, be it in outer silence or be it in outer unrest.

After the recognition of egocentricity, the practical letting-go of egocentricity and overcoming it is best learned and practiced in daily life. The pupil is confronted with the reality of his being in daily life. The reactions of the outer world towards him and his reactions to the outer world show him clearly enough where he still lives egocentrically. The pupil must prove himself in daily life supported by the spiritual forces active in him. If he only lets go of his ego in the thought realm and meditatively, then there would be the danger that the ties would still be maintained and at most repressed.

Prayer

The pupil of the Spiritual School of the Rosycross also examines the various kinds of prayer very carefully. A prayer going out from the ego and its interests that intends to connect the human being with the spiritual world will necessarily miss its goal. Egocentricity is behind it after all. Should it be possible that God, the invisible spirit, would let itself be harnessed for egocentric interests of the human being, be they directed to one's own life, be they directed to the life of others? A prayer that connects the human being with the spirit has to go out from the spirit in the human being, from the true self. "God is spirit, and those who worship him must worship in spirit and truth," it says in the Gospel of John.[89]

Thus, a prayer that stimulates the spiritual forces of the true self in the human being and connects them with the cosmic spiritual forces can only go out from the true self of the human being—taking for granted that the egocentric being is silent. Such a prayer can only have the goal that the world of the spirit is to become active in the human being and in humanity. The first three requests of the Lord's Prayer refer to this goal.

The prerequisite for this is again that all egocentricity that stands in the way of the working of the spirit disappears. Therefore, a prayer going out from the spirit in the human being also includes the request that all egocentric ideas, desires, and ideals may disappear. The four last requests of the Lord's Prayer give expression to the different aspects of this great request.

But if such a prayer is to be meaningful, then it may not just occur within the human being. The human being must also act in accordance with it in the outer world. If he does not let go of his egocentric ties in daily life, if he does not always place the impulses from the spirit spark, the true self, in the foreground, then all reflection will be of little help to him. For this reason, the practice of the spiritual path is the real prayer of the pupil of a spiritual school.

Jan-van-Rijckenborgh Temple in Bad Münder and accommodation building in the north German working field

The Structure of the Spiritual School

> *Such a hierarchical body is not an order of administrations, but a well prepared organism formed out of the being of the Gnosis, with the help of which the great holy work can be accomplished. Such a gnostic living body contains the elements of all the gnostic mysteries, the characteristics of a Spiritual school.*
> (Jan van Rijckenborgh, *The Gnosis in Present-Day Manifestation*)

The basic composition of the Spiritual School of the Rosycross, its goal, its structure, and its methods were established by the founders in accordance with the structure of the spiritual field that had became manifest in the founders. From this structure followed the outer step-wise structure of the Spiritual School corresponding to the inner steps that follow each other on the spiritual path.

At the head of the Spiritual School are presently thirteen persons who form the Spiritual Directorate. In the various work fields, there are National Directorates with the task of coordinating the work within their region. The next-smaller organizational entities are the large-city Centers. In these Centers are held public lectures and introductory courses on the universal doctrine, as well as communal events for the pupils living in the surrounding area.

Entry into the Lectorium Rosicrucianum

Pupilship

How does an interested person become a pupil of the Spiritual School of the Rosycross? Every interested person can attend the public lectures of the Lectorium Rosicrucianum, public temple services, and an orientation course in the philosophy of the Rosycross. Rosicrucian literature including the magazine of the Spiritual School, the *Pentagram*, is also available for study. In this way, he will notice if an echo of the teachings and the force of the Spiritual School resounds in him. Especially in the orientation course, he will be able to test if the path shown by the Spiritual School could also be his path. In this course, the main points of the universal doctrine, the goal, structure, and work of the Spiritual School are presented by pupils in the form of short lectures followed by discussion. The course usually runs about 12–13 evenings, one per week. In this way, the interested person can in complete freedom get a picture of the School and its teaching. The course can also be taken by mail.

If the interested person has taken the introductory course and meets certain elementary requirements, then he can request membership. After about six months of membership and having attended some conferences, he can request pupilship. If there are no serious obstacles in the way of the realization of pupilship, he will be received in the School. This reception is a free tie between the new pupil and the Spiritual School. "The School of the Rosycross is prepared to make contact with all those who are interested on a free, democratic basis."[90] It offers him a field in which he can freely unfold his true self. The Spiritual School and its coworkers make no judgment of the kind of connection between the pupil and the world of the spirit. This is a matter entirely between the pupil and the truth and power as represented to him in the form of the universal doctrine.

After the introductory course, if the interested person is considering membership and perhaps eventual pupilship, he is offered the possibility to more closely examine this decision. Over a period of several months, he can participate in some events for members and pupils, especially conferences, in order to more intensively investigate how he reacts inwardly to the work and the power field of the School. Once he has definitively made a positive decision, he can become a member and after about six months a preparatory pupil, which generally lasts about a year and a half. During this time, the pupil further orients himself in the power field and in the teachings of the Spiritual School. He consciously works on the spiritual, inner task that is typical for the first phase of the path of the pupil, for the beginning state of the pupil: to gain insight into his present state and the spiritual goal to which he is on the way.

After the period of preparatory pupilship, provided he has used the possibilities offered to him, he is invited by the School to go further and to occupy himself intensively with the task of the second phase of pupilship, that is, to consciously continue with the inner process of change. He now recognizes that as a consequence of the spiritual goal, a certain way of life follows. The above-mentioned modes of behavior, among them vegetarianism and abstinence from smoking and alcohol, become obligatory for him. If in the first phase of the path, a state of receptivity for spiritual forces has developed in the pupil, then he will recognize these outer consequences as necessary and be able to accept them as a free decision without any great problems. "When the relationship between the School of the Rosycross and the interested person develops on this basis there is no question of authority or mindless docility. There is an inner recognition, a conscious following of a path, authenticated within one's own self."[91] Continuing in this manner, new inner understanding and forces come to the pupil from the world of the spirit, allowing a new consciousness and new psychic states to grow in him corresponding to succeeding steps of pupilship.

Withdrawal

Every pupil also has the freedom on every step of the path to immediately leave the Spiritual School of the Rosycross without complications. No obstacle is placed in his way in this regard.

Membership

Attached to the actual community of pupils, the Lectorium Rosicrucianum, is a circle of members and the "youth work." The circle of members consists of people who after attending the introductory course want to have a loose connection with the Spiritual School. They may do this without taking the spiritual path of the pupil with the consequences and processes of change that go with it. The Spiritual School of the Rosycross sometimes offers to members of this circle special lectures, written material, conversational opportunities, temple services, and conferences.

The members of this circle are seekers who are touched and attracted by the power field of the School and have opened themselves to the truth of the spirit. Some may want to gain more certainty that the path of the Spiritual School of the Rosycross is also their path before they definitively begin with pupilship. They may also want to further orientate themselves in the power field and learn about the power field of the School in order to achieve a firm inner foundation for the path. Others may prefer to remain in this circle for an indefinite time. Every member can become a pupil at any time after six months of membership and provided the corresponding prerequisites are met.

Countless human beings today feel that traditional religious and esoteric teachings and communities no longer give them satisfactory answers to their existential questions, and so they seek a new orientation to life. In this circle of members, they can find a philosophy of life satisfying to mind and heart.

The Youth Work

The youth work of the Lectorium Rosicrucianum has the task of holding open the possibility for children to go the spiritual path. This applies to children of pupils and members or of sympathizers. The youth work tries to transmit to the children an objective view of the given facts of the world and the human being and to offer them an atmosphere in which the deepest needs of their soul can be met. Thereby the children themselves can develop an inner yardstick in order to recognize what inner and outer factors correspond to their true being and what could obscure or obstruct this being.

"Noverosa" (new rose). Temple of the youthwork in Doornspijk, the Netherlands

Of course, the children in the youth work do not yet go a spiritual path. Such a path would presuppose independence and a developed mind, which is why a youth may only request membership and pupilship starting at age 18 after taking the orientation course. Children first have the task to develop their earthly personality, to unfold and develop their talents, to struggle with their immediate and more distant environment, and to gradually find their identity as an earthly personality. But they also have the task of embedding this identity in a more comprehensive frame of reference—a world view and the greater identity of the true self. In the youth work, the children are given help to fulfill these tasks. They can decide for now or for always to employ all their forces for the development of their earthly personality. But the youth work also offers the soil in which the child can unfold and become conscious of his deepest talents of soul until he eventually takes the spiritual path as an adult.

Like the Lectorium Rosicrucianum itself, the youth work is also active internationally. It has its own international conference center in the Netherlands.

A child can become a member of the youth work as of age six. He has to be registered by the parents or legal guardians. If the parents do not belong to the Spiritual School, a written declaration of consent is necessary from them. The youth are divided into four age groups: 6–9, 9–12, 12–15, and 15–18 years. In general, there are special temple services, discussions, conferences, and recreational activities for the children and youth.

The themes of these events are always age-respective. Thus, the youth temple services for the younger ones (6 –12 year-olds) are built up in such a way so that the heart of the child is addressed. For example, a story or a fairy tale is told that depicts contents from the universal doctrine. The youth temple services for the 12–18 year-olds, on the other hand, are more philosophically orientated, and on the basis of the experiences that the youth has with himself and the world, they stimulate his own thinking and faculty of judgment.

Furthermore, recreational events and conferences, which include games, conversations, and joint projects, give the children and youth the opportunity to experience joy, harmony, and friendship and to develop spontaneity, creativity, and openness for others. Every child is a personality with his own rights, a microcosm with his specific karma and his more or less awake spirit spark. He must have the freedom to unfold his talents and live through difficulties at his own tempo and with his own decisions. But he needs help to do this and will accept help if it is given with regard for his individuality and with love and understanding. If it is met in this way, he will also learn to meet others with respect and love.

Aspects of the outer Organization

The Spiritual School of the Rosycross is a community whose members go an inner, spiritual path. As this path is walked communally, the School also needs an outer organization. This is based on the seven-step structure of the Spiritual School, which reflects the spiritual path.

The true self of the pupils and coworkers of the Spiritual School of the Rosycross unfolds in the forces of the spirit, gains an increasing share of these forces, and applies them for others. These forces are called freedom, unity, and love. All problems of the outer organization can only be solved through these forces. The outer organization is a means to an end, a frame in which the pupils go their path, and through which they can transmit the spiritual forces for others in the material world. As a means to an end, the outer organization is in principle determined by the great goal of the Spiritual School of the Rosycross and all its pupils: a life in freedom, unity, and love.

Directed in Freedom

Every organization has goals and a structure and needs human beings who keep the goals and structure alive.

The goal of the Spiritual School of the Rosycross, like that of every spiritual school, is not dependent on personal arbitrariness. Its founders articulated this goal out of their living experience of the spiritual field and built up the sevenfold structure of the Spiritual School of the Rosycross according to the lawfulness of the spiritual path.

Installation of Co-Workers

In the installation and choice of coworkers by the Directorate of the Spiritual School, it is vital that the coworkers are so steeped in the forces of freedom, unity, and, love, so that their decisions will not be determined by personal interests. On the spiritual path, the true self develops not according to personal sympathies and interests but in freedom of action and in recognition of the freedom of others as well.

Leading coworkers in the Spiritual School of the Rosycross become conscious of their personal limitations and learn to replace them by objectivity and matter-of-factness. A leading coworker who is responsible for other coworkers leaves them the freedom to unfold according to their own inner laws, to do their work in their own way, and also to learn to act objectively and matter-of-factly out of the forces of the spirit. Here these words from the *Tao Te Ching* are applicable according to their meaning: "If princes and kings were able to sustain it [Tao—the law of the spirit—] …the people would enter harmony spontaneously, without needing to be told."[92]

In principle, the members of the Spiritual Directorate and their coworkers choose the coworkers according to their suitability for the respective office—that is, from above and not from below. Suitability means: Is the person concerned in a position to exercise the functions of the office according to his personal abilities? That he is faithful to his goal and the goal of the Spiritual School and learns ever more to place his personal interests aside and to work out of the forces of the spirit is presupposed for every pupil and potential coworker.

The reason for the choice from above is because whoever is to call pupils to work on a particular step of the Spiritual School has to know this step himself along with its possibilities and problems. He has to have experienced the inner state that comes with this step. Whoever has not experienced this state himself—and these are, in principle, all pupils on the previous steps—cannot judge which pupil is suitable as a coworker. Thus, the more experienced must choose the less experienced.

Purity of the Doctrine

Beside organizational decisions, the essential task of the coworkers of a spiritual school is the transmission of the universal doctrine to pupils and to outsiders. The goal of the Spiritual School of the Rosycross and its pupils is becoming conscious of and unfolding the true self in the human being. This can only occur with the pupil's own experience and insight. It is not a matter of the transmission of creeds, dogmas, and moral principles. It is primarily a matter of the free flowing of spiritual and soul forces, of the vivification of inner states through words, symbols, and rituals. In the Spiritual School of the Rosycross, words, symbols, and rituals bring to expression the lines of force from the world of the spirit that characterize the state of the true self.

When the community of pupils lives out of the Christ-centered power field, reacts to it in freedom, and transforms it inwardly and outwardly, living processes and experiences of becoming conscious develop corresponding to this power field. Every coworker and pupil is himself responsible of seeing that his connection with the power field remains viable while he himself remains inwardly and outwardly alive.

For this reason, there is no training of coworkers according to a plan of instruction in the Spiritual School. What is decisive is their state on the spiritual path, and this state cannot be taught. It depends on the possibilities of the coworker to go the spiritual path and on the communal transformation of spiritual forces through all pupils. The experiences in life and in the power field of the School from stage to stage are the "training" through which the coworker goes.

Also in regard to keeping the teaching alive, the sentence previously cited from the *Tao Te Ching* applies: "If princes and kings were able to sustain it [Tao] …the people would enter harmony spontaneously, without needing to be told."

Freedom of the Pupil

When love, freedom, and unity take form in the leading personalities, coworkers, and pupils of the Spiritual School, there can be no breach of confidence and no misuse of freedom. The Spiritual School of the Rosycross works out of the Christ-centered spiritual field in which personal interests have no place. Therefore, all pupils, coworkers, and leading personalities have the responsibility to behave in such a way that no personal interests are pushed into the foreground. They strive for this ideal situation. So a kind of "exercising of office" is established in principle in the Spiritual School that corresponds to the essential being of humanity. It is like in an orchestra: All, beginning with the conductor, serve the common task—the performance of the piece of music. Everyone plays his part independently and freely and in such a way that he contributes his best to the whole.

The pupil also does not bind himself personally to a master and does not accept any instructions or counsels for the spiritual path that are designed especially for him. The master of every pupil and coworker is also the master of the founders of the Spiritual School: the Christ-centered power field, which works within and outside of the human being.

Diversity in Unity

The inner state of a pupil determines what worth and rank comes to him in the spiritual world. If he acts responsibly in the field of the Spiritual School, out of the laws and forces of the spirit, then his true self is active and serves all others. The abilities of his personality are a benefit to others without egocentricity. Such a pupil embodies pure service; he does not have to push himself into the foreground nor to strive for recognition and honor.

The true self of a human being is distinct from that of anyone else as concerns his tasks in the total development of humanity. The personal abilities of every human being are different from those of all others, but all human beings are unbreakably bound to one another according to their true self, which mirrors the structure and forces of the one spirit. And when without striving for recognition, they put their personal abilities at the disposal of the impulses of the spirit, then all differences of personalities are also joined in unity.

Despite all personal differences, every pupil of a spiritual school can experience the unity in the spirit, which connects him with all other pupils. All other pupils have the same goal that he has: The true self wants to unfold in all, and everyone goes the spiritual path with his own special personal difficulties and understanding. When by reason of the tasks on the spiritual path with which he is presently inwardly occupied, a pupil takes a particular step in the structure of the Spiritual School, then this is not a personal merit. It is only the expression of the fact that he is going through a particular phase of soul work. The work in every phase is to the benefit of all other pupils and only has the intention to free the true self. The true self is as it is and does not need to make itself bigger or smaller.

Thus, a spiritual school that has developed and is working out of the laws and forces of the spiritual field can become a community that shows real unity—a pattern for the community into which all of humanity will eventually grow according to their inherent aim. Paul compared such a community with the body of Christ.[93] In Christ, the spirit, all coworkers and pupils are one in accordance with the true self. Like different cells and organs in one organism, they have different tasks in this community according to their personal abilities. No cell, no organ will go its own way and fancy itself as more than another; otherwise the harmony of the whole is disturbed. Only when all act out of the law of the organism, which is Christ, and perform their functions without ego, does this law unfold.

Owned in Love

Material Property

Concerning outer, material property, the Spiritual School of the Rosycross has conference buildings and land in every working field. The centers in larger cities are in some places rented rooms, and in others the pupils have their own buildings or rooms at their disposal. They are maintained by the contributions of the members and pupils and voluntary donations. Public activities that require, for example, the renting of rooms and spreading of information are financed in the same way. Orientation courses for interested persons may have a minimum charge and internal courses for pupils are free. Only the director attendants of larger conference centers and the staff working there have permanent positions paid from the means of the School, depending on the size of the buildings. All other coworkers do their tasks voluntarily. The contributions and donations are measured in such a way that eventual additions to the buildings, the maintenance of existing buildings, and the running costs are just covered. In this sense there is no wealth that would yield long-term profits.

The Spiritual School of the Rosycross has the legal structure appropriate to the respective countries in which it operates. In Germany, for example, it is a registered society recognized as useful for the common good in promoting religion. In the United States of America, it is non-profit religious organization.

Besides the School, there is in Holland an independent enterprise, the publisher "Rozekruis Pers" (Rosycross Press) with its seat in Haarlem. It publishes the literature of the Spiritual School, related literature, and the bimonthly journal—*Pentagram*—for various countries. It works on the basis of a balanced financial statement.

Besides this publisher and smaller publishers in some countries, there are no other businesses that have a direct or indirect influence on the Spiritual School of the Rosycross. The Spiritual School of the Rosycross does not receive any subsidies from the economic realm, state associations, or cultural foundations.

The motivation of why a pupil is in the Spiritual School of the Rosycross and why this School itself works in the world is to unfold the true self. Material wealth and property have a good potential to support the activity of the spirit in the world provided this support is free of personal interests and in clear recognition of what is necessary in a given situation. A person can use wealth and property for his own grandeur and power or cling to it in fear. But he can also use them without being tied to them and on his own responsibility so that they serve the development of humanity.

Such a disinterested, impersonal use and flowing of material forces is true love that is to the benefit of all human beings without personal sympathies and antipathies stepping in between. The pupil learns to regard his personal property in this light, just as the coworkers of the Spiritual School of the Rosycross work for others with the means of the community responsibly and without personal interests.

Immaterial Property

This is even more valid of the immaterial resources of the community—its treasures of symbols, knowledge, and experience. Also in this regard, the Spiritual School of the Rosycross strives towards a community that realizes what will eventually be realized in all of humanity: the communal reception and release of spiritual forces in the conscious recognition of the tasks for which these forces exist.

The accounts in the gospels about the feedings through Jesus and his disciples are good descriptions of these processes.[94] The spiritual forces of knowledge and love symbolized by the bread and fish that Jesus and his disciples distribute flow inexhaustibly when they are distributed in constant connection with the spiritual field and without self-interest, yes, they even multiply due to the reactions of the recipients. For knowledge and love arise in them when they are touched by knowledge and love.

Spontaneity and Crystallization

The laws at the basis of the structure and development of the spiritual world are unchanging and static, yet the forces of the spiritual world are alive and dynamic. A community like the Spiritual School of the Rosycross, which lives out of the laws and forces of the spirit, will therefore be filled with life and movement.

The life and movement of the unfolding spirit are active in the true self of every pupil and in the community as a whole. This means in principle that the freedom of the true self, which grows in accordance with the spiritual law, ever increases; that the pupils grow ever more into unity on the basis of the true self; and that the forces of love liberated in them flow ever more strongly.

The structures and working methods of the Spiritual School must have a certain firmness and durability; otherwise all work would be impossible. These firm structures only fulfill their purpose when they are vessels for and expressions of the forces and laws of the spiritual field, which must develop in the frame of a spatial-temporal organization and the physicality of the human being when the bridge between spirit and matter is to be built.

The more the spiritual power field is alive in the pupils and coworkers and the more the outer organization becomes the streambed for the spiritual forces, the less it can develop a life of its own. It is an aspect of the spiritual path that the pupils and the leadership of the School recognize the danger of the crystallization of structures in the individual and in the community and are watchful to constantly remain inwardly alive.

Doctrine

When the true self of the pupils unfolds in unity, freedom, and love and the community of pupils lives out of the spiritual forces, then the dynamism of the living experiences of the pupils with the spiritual world and their confrontation with the obstacles on the spiritual path will increase. This will become apparent in the addresses, events, and the current literature of the Spiritual School of the Rosycross. The universal doctrine will be presented ever more powerfully and clearly.

When the longing arises in every pupil and in the Spiritual School as a whole for the true self to grow ever more in spirit and for the obstacles on the path to be ever better perceived, then the doctrine stays alive and gains in power. The forces of the spirit itself then break up all tendencies towards crystallization and fill the spoken and written words of the coworkers and pupils with life.

The Individual and the Spiritual Community

A community like the Spiritual School of the Rosycross, which developed out of the spiritual field and leads back into the unity of this spirit, shares the anticipation of the community of all human beings in spirit. The pupil of a spiritual school seeks to realize what is a concern in every human being—the unity with all other human beings in the spirit. He will therefore affirm the community of all pupils, because he understands that this unity on the basis of the spirit is at least realized in principle, though some may perhaps often be still far removed from it.

As a rule the individual is not capable of recognizing and defining his spiritual goal on his own, not to speak of finding and going the path to that goal. But, as Jan van Rijckenborgh writes, "From the point of view of the separatist there are, of course, many objections to this way in the beginning. Before everyone is able to understand the purpose and to join with insight the new group-unity, there is, according to the style of this world, so much striking and kicking, taunting and mocking, so much merciless criticizing that very great pain and suffering result from it. But as more are willing to make a sacrifice, to let themselves be struck, taunted and criticized for the sake of the great purpose, we will have struggled more quickly through the pool of tears and thereby be able to enjoy the happiness of the new day together with the others....A magnetic body must exist to be able to set out and complete the homeward journey; a body that is completely organized, prepared and all providing."[95] In such a "magnetic body," the pupil finds the most favorable conditions for his path:

First: Community in Spirit

A group of like-minded human beings striving for the same goal is an incentive and encouragement for the pupil. Only with such like-minded people will it be possible for him to strive for the future community in the spirit. Only in a spiritual community as represented, for example, by the Spiritual School of the Rosycross can he hope to realize unity, freedom, and love in the spirit.

Second: Enhanced Exchange of Forces

Furthermore, the pupil in a spiritual community has a possibility that he would not have in the same measure as an individual: to place his inner development and new forces directly at the disposal of others who are receptive to them—be they other pupils, be they other truth seekers within the framework of the public work of the community. Conversely, the forces and experiences of all other pupils with whom he is connected flow towards him. And this means a lot in a world in which the individual is constantly exposed to diverting influences, which he often does not even recognize as such.

Third: Growth of Responsibility

The group dynamics developing through the reciprocal exchange of experiences mean that the pupil is not only responsible for himself but also for the development of the whole group—within the bounds of the possible. How could it be otherwise, and how could he want it otherwise, as the gradual overcoming of isolation that is the result of the urge for self-maintenance is a sign of the spiritual path, whereby a conscious and responsible giving away of all new forces to others becomes possible.

The individuality of the pupil does not dissolve through the membership in a community living out of and towards the spirit. On the contrary: The true self of the pupil, his real identity, comes only clearly to the fore through the touch with the true self of all other pupils. The pupil sacrifices his egocentricity not to foreign interests and powers but to his true self through which all his personal abilities become active in a new way. He does not become thereby a uniform member of the community but becomes ever more an independent, responsible helper in the community who, without asserting himself, freely receives the spiritual forces and lets them flow. Only in this way is spiritual development possible, not through persisting in isolation.

Fourth: Self-Realization

The pupil has a better chance of recognizing and overcoming his hindering characteristics in a community than as a single individual, for he sees them partly in his reactions to other pupils, partly in the reactions of other pupils towards him. But since in a spiritual school, otherwise than in ordinary life, all try to react with understanding, not with retribution, it will easier for him to understand his own weaknesses in this atmosphere of understanding and in the long run to overcome them.

Should a truth seeker in fear of the crystallization tendencies in a group renounce the favorable conditions that just such a group offers for the spiritual path? Would it not on the contrary be sensible to make use of these favorable possibilities but thereby to clearly see the dangers and endure them? And who as an individual is safe from crystallization tendencies within his own being? A pupil of the Spiritual School of the Rosycross can become conscious and dissolve crystallization tendencies in his own being much better on the spiritual path in the forces of the spirit.

Relationship of the Sexes

In the personality of the present-day human being, the spirit and the spirit-determined soul are latent. The goal of the spiritual path is above all to awaken again the latent spirit-soul to consciousness and activity so that it can consciously receive the spirit and transmit its forces. From the working together of the conscious and active soul and the spirit develops the new, transfigured personality. Such a human being rests in the spiritual world and is autonomous.

There are two expressions of this autonomous human being: one in which the spirit is "within" and the soul on the "outside," and one in which this is reversed (see the earlier section on the relationship of the sexes in the chapter "The spiritual roots of the Lectorium Rosicrucianum"). Both expressions work together to strengthen their respective possibilities. Such a working together took form in the Spiritual School of the Golden Rosycross through Jan van Rijckenborgh and Catharose de Petri.

What matters on the spiritual path is that the pupil awakens the spirit-soul-unity inherent in him from its latency. He will try to practice what the goal of this path is already while on the path: the working together between man and woman as the two expressions of the spirit-soul human being who has become autonomous. These attempts are a decisive factor in the development of a group of pupils. Therefore, women and men, who represent different expressions of the spirit-soul human being, must work together in a spiritual school.

Working Together with Equal Rights

From the basic principle of autonomy of the spirit-soul human being follows that absolutely equal rights reign between the two expressions. For both expressions possess the spirit as well as the spirit-soul, only just differently polarized and functioning. Women and men in the Spiritual School have in general different functions but have equal rights and work together on this basis. This is, for example, mirrored in the temple services, which are as a rule given by a man and a woman together, whereby the man represents more the philosophical aspect that speaks to the mind and the woman represents more the ritual and symbolic aspects that speak to the heart.

But there can be truly lived equal rights between women and men only when their egocentricity gradually disappears and new souls and personalities arise that are again truly autonomous in the connection with the spirit. Also in this sense, a community like the Spiritual School of the Rosycross is the anticipation of a human community that corresponds to the inherent potential and destiny of the human being.

Foyer Catharose de Petri in Caux: temple and accommodation building of the Spiritual School in the Swiss working field

The Spiritual School of the Golden Rosycross in Society

Declaration of the Brotherhood of the Rosycross

The religious community of the Lectorium Rosicrucianum aims at the restoration and the revitalization of the original threefold temple of God, which existed in human pre-history and which manifested itself to all of humanity and aimed to serve it.

This threefold temple brought to humanity the original royal and priestly Religion, the original Science, and the original Art of Construction.

In the course of history, and for the last time about 700 years ago, time and again attempts were made to forge, enliven, and maintain this threefold connecting link between the nature of death and the original Divine Nature. But time and again these activities were prevented, destroyed, and stifled in blood baths by various adversaries of the ultimate restoration of mankind.

However at the end of a day of manifestation, there always emerges a clearly discernable swing in this continuous struggle between Light and darkness, through the permanent establishment and the unshakable restoration of the Universal Temple, which reveals itself in power and shows itself to be invincible.

The Lectorium Rosicrucianum is the commencement of this festival of victory.

It brings to humanity, firstly, a community of seeking souls who want to orient themselves on the original Universal Doctrine. This community is continuously protected and surrounded by a mighty all-penetrating radiation field, in order that the light, the life, and the future of the liberating path can be visualized clearly by all who belong to this community.

Behind this community of the forecourt, there is, secondly, the Mystery School of the Lectorium Rosicrucianum, in which all those are accepted who make the decision to actually walk the path of liberation from the wheel of birth and death. The same radiation field or Living Body completely assists every seriously striving pupil so that no truly determined pupil needs to fail.

Thirdly, behind the Mystery School there is the Community of the Inner Degrees, the Universal Chain of all preceding Gnostic Brotherhoods, which accepts all pilgrims to the liberating life and welcomes them into the realms of immortality and resurrection.

With this declaration the Lectorium Rosicrucianum aims to formulate its mission clearly, and arouse all those concerned in seeking life's fulfillment, to take the decision of making themselves known to the Lectorium Rosicrucianum.

Catharose de Petri and Jan van Rijckenborgh
Haarlem, December 21, 1960

Developments in Recent Decades

After 1945 the Spiritual School of the Rosycross began to spread from Holland to other countries. In Europe in the 1950's, branches first formed in Germany, Switzerland, Sweden, and France; later in Spain, England, and Italy.

In 1958 the "Noverosa Temple" was erected at Noverosa for the International Youth Work. The following consecrations took place: also in 1958 the "Christian-Rosenkreuz-Heim" in Calw, Germany; in 1965 the "Jan-van-Rijckenborgh-Heim" in Bad Münder, Germany; in 1978 the "Foyer Catharose de Petri" in Caux, Switzerland; in 1989 an Austrian conference center at Neustein Castle near Steinfeld on the Drau; and in 2000 a third German conference center "Christianopolis" in Birnbach near Altenkirchen.

Since the opening of the Iron Curtain, the School also officially works in the countries of the former Eastern Block. It has, moreover, established bases in Africa, North and South America, Australia, and New Zealand—that is, worldwide wherever there is Western culture and civilization. For the Rosicrucian impulse is especially suited to Western culture and civilization, although it is basically responsible for the development of spiritual laws valid for all of humanity.

In the midst of the manifold work with new pupils and new nationalities, new books were released consisting mostly of addresses by the two founders, thus enlivening the work and giving new impulses to the development of the School. In 1953 *The Coming New Man* by Jan van Rijckenborgh was published, which depicts the characteristics of the transfigured human being and the way of transfiguration, followed in 1955 by *The Gnosis in Present-Day Manifestation* by Jan van

Rijckenborgh, which describes the lawfulness in the building and inner development of a spiritual school. From 1961 to 1966 the four volumes of *The Egyptian Arch-Gnosis* by Jan van Rijckenborgh appeared. These represent an interpretation of 18 texts attributed to Hermes Trismegistus in which ancient Egyptian mystery traditions were set down in the first centuries of the Christian Era, partly clothed in Neo-Platonic, Gnostic thought. Two more books by Jan van Rijckenborgh were published posthumously: in 1987 *The Chinese Gnosis*, a work on the first 33 verses of the Tao Te Ching of Lao Tzu, and in 1991 an interpretation of a portion of the Gnostic Gospel *Pistis Sophia* entitled *The Gnostic Mysteries of Pistis Sophia.*.

Jan van Rijckenborgh died on July 17, 1968, after a long illness. He left an extensive, future-oriented literary work created while working together with Catharose de Petri. Building on the works of Blavatsky, Steiner, and Heindel, this work develops and explains in detail the spiritual path of Christianity for the modern, scientifically-oriented human being, and it includes the spiritual and mystery traditions of all epochs of world history. He left an organization active worldwide (the outer, material garment for an inner organism, a "living body") whose structure and function he designed and, in the form of teachings and rituals, enlivened together with Catharose de Petri and his coworkers drawing directly from the ever-flowing sources of the Universal Brotherhood. It is the living body with seven grades corresponding to the seven steps of the spiritual path, in which human beings open thereto can go this path. Jan van Rijckenborgh left numerous coworkers and pupils who themselves went the path with earnestness and enthusiasm, and who by their devoted work enabled others to go this path and thereby spread the work in the whole world.

Four volumes of the "Egyptian Arch-Gnosis," an interpretation by Jan van Rijckenborgh of the gnostic texts attributed to Hermes Trismegistus

Immediately after Jan van Rijckenborgh's death, this community experienced a severe shake-up. More than a year before, Jan van Rijckenborgh had appointed his son Henk Leene as his successor. Shortly before his death, however, Mr. van Rijckenborgh had installed seven persons, his son and his closest coworkers, as International Spiritual Directorate. Henk was evidently still influenced by his father's earlier remarks and wanted to continue leading the Spiritual School in accordance with his own ideas. Meanwhile, he did not gain the support of Mrs. de Petri and the other six members of the Spiritual Directorate, so he left the Spiritual School of the Rosycross with a number of pupils and founded a new organization called "Sivas."

Together with the remaining close coworkers of Jan van Rijckenborgh, Catharose de Petri continued the work. She completed the rituals, clarified some aspects that had remained indistinct, and explained and showed through her example how all individual conflicts and doubts as well as all possible conflicts in a society can be overcome through inner clarity, wakefulness, and harmony arising from the connection with the spiritual world. She set down her experiences in this regard in several books, one of which also contains correspondence with pupils. Over the course of time, she concentrated more and more on the spiritual work while leaving the organizational tasks to her coworkers. The final inner structure of the Spiritual School of the Rosycross exists thanks to her untiring activity into old age. Before her death in 1990, she arranged her succession and the directorship of the School so that 13 coworkers (in general the directors of the large working fields) were to direct the fate of the School.

The Spiritual School of the Rosycross in its Environment

The members of a spiritual school and spiritual schools as a whole try to live out of a dimension that fundamentally differs from the forces of this world and the beyond—forces that are oriented to success, wealth, and power. So it is understandable that there could be problems in the relationship of such an institution and its members to society and its institutions and currents. The members of such a school and the school as a whole will above all concentrate on their path, which by itself results in a distance from society as far as the latter is determined by egocentric goals.

On the other hand, the School acknowledges the societal environment in which it and its members live as a necessary framework for its own existence and work, and behaves in such a way that this environment remains in as good a condition as possible thus avoiding points of friction. Indeed, positive influences will go out to society from the School without it especially striving for this. Striving for success, wealth, and power always calls up conflicts and chaos, whereas a lack of this striving enables objectivity and tranquility. Thus, a general overview and a new point of view in the shaping of the world's concerns also results.

Even the first step on the spiritual path, insight and neutrality, can have enormous consequences in this regard, for the pupil in the state of neutrality does not add any new fuel to the countless conflicts that constantly develop in the world through opposing interests. He does not stir up unrest by feverish activity and counter-activity; nor does he lazily let himself be dragged along by circumstances, for he possesses the distance of alert tranquility and is rooted in the spiritual dimension of being. Thereby a clear recognition of what is taking place in the world becomes possible.

Political Neutrality of the Spiritual School of the Rosycross

In principle, the Spiritual School of the Rosycross never interferes with political, social, and economic processes of decision. It does not maintain any connections to political, social, and economic institutions and does not build up such institutions. It remains independent and is not tempted to fall into the turmoil of the struggles of relative interests and views. "However, the Rosycross warns its pupils not to take sides in the vast whirlpool of dialectical activities... It should be understood that we are not asking you to withdraw from dialectical life, but that the point of view of the Rosycross is simply the consequence of the path which it proclaims...the path that leads to being 'in this world but not of this world'. First of all, the pupil should see to it that he is no longer of this world. Then he will be able to act in the world according to the demands of the Hierarchy. Then he will be a master, a possessor of the stone."[96]

The Spiritual School of the Rosycross does not observe the events in the world with indifference. It sees the immeasurable suffering, which is the result of opposing interests and conflicts. It tries to realize a community with its pupils in which the urges for power, recognition, and possessions are dissolved, so that a community of free and independent human beings develops, which lives out of the spirit that brings unity. Thereby it believes that it is contributing to the life of a future humanity in which the spiritual destiny of the human being is the primary goal. "The possessor of the stone ... is neither conservative nor reactionary, he is not inclined either to the right or the left. With the faculties of the mind ... and the faculties of the soul ... he places himself solely in the service of the divine government, in other words, he knows and serves the work of the Christ-Hierarchy in dialectics."[97]

The Spiritual School understands very well why human beings struggle for better living conditions and why they hope to eventually find happiness through dogmatic-religious and ideological institutions or by staking all their forces on gaining influence and prosperity. It comprehends very well why people violently resist developments unworthy of them. But it also knows that such ways of behaving do not alter anything of the causes of the problems. The causes are that the human being does not live according to his spiritual destiny or does not even recognize it. All political, social, and economic structures must remain inadequate, often even unworthy of human beings, as long as they do not remove these actual causes. Forced political measures, however, would only further increase the entanglements. For this reason, the Spiritual School of the Rosycross concentrates on allowing a new spiritual basis to grow in its community through which the causes of conflicts are gradually dissolved at their roots.

The appearance of a spiritual school strengthens the laws and forces of the spiritual field that influences human beings. It tries to respond positively to this spiritual field and thereby to support developments in the direction of the destiny of humanity. When on the basis of a conscious union with the spirit and together with its pupils, it builds a community free of political power and special interests, then it contributes to the formation of a greater community that corresponds to such principles on the national and international scale.

"The Call of the Rosycross—Four Centuries of Living Tradition," title page of the catalog for an exhibition of books relating to the Rosycross in Amsterdam, which was jointly organized in 1998/99 by the Royal Library in Den Haag and the Bibliotheca Philosophica Hermetica (Amsterdam).

Thus, when a pupil of the Spiritual School of the Rosycross concentrates above all on his spiritual path, then he is not fleeing from the world. He withdraws from the world in as far as it places itself as absolute and follows material and ideological interests. He tries to gain a new inner basis by going the spiritual path. From this basis, not by force but through his own changes in consciousness and being, he contributes in the framework of what is possible to the gradual construction of a new social and state order or to changes within an existing order that better correspond to the spiritual life.

He behaves like the man in a famous parable of the Buddha. The man leaves a burning house and can now, from a safe distance, bring water and extinguish the fire. If he would stay in the house and try with the little usable water therein and without the necessary distance to save the house, then he would fail and perish with all other inhabitants together with the house.

In this sense, the classical Rosicrucians spoke of a general "reformation of the world": beginning with the sciences over art and religion up to the new ordering of the political, economic, and social environment.

The Lectorium Rosicrucianum and the Sciences

A New Picture of the World

Modern science with few exceptions is materialistically orientted. It tries to explain the world by chemical-physical laws: This is true for the natural sciences, from astrophysics and physics to biology, but also to a large extent true for psychology, anthropology, and the social sciences. Even the arts and humanities want less and less to explore their fields according to the fields' own inherent laws and instead prescribe formal, statistical, and mathematical methods. Furthermore, modern science serves almost exclusively the desires of the human being of this side for prosperity, happiness, and dominion over nature and other human beings.

A totally different science and totally new perspectives on all aspects of life develop out of the laws of the spirit, however. The world view of the Spiritual School of the Rosycross is stamped by the experience that at the basis of all appearances and of matter itself lie spiritual laws. From this follows that a new science would serve humanity's destiny, which consists of the freedom, unity, and love of all human beings based on spiritual laws.

Natural Sciences

Human beings with spiritual sight have from earliest times up to the present described the development of world and humanity in a far more encompassing perspective than today's natural science. The cosmology and anthropology in the works of, for example, H. P. Blavatsky, Rudolf Steiner, and Max Heindel describe not only the gross-material form side of the evolution of world and humanity but also the inner, subtle-material side and illuminate thereby totally different connections.[98] Jan van Rijckenborgh also places the gross-material and subtle-material side of things emphatically opposite the original spiritual world; this results in the true valuation of the gross-material and subtle-material developments. From this horizon, the data of modern scientific research and the laws ascertained through this data receive their true meaning. If natural science would be based on such perspectives, then a totally new physics, chemistry, and biology would develop.

A New Medicine

A new medicine could also develop and would study the psychosomatic processes much more thoroughly than up to now, as is already partly happening today. It would recognize that most diseases of the body arise from thought patterns, emotional patterns, and energy flows that are not in harmony with the law according to which the human being has appeared. Indeed, they will recognize that many psychic and mental illnesses—that in turn can call forth physical illnesses—come about as a result of disturbances of the spiritual lines of force that are active in the human being and urge him to the realization of the true self.

When a human being does not react or reacts incorrectly to the impulses of the spiritual world that want to be active in him, then his whole constitution—thinking, feeling, energetic matrix, and physical body—will suffer. Such disturbances and incorrect reactions are recorded in the spiritual world. These records are as a rule longer-lived than only one bodily form of this human being. They can affect many succeeding bodies, many reincarnations, so that a human being comes into the world with organic or psychic illnesses, for example, that are the effects of earlier incorrect reactions.[99]

A new medicine could explore these connections and above all develop new yardsticks for what is healthy and what not. For real health only exists when the human being in spirit, soul, and body lives and develops in harmony with the laws inherent in him.

A New Psychology

The same is true for psychology. A new psychology would first of all take into consideration that from eternity, spiritual and psychic laws are inherent in the human being and in humanity, and furthermore, that events from many earlier incarnations are also being worked out. It is not only a matter of locating and healing psychic conflicts from childhood or the present adult life. Most often such conflicts are after all expressions of much deeper disturbances in the soul-spiritual workings of the human being. Long-term and real psychic healing can only result from the human being again connecting with the spiritual world, its laws and forces, and in such a way that he experiences and realizes this connection within himself. The only path to the real healing of the human being is a spiritual path.

A connection of the human being with the spirit within himself and the processing of conflicts on the basis of the true self can only be promoted by a psychologist who himself lives out of the connection to the spirit. A psychologist (psyche—soul) would need to be at the same time a "pneumatologist" (pneuma—spirit) and not only know soul and spirit but also experience them. For the soul receives its life and its goals from the spirit. How else could someone who does not know and live by the laws and forces of the spirit help a human being to find the goal of his soul, the meaning of his life, and thereby psychic health?

Social Sciences

The social sciences: jurisprudence, economics, political science, and sociology restrict themselves these days either to the determination of what is or judge what is at hand with the yardstick of the democratic state under the rule of law or on the basis of models of ideal societies. It is only too understandable that ever new social plans are developed, for the world is full of injustice, subjugation, and poverty, and therefore the personality on this side cherishes the hope of removing these unendurable situations through a new organization of society. But even more important is that in every human being, the true, spiritual self is active the nature of whose being is justice, freedom, and abundance and which longs for the outer world to correspond to the inner, spiritual world.

But instead of the true self being developed within, from which a corresponding outer order would follow, the human being believes that he is able to fulfill his deepest longing alone by changing circumstances. He projects the perfection of the true self outwards in newly erected social structures without wanting to carry out a basic change of being.

A new social science would have to illuminate these connections. It could show out of which misunderstandings and false projections of the impulses of the spiritual world ideological designs for society develop. It could show that the underlying need for a social order based on truth, justice, and freedom is justified and originates from the true self, which wants to unfold. On this theoretical basis, it could altogether correctly understand the totalitarian ideological systems of the recent past and thereby make a contribution towards coping with the past and present. For these systems, fascism and communism, are not to be explained primarily out of sociological, economic, and political deficits. Poverty and subjugation, social uncertainty and national resentments have surely played a great role in their origin and their growth and delivered a part of the psychic energies for their development.

But decisive is the longing for the realization of the true identity of the human being, which runs as a motor behind such ideologies. It is this primal longing of the human being that can first explain the thrust of these movements and makes comprehensible the enthusiasm, even total devotion, with which many human beings at least in the beginning supported these streams.

The new human being, the true spiritual human being, can only develop in the structures and forces of the spirit and only when all self-maintenance and all expectations that the material world could become a paradise have vanished. Instead, totalitarian systems try to construct the "new society" and the "new human being" on the basis of the being of this side and in the realm of this world.

They project the spiritual community of human beings living out of the spirit onto communities founded on this side. One system awaits the absolute unity of human beings of a "community of the people and blood," that is, biological connections. Another system wants to realize absolute justice, freedom, and equality in a "classless society" through economic and social connections. And totalitarian systems project spiritual human beings living out of spiritual laws and forces onto present human beings. In a "community of the people and blood"—under biological signs—this "new human being" is a human being of pure race who follows his "unspoiled" natural instincts and is a warrior towards the outside of the community, a "people's comrade" within the community. In a "classless society"—under socioeconomic signs—the new human being is the free "proletarian" who, connected internationally with all other proletarians in solidarity, justly administers the means of production.

A new economics could also develop. It would show that the purpose of economics cannot be to attain ever greater individual or collective prosperity without regard to human beings and the environment.

The purpose of economics is above all to create the material prerequisites for the necessary cultural and spiritual developments of the human being. For the real goal of the human being lies in the fulfillment of his spiritual destiny. The new economic science would demonstrate that with this goal in the background, economic activity cannot be determined by the principle of the self-maintenance of human beings against other human beings and against nature. Sustainable economic activity could only be based on the cooperation of human beings with each other and with nature.

The Lectorium Rosicrucianum and the Arts

Through a spiritual path such as the one walked by the pupil of the Spiritual School of the Rosycross, the bases for a new music, literature, and fine arts can arise in the talented pupil, and impulses for a new art can go out into society from such a school.

Fine arts, literature, and music can serve many purposes: entertainment or recreation, benumbing the human being or tearing him out of his habits, the defense of the *status quo* or social criticism, but above all also the realization of the spiritual world. The arts can show how the latter purpose is expressed in things and beings purely or—distorted through misunderstandings and false projections—impurely. When they transmit realization in this way, they contribute to the human being becoming conscious of his inherent aim, finding suitable paths to the realization of the laws of the spiritual world, and avoiding wrong tracks. Conversely, art can also be used consciously or unconsciously to hinder such a becoming conscious.

The function of art of furthering insight was in earlier times its highest function; indeed, from this they first received their real justification, and yardsticks as to what was art and what not were derived from this. Today, this function has almost wholly disappeared. The arts in today's chaotic situation should have an even greater task of feeling out and describing the force lines of the spiritual world that are becoming active seismographically and atmospherically, that are waiting for their realization in the human being, and that are urging him towards a new order in thinking, feeling, and doing.

One of the highest abilities of the human being, the creative-formative faculty, would thereby be freed from the lack of orientation and obligation from which it currently suffers and would again contribute to the goal, which basically all human talents should serve: the realization of the destiny of the human being.

The Lectorium Rosicrucianum and Religion

For the Lectorium Rosicrucianum, religion is the reconnection of the spiritual nucleus in the human being with the spiritual world through the spirit in the human being becoming conscious and active. In this sense, the view of the Lectorium Rosicrucianum differs from all conceptions that understand religion as the reconnection of the human being of this side with the spiritual world. Isn't such a connection impossible? Does not the Bible say: "Flesh and blood cannot inherit the kingdom of God"?[100] The human being of this side cannot be awakened from the dead, not even on the Last Day and in a changed form, and live eternally. What is constructed from transient nature will again dissolve in transience. "There is a different 'dead man' to be awakened, however, one who has been 'dead' within us for eons past, namely, the true man with his heavenly vehicles, the citizen of the Kingdom of Heaven."[101]

From this also follows that for the Spiritual School of the Rosycross, the relationship of the human being to the spiritual world is not the personality of this side facing a personal God who embodies all perfection imaginable and unimaginable by the human being of this side. It is much more the spiritual human being becoming consciously embedded in the spiritual world from which it came forth, in which it lives, and of which it again becomes conscious. The relationship of the spiritual human being to the spiritual world is analogous to the relationship of the thought to thinking, or the cell to the organism, or as the Bible expresses it, the branch to the vine.[102]

The Universal Church

The resurrection of the true self is its awakening from latency. This is nothing other than salvation: liberation of the true self from its imprisonment in karma and in the crystallized ego-personality separated from the spirit. Salvation happens through the spirit becoming conscious in the true self, through realization or illumination. Thereby the personality is also transfigured and released from its imprisonment by the ego.

Although salvation of the true self happens with the cooperation of the personality of this side, the human being cannot accomplish it by his own power. The founders of the original religions and mystery schools place the forces necessary at his disposal. In this sense they are saviors. Every human being who has restored the connection to the divine world becomes in this sense a savior for others. He transmits forces to them in which they can go their path to reconnection.

The Spiritual School of the Rosycross is also part of this chain of endeavors to save humanity. All those reconnected with the spirit and those human beings found on the way to this goal form the Ecclesia, the true church, the Brotherhood of Life, which works out of and with the Christ forces, the redeeming forces of the divine world. Therewith, the Spiritual School of the Rosycross finds itself in harmony with all other religions of the world as concerns their inner core—not their dogmatic shell: with the inner core of Hinduism contained for example in the Upanishads; the core of Buddhism as it is proclaimed in the *Dhammapada*; the Jewish Kabbalah; Islamic Sufism; and the original Christianity that was continued in the Gnosis. For at their core, all world religions strive for the one goal of the reconnection of the true self of the human being with the spiritual world—through becoming conscious. And in all of them the redeeming Christ forces are more or less active. "In all world religions the Christ Hierarchy speaks, testifies and works, but only in the last link of this chain do we celebrate the victory in Jesus the Lord.... In the seven great religious impulses of that period the accomplishment of a work was at stake which, although showing cohesion, was at the same time aimed at one thing only, namely, building in succession the seven steps of a stairway that was to lead up to the ultimate manifestation of God in the flesh, Jesus Christ."[103]

Thus one can see the chain of religions and mystery schools and their founders in such a way that they all came out of the one light and the one power of the spirit, but that ever more light and power was revealed in the measure that the involution of the spirit spark progressed into matter. In the same measure, ever more layers of the personality were taken up in the processes of change initiated by the spirit: at first only the finer parts, like thoughts and feelings, but finally also the material body with its sense-consciousness and ego-awareness. There came a moment when the spiritual world revealed itself in its fullness to a human being, into the deepest sunken state of the human being, but also in such a way that the deepest sunken state could be reversed thereby. The Christ, the light of the divine world, the son of the invisible spirit, connected itself directly with the human being Jesus and filled him so that he could bring about the transfiguration even into the material aspects of the personality. Since then this possibility is anchored in principle in humanity. In principle, all of humanity has become the spiritual school.

The Spiritual School of the Rosycross connects to this situation, and it teaches and carries out the reconnection with the divine world through transfiguration as far as into the material aspects of the personality. It regards itself as expression of the redeeming endeavor of Christ for humanity. And since the modern human being, due to his ego-consciousness active in the world of the senses, is principally capable of and destined for independent thinking and self-responsibility, the Spiritual School of the Rosycross formulates this Christ endeavor in a way that can be comprehended by the mind.

The Sacred Scriptures

Correspondingly, for the Spiritual School of the Rosycross, the sacred scriptures of all religions are witnesses of the experiences of human beings on the path to the reconnection with the spiritual world and descriptions of the help that the spiritual world gives to humanity in this regard. The sacred scriptures of the religions can only be understood if one reads them above all as expressions of the experiences of the true self on its path through the transitory world.

The New Testament describes how a human being, Jesus, is connected with the Christ—he becomes the "Anointed" who goes the path of the transfiguration of the personality in the power of Christ and makes this path possible for others as savior. The death on the cross is the consequence of this mission.

The life and the death of Jesus are exemplary for all cases in which a savior comes into the world or a human being goes the path of transfiguration in the power of this savior. Ever and again the light of truth is persecuted and crucified, be it in the individual human being who resists the light with his nature or be it that society does not accept a human savior. The death of Jesus on the cross becomes in this sense a picture of how Christ in the human being of this side and in this society is always persecuted and killed. He also becomes a picture for the decisive condition for the reconnection of the true self with the spiritual world. For only when the old ego-personality "dies," is "crucified," can the true self become conscious and active. Only then can the true self resurrect and construct a transfigured, immortal personality that leaves the "grave" of earthly nature.

The resurrection of Jesus is a process that the Christ, the true self, which was as if "dead" in Jesus' personality of this side of flesh and blood, again becomes conscious and active, that is alive. Thereby it also becomes possible that the personality transfigures and a new "spirit body" arises in the old personality. As the means of expression of the true self, this spirit body is also eternal and resurrects with it. The rest of the old personality, on the other hand, goes the way of all flesh. Resurrection is consequently not a sense-perceptible fact but nevertheless a soul-spiritual fact whose transformative power extends even into the material.

Every human being who goes the spiritual path will in following Jesus reach this resurrection of his true self and of a new body. Resurrection is not a one-time historical event but a soul-spiritual-material process, a lawfulness that can become historical again and again. But since Jesus carried it out exemplarily, his resurrection can serve as a picture and symbol for every succeeding one.

For this reason, the classical Rosicrucians said of the Bible: "Rather, we desire to testify that not since the beginning of the world has man been given a greater, more admirable or more beneficial work than the Holy Bible: Blessed is he who possesses it; more blessed is he who reads it; most blessed is he who becomes thoroughly acquainted with it; while he is most like unto God who obeys as well as understands it." The modern Rosicrucians of the Lectorium Rosicrucianum agree with this declaration. In their works, Catharose de Petri and Jan van Rijckenborgh cite countless times from the Bible and show that and how the living truth comes to expression in it. It is only necessary to find the inner key, that is, to recognize the consciousness out of which the authors of the Bible wrote. Then the texts are unlocked in their richness and spiritual substance. This is not negated by the fact that Jan van Rijckenborgh also repeatedly made statements about the willful falsification of the New Testament. Here he adopted views of authors who were not at the present level of text-critical research. According to the findings of modern biblical science, the texts of the New Testament as we have them are essentially transmitted as they were composed or edited in the decades between about 40 AD and 100 AD. When falsifications occurred, then this happened above all through dogmatic interpretations that disguised the real meaning of the texts.

The Lectorium Rosicrucianum and the Churches

Regarding his relationship to the churches, the pupil of a spiritual school understands well what can give a human being the belief that humans on this side would be saved by a redeemer and live eternally. For the human being of this side does not wish for anything more longingly than to be lifted out of the pain and the guilt of this transitory world. But the pupil of a spiritual school has also experienced that this belief does not satisfy his deepest yearning and foreboding. He knows that the deepest longing is only stilled when the true self has become one with the spiritual world.

The pupil of a spiritual school also understands very well what the relationship to a personal God means for the human being of this side. After all, he is himself a human living on this side and knows his need to be sheltered in a personal relationship. But at the same time, he also experiences that it is human destiny to experience the unity of the true spiritual self with the spiritual world, the unknowable "father principle" from which the true self is born, and to be embedded in it like a living, conscious cell in a living, conscious organism.

From this knowledge and striving of the Lectorium Rosicrucianum follows that a pupil of the Spiritual School of the Rosycross cannot at the same time be a member of a church. Even such relatively minimal differences in outer belief as for example between Protestants and Catholics preclude simultaneous membership in the Catholic and a Protestant church. For one cannot believe in two dogmas incompatible with each other.

It is even more self-evident that someone who wants to reach beyond the limitations of the human being of this side to the unity with the spirit cannot simultaneously remain imprisoned by these limitations. The forces of the spirit in the true self dissolve the tendencies in the being of this side to want to resurrect and live eternally. A pupil of the Spiritual School of the Rosycross who surrenders to the spiritual forces cannot at the same time continue to follow the tendencies of the human being of this side.

"The Mystery of the Beatitudes," a book, which was compiled from addresses given by Jan van Rijckenborgh in the years 1945–1947

Every pupil who enters the Spiritual School of the Rosycross has a year and a half to occupy himself with these circumstances and this lawfulness in his own being and in the world. If he becomes convinced that he should seek his life goal and his salvation after all in a traditional religion and church, then he can freely and without obstructions leave the Spiritual School of the Rosycross. If he is not a pupil but a member, then he has the freedom to simultaneously be a member of a church for as long as he wants to.

The Lectorium Rosicrucianum and Esoteric Movements

The great life accomplishment and legacy of the founders of the Spiritual School of the Rosycross is to have lain bare in the chaos of the esoteric streams of the present the path that liberates from all determination by this world and the beyond, to have explained this path by means of a philosophy, and to have anchored this path in this world through a modern spiritual school. It was their realization that a path that leads directly to the destiny of the human being, the restoration of the unity of the human being with his divine origin, can only consist in a transfiguration of the human personality. This path is already laid out in the original Christianity. It is the Christian mystery path and initiation path that Jan van Rijckenborgh described in *Dei Gloria Intacta*.

From this perspective follows a comprehensive view on the numerous esoteric movements and groupings of the present.

First:

Among the esoteric paths that really strive for regaining the unity of the human being with his divine origin, only transfigurism still leads to the goal. The path of the pupil connects directly to his spirit spark, the representation of the divine world in him. It consists of the construction of a new personality living out of the spirit with the simultaneous demolition of the old, egocentric human being. Traditional esoteric paths of the East as well as the West, which once may have been liberating, can no longer have a liberating effect for the present-day human being, at most still a preparatory function. This human being is anchored too much in the gross- and subtle-material and in egocentricity.

A "higher development" of the earthly human being into the spiritual world is no longer possible. As much as he may refine his bodies—and may they also quantitatively reach the vibrations of the original soul world stamped by the spirit: They are still qualitatively ruled by egocentricity and therefore cannot correspond to the new life field, which is free of egocentricity. In the *Alchemical Wedding of Christian Rosycross*, several seekers reach the "wedding room" on account of methods of refining their earthly bodies. But they are sent away again because they cannot withstand the spiritual forces that are free of egocentricity.

Also, a qualitative change of the higher subtle bodies, whereby the lower bodies remain as they are, can no longer be liberating. The lower bodies constantly hold back and obstruct the higher bodies even should these correspond qualitatively to the new life field.

Thus, only a complete abandonment of egocentricity in all bodies on the basis of the spirit spark in the human being leads to the goal. For new bodies that correspond to the new life field can only be built up in this way.

Second:

There are presently many esoteric systems and paths that give as their goal the reconnection of the human being to the divine world but that confuse the subtle material realms of the transient earthly world with the divine world of the original spirit. For this reason, the founders of the Spiritual School of the Rosycross distinguished so sharply between the two "nature orders": the beyond and this side on the one hand; the supernature, that is, the divine world on the other. Many esoteric groups speak of "divine" energies and masters who in reality belong not to the divine world but the subtle material regions. These groups also demand the abandonment of egocentricity—for also someone who wants to unfold the higher ego in the beyond has to let go of the lower ego on this side. If the human being goes such a path, however, then he loses his lower ego not to the benefit of his innermost essential core, his true self, his spirit spark, but to the benefit of an authority or ideology that connects to his higher ego and is foreign to the true self. He becomes imprisoned by an authority or ideology foreign to his real identity. On the transfiguristic path, on the other hand, the pupil gives up his lower ego as well as his higher ego to the benefit of his true identity, his immortal spiritual principle.

Third:

Beyond these there are esoteric paths that directly speak to the human being's desire for power and happiness, that is, his egocentricity, and promise him mastery of life in the gross-material or subtle-material regions of the world. The founders of the Spiritual School of the Rosycross have repeatedly also referred to this fact.

Such paths use esotericism for relaxation, conflict resolution, healing, and harmonization of the human being or for expansion of consciousness into the subtle-material regions whereby the human being is to become master over destiny, chance, and other human beings. But this downright contradicts the real goal of every true esoteric path, namely, the reconnection of the true self of the human being with the divine world.

All such paths may be the first steps of a seeker who in the end realizes that they do not satisfy his inner need after all and sometimes have even created considerable damage to his possibility to go a really liberating path. In this sense, they have their legitimacy as perhaps necessary experiences on the path of the truth seeker. If he decides after possibly many such experiences for a spiritual school like the one of the Rosycross, then it is clear from what has been said that he cannot simultaneously be a pupil of this school and another esoteric community or that he can continue to use esoteric methods that only strengthen his personal interests or that want to connect him with the beyond. He will recognize this incompatibility himself when he has gained the power of discrimination and experienced that all such methods tie him to the interests of his lower or higher ego-personality from which he wants to be freed after all.

The becoming awake and conscious of the true self presupposes the becoming free of such interests. For the true self is anchored in the laws and forces of the spirit that encompass humanity and give themselves away, while the lower and higher ego-personality are always seeking for themselves and their power be it ever so sublime.

Renova Temple (Temple of Renewal) in Laage Vuursche in the Dutch working field

The Revelation of Christ

The Christ, the true human being, existing potentially in every individual and in humanity as a whole wants to be revealed. Countless catastrophes and conflicts in individuals and peoples develop from the—negative—reactions of human beings to the image of the true human being in them urging to be revealed. The image of God, the Christ in them, wants to unfold urged by the cosmic Aquarius impulse.

The human being can react positively to this image pressing to be revealed in him and consciously go a path in which he discards tendencies hindering the unfolding of the image. He can also react negatively and call up immense suffering and disappointments. Thereby he learns.

So, the Christ gradually pushes aside the veils of the self-maintaining ego that want to hinder his appearance in the human being and in humanity.

The Spiritual School of the Rosycross tries to react positively to the true self urging to be revealed in the human being and to the cosmic spiritual impulses. In the measure that the veils hiding the Christ, the true self, are dissolved in the pupils through insight and inner work, the contours of the Christ show themselves in them and in the Spiritual School. For what is the coming of Christ other than the manifestation of the true, spiritual being inherent in the individual and in humanity?

When it says in the Bible that Christ will come "in clouds,"[104] then the "clouds" are an indication of the cosmic spiritual field that influences all of humanity and develops a special strength in the power field of the Spiritual School and in the spiritual field of the individual pupil.

The true human being, the Christ, became visible in the founders of the Spiritual School of the Rosycross. He took form in the construction and work of the Spiritual School of the Rosycross. After the founders laid aside their material bodies and are still active out of the spiritual field, he only becomes gradually conscious and active in the pupils. He shows himself above all as longing and in the inner struggle of the pupils for the right power of discrimination as well as for the liberation from the veils covering the true human being. Will the Christ forces sometime totally reveal themselves in the pupils? Will they become fully conscious of the Christ and consciously experience the spirit that comes forth from him? They strive for this. And already the contours of the Christ, the true self, that shimmer through all the inner struggles can accomplish much in the individual pupils, in their community, and in the world.

"There are thousands of people who say they know Christ. They mouth his words with their lips, but their hearts remain unmoved and their minds do not understand him. They know of a holy sacrifice in an ancient past, but of that face with the crown of thorns which can now be seen on the horizon they know nothing at all.... That is why the mission of the Order of the Rosycross is to tell you what, who and how the Christ is, what this tremendous Sun-Spirit desires for you, does for you, and wants from you: ...not the negative expectation that He will make everything right. No, you must do it yourself! ... The flames of the love of the spirit must burst forth in you.... Christ is a power, the Logos.... He is all in all, provided you react consciously and dynamically to the spirit of God."[105]

Notes

All books by Catharose de Petri and Jan van Rijckenborgh are published by Rozekruis Pers, Haarlem, The Netherlands.

---

[1] And God said: "Let us make humankind in our image…" (Genesis 1:26 NRSV)
[2] *Tao Te Ching*, verse 2
[3] Majjhima Nikayo I, 22nd sutra
[4] See Friedrich Weinreb, *Vor Babel* (Before Babel), Weiler 1995
[5] Mark 8:35
[6] Jan van Rijckenborgh, *Dei Gloria Intacta*, 1962, pages 51-52
[7] In this book, the designations "Lectorium Rosicrucianum" and "Spiritual School of the Rosycross" are used more or less synonymously. At most one could say that "Lectorium Rosicrucianum" emphasizes more the outer organization, "Spiritual School of the Golden Rosycross" more the inner work.
[8] Jan van Rijckenborgh, *The Elementary Philosophy of the Modern Rosycross*, 1984, pages 10-11
[9] Jan van Rijckenborgh, *Dei Gloria Intacta*, 1962, page 198
[10] Jan van Rijckenborgh, *Elementary Philosophy*, 1984, page 10
[11] Catharose de Petri, *Transfiguration*, 1995, page 9
[12] Jan van Rijckenborgh, *Elementary Philosophy*, 1984, pages 13-14
[13] Jan van Rijckenborgh, *Dei Gloria Intacta*, page X
[14] Rupert Sheldrake, *A New Science of Life—The Hypothesis of Morphic Resonance*
[15] Eugen Heinrich Schmitt, *Die Gnosis* (The Gnosis), Aalen 1968

[16] See Rudolf Steiner, *How to Know Higher Worlds* (*Knowledge of Higher Worlds and its Attainment*) and *An Outline of Esoteric Science* (*Occult Science—An Outline*)

[17] For Max Heindel see "The Birth of the Rosicrucian Fellowship" published by the Rosicrucian Fellowship, Oceanside, CA.

[18] Jan van Rijckenborgh, *Elementary Philosophy of the Modern Rosycross*, 1984, page 51, 50

[19] See Psalm 138:8

[20] Jan van Rijckenborgh, *Dei Gloria Intacta*, 1962, page 174

[21] J. W. Jongedijk, *Geestlijke Leiders van ons Volk*, 1962, page 172.

[22] See the lecture by A. H. van den Brul given at a symposium in Wolfenbüttel November 23–25, 1994, printed in *Pentagram*, No. 4, 1995, article: "Jan van Rijckenborgh—a modern Rosicrucian and Hermetic Gnostic" and in *Rosicrucians through the Ages* (Rozekruis Pers, Haarlem, 2005), chapter 16

[23] Galatians 2:20

[24] The following account is based on a brochure by the Leene brothers from the year 1936: "Enige grepen uit de geschiedenis van het Nederlandse Rozekruisers Genootschap" (Excerpts from the History of the Dutch Rosicrucian Fellowship) and a manuscript by G. Westenberg from July 24, 1987: "Een korte schets van het ontstaan van het Lectorium Rosicrucianum en haar leestellingen" (Short History of the Origin of the Lectorium Rosicrucianum and Its Teachings)

[25] Luke 7:28

[26] Jan van Rijckenborgh, *Elementary Philosophy*, 1984, page 201

[27] Leene brothers, "Excerpts from the History of the Dutch Rosicrucian Fellowship"

[28] G. Westenberg, "Short History of the Origin of the Lectorium Rosicrucianum and Its Teachings"

[29] Jan van Rijckenborgh, *The Gnosis in Present-Day Manifestation*, 1980, page 132
[30] J. W. Jongedijk, op cit, page 178
[31] Catharose de Petri, *The Treasure of the Cathars (24. December 1980)*, page 7
[32] J. W. Jongedijk, op cit, page 179
[33] Jan van Rijckenborgh, *Dei Gloria Intacta*, 1962, page 8
[34] Ibid, pages 4-5
[35] Ibid, page 2
[36] Ibid, page 5
[37] Ibid, page 6
[38] Matthew 6:33
[39] Catharose de Petri, *The Living Word*, page 83
[40] Jan van Rijckenborgh, *The Gnosis in Present-Day Manifestation*, 1980, page 137
[41] Ibid, pages 146 - 147
[42] See also Rudolf Steiner, *Esoteric Christianity and the Mission of Christian Rosenkreutz*, London 2000.
[43] Revelation 21:1
[44] *Fama Fraternitatis* (1614), *Confessio Fraternitatis* (1615), *Chemical Wedding of Christian Rosycross: Anno 1459* (1616)
[45] Carlos Gilly, Catalog of an Exhibition at the Bibliotheca Philosophica Hermetica, Amsterdam 1986, page 67.
[46] Joseph R. Ritman, "The Key to Hermetic Philosophy" in *Das Erbe des Christian Rosenkreuz* (The Heritage of Christian Rosycross), Amsterdam 1988, page 205
[47] Jan van Rijckenborgh, *The Call of the Brotherhood of the Rosycross*, 1988, page 35
[48] Carlos Gilly, op cit, page 73
[49] Ibid, page 65 and following
[50] Printed in Wakefield and Evans, *Heresies in the High Middle Ages*, New York 1969, 1991

[51] The "pure ones" = "Katharoi" in Greek.
From this word came the German word for heretic: "Ketzer."

[52] See Lothar Baier, *Die grosse Ketzerei* (The Great Heresy), Berlin 1984

[53] See Antonin Gadal, *On the Path to the Holy Grail*, Haarlem 2006

[54] On alchemy, see Titus Burckhardt, *Alchemy*, 1997

[55] 1 Corinthians 13:12

[56] Jan van Rijckenborgh, *The Alchemical Wedding of Christian Rosycross, Part 2*, 1992, page 206

[57] "Spirit" and "soul" are not identical with the "animus" and the "anima" of C. G. Jung. Animus and anima are soul forces of the personality of this world, while the spirit and soul of the alchemists are factors of the spiritual world that have become latent in the human being. When these factors become active again, then the human being lives as spirit and spirit-soul, as "spirit-soul human being," out of the spiritual world. His personality is renewed and transfigured by both factors so that it again becomes an expression of the spiritual world.

[58] Jan van Rijckenborgh, *Elementary Philosophy*, 1984, page 159

[59] Ibid, page 162

[60] For the origin of the Gnosis, see Konrad Dietzfelbinger, *Mysterienschulen* (Mystery Schools), Munich 1997

[61] Romans 6:6

[62] John 10:30

[63] John 8:12

[64] John 12:36

[65] The Wisdom of Solomon, 2 and 3 (apocryphal—not found in all Bibles)

[66] 2 Corinthians 4:4

[67] John 10:30 and Matthew 5:48

[68] Jan van Rijckenborgh, *The Gnostic Mysteries of Pistis Sophia*, 2006
[69] Vollständige Texte aus Nag Hammadi in 4 Bänden (Complete Texts from Nag Hammadi in 4 volumes), published and commentated by Konrad Dietzfelbinger, Andechs 1988–1994
[70] The Hermetic writings were doubtlessly composed in the 1st or 2nd century CE in Alexandria and are a precipitate and re-enlivening of ancient Egyptian mystery traditions—hence Hermes, the Egyptian Thoth—that are here depicted with the help of Greek, especially Platonic, philosophy.
[71] Jan van Rijckenborgh, *The Gnosis in Present-Day Manifestation*, page 147 - 148
[72] John 8:32
[73] Matthew 5:3. The literal translation from the Greek.
[74] Mark 8:35
[75] 1 Corinthians 13:12
[76] Jacob Boehme, *Aurora—That is, the Day-Spring or Dawning of the Day in the Orient*. Holmes Publishing Group, 1992.
[77] Jan van Rijckenborgh, *Elementary Philosophy*, 1984, page 45
[78] Jan van Rijckenborgh, *The Coming New Man*, 2005, page 196
[79] Ibid, pages 32–33
[80] Ibid, pages 40–41
[81] Ibid, pages 46 and 322
[82] Ibid, page 199
[83] Ibid, pages 199–200
[84] Ibid, pages 218 and 220
[85] Ibid, pages 235 and 236
[86] Jan van Rijckenborgh, *Dei Gloria Intacta*, 1962, page 103
[87] Ibid, page 100
[88] John 2:19–20
[89] John 4:24
[90] Jan van Rijckenborgh, *Elementary Philosophy*, page 14

[91] Ibid, page 10–11
[92] *Tao Te Ching*, verse 32 in Jan van Rijckenborgh and Catharose de Petri, *The Chinese Gnosis*, page 432
[93] Romans 12:4
[94] for example Mark 6:30–44 and 8:1–9
[95] Jan van Rijckenborgh, *The Gnosis in Present-Day Manifestation*, pages 141–142
[96] Jan van Rijckenborgh, *Elementary Philosophy*, page 172
[97] Ibid, page 173
[98] For example, Rudolf Steiner gives a description in his *Occult Science—an Outline* (*An Outline of Esoteric Science*) or Max Heindel in *The Rosicrucian Cosmo-Conception*
[99] Of course, they can also be the consequences of the environment or the incorrect behavior of the parents. The passage in John 9:1–3 alludes to both of these possibilities.
[100] 1 Corinthians 15:50
[101] Jan van Rijckenborgh, *Dei Gloria Intacta*, page 16
[102] John 15:1
[103] Jan van Rijckenborgh, *Dei Gloria Intacta*, page 28
[104] Mark 13:26
[105] Jan van Rijckenborgh, *The Confession of the Brotherhood of the Rosycross*, page 7–8

Most of the books of Catharose de Petri and Jan van Rijckenborgh in English are available from Amazon.com.

For public activities and additional materials, such as the Orientation Course and the bi-monthly journal Pentagram, *contact a center of the Lectorium Rosicrucianum near you. These can be found through the website www.lectoriumrosicrucianum.org.*

About the author:

Konrad Dietzfelbinger, born in 1940, with degrees in sociology and Germanic studies, worked from 1980 to 1990 as reader and manager at a publishing firm and is since independently active as translator, publisher, and author in Munich.

Besides other works, he published the Nag Hammadi texts with introductions and commentaries in four volumes (1988–1995) and authored the books *Kafkas Geheimnis* (Kafka's Secret), *Schopenhauers Vermächtnis* (Schopenhauer's Legacy), *Mysterienschulen* (Mystery Schools), *Der spirituelle Weg des Christentums* (The Spiritual Path of Christianity), and *Die Geburt des wahren Selbst im Menschen* (The Birth of the True Self in the Human Being).

CPSIA information can be obtained
at www.ICGtesting.com
Printed in the USA
LVOW04s1425171216
517723LV00006B/92/P

9 781439 268988

HISTORICAL RECORDS AND STUDIES

UNITED STATES CATHOLIC HISTORICAL
SOCIETY

MONOGRAPH SERIES XVIII

Adventures of Alonso:
CONTAINING SOME STRIKING ANECDOTES OF THE PRESENT PRIME MINISTER OF PORTUGAL — IN FACSIMILE

ANONYMOUSLY PRINTED IN LONDON IN 1775, AND NOW ATTRIBUTED TO THOMAS ATWOOD DIGGES (1741-1821) OF WARBURTON MANOR, MARYLAND

THE FIRST AMERICAN NOVEL
by
ROBERT H. ELIAS

Edited by
REV. THOMAS J. McMAHON, S.T.D.

NEW YORK
UNITED STATES CATHOLIC HISTORICAL SOCIETY
1943

Copyright 1943

THE UNITED STATES CATHOLIC
HISTORICAL SOCIETY

PUBLICATION COMMITTEE

Rev. Thomas J. McMahon, S.T.D.

S. Sterns Cunningham   Richard Reid

Rev. W. Eugene Shiels, S.J., Ph.D.

OFFICE OF
THE EXECUTIVE SECRETARY OF THE SOCIETY
346 Convent Avenue, New York

UNITED STATES CATHOLIC HISTORICAL SOCIETY

Honorary President
MOST REVEREND FRANCIS J. SPELLMAN, D.D.

President
ARTHUR F. J. REMY, PH.D.

Vice-President
VERY REV. MONS. PHILIP J. FURLONG, PH.D.

Treasurer
CHARLES H. RIDDER

Corresponding Secretary
LEO R. RYAN, PH.D.

Recording Secretary
GEORGE B. FARGIS

Executive Secretary
ELIZABETH P. HERBERMANN

Librarian-Archivist
REV. THOMAS J. MCMAHON, S.T.D.

Trustees

RT. REV. MSGR. A. J. SCANLAN, S.T.D.
WILLIAM THOMAS WALSH, PH.D.   ARTHUR KENEDY
REV. FRANCIS X. TALBOT, S.J.   WILLIAM J. AMEND
REV. EDWARD J. KERN, PH.D.   RICHARD REID

Councillors

JOSEPH C. DRISCOLL   REV. BRO. EDWARD, F.S.C.
JOSEPH H. MCGUIRE   JOHN J. FALAHEE
REV. JOHN K. SHARP   S. STERNS CUNNINGHAM
        REV. W. EUGENE SHIELS, S.J.

[v]

THE MONOGRAPH SERIES

I. The Voyages of Christopher Columbus, as told by the Discoverer.
II. Unpublished Letters of Charles Carroll of Carrollton and of His Father, Charles Carroll of Doughoregan.
III. Forty Years in the United States of America (1839-1885). By the *Rev. Augustus J. Thébaud, S.J.*
IV. Historical Sketch of St. Joseph's Seminary, Troy, New York. By the *Right Rev. Henry Gabriels, D.D.*
V. The Cosmographiae Introductio of Martin Waldseemüller—in Facsimile.
VI. Three Quarters of a Century (1807-1882). By the *Rev. Augustus J. Thébaud, S. J.* Two vols.
VII. Diary of a Visit to the United States of America in the Year 1883. By *Charles, Lord Russell of Killowen,* late Chief Justice of England.
VIII. St. Joseph's Seminary, Dunwoodie, New York, 1896-1921. By the *Rev. Arthur J. Scanlan, S.T.D.*
IX. The Catholic Church in Virginia (1815-1822). By the *Rev. Peter Guilday, Ph.D.*
X. The Life of the Right Rev. John Baptist Mary David (1761-1841). By *Sister Columbia Fox, M.A.*
XI. The Doctrina Breve—Mexico, 1544—in Facsimile.
XII. Pioneer Catholic Journalism. By *Paul J. Foik, C.S.C., Ph.D.*
XIII. Dominicans in Early Florida. By the *Rev. V. F. O'Daniel, O.P., S.T.M., Litt.D.*
XIV. Pioneer German Catholics in the American Colonies (1734-1784). By the *Rev. Lambert Schrott, O.S.B.*—The Leopoldine Foundation and the Church in the United States (1829-1839). By the *Rev. Theodore Romer, O.M.Cap., S.T.B., M.A.*
XV. Gonzalo de Tapia (1561-1594), founder of the first permanent Jesuit Mission in North America, by the *Rev. W. Eugene Shiels, S.J., Ph.D.*
XVI. Old St. Peter's (1785-1935), The Mother Church of Catholic New York. By *Leo Raymond Ryan, A.B., M.S. (E.)*
XVII. The Quebec Act: A Primary Cause of the American Revolution. By *Charles H. Metzger, S.J.*
XVIII. Adventures of Alonso: Containing Some Striking Anecdotes of the Present Minister of Portugal (London, 1775)—by *Thomas Atwood Digges* (1741-1821), of Warburton Manor, Maryland. In Facsimile.

FOREWORD

The United States Catholic Historical Society is privileged to publish this facsimile edition of the first American novel, *Adventures of Alonso,* by Thomas Atwood Digges (1741-1821), a Catholic and a native of Maryland. Today, because of its variant title page, this work belongs to rare Americana, but even if this were not so, its Catholic authorship, together with the fact that it is the first novel written anywhere by a citizen of the United States as well as the first to be translated into another language, would be claim enough on the munificence of our Society.

There is another reason for producing this monograph, and that very personal and intimate. In doing so, we are carrying out what was for us the last will and testament of our later revered President, Thomas F. Meehan, K.S.G. (1854-1942). Mr. Meehan, eminent Catholic journalist and historian, was editor of our publications since 1916. The many volumes of Monographs and Historical Records and Studies will always be a lasting monument to his lifelong zeal for the cause of Catholic history. To him must be given the credit for planning the present publication, for he wrote at the end of his last volume:

> According to Philip Brooks, editor "Rare Books", *New York Times Book Review* (September 14, 1941), Robert H. Elias of the University of Pennsylvania has compiled conclusive evidence that the first American novel published anywhere and written by a native of the United States, was *Adventures of Alonso: Containing Some Striking Anecdotes of the Present Prime Minister of Portugal;* published in London in 1775 and written by Thomas Atwood Digges of Warburton, Maryland. . . . That the name of a Catholic should "lead all the rest" of American novelists is a find that ought to set research students in a very busy mood.
>
> The author was a member of one of the pioneer Catholic families of the Maryland Calvert colony. William, John and Charles Digges were among the insurgents led by the Carrolls, who threatened a mass emigration in 1728 in protest against the penal laws and intolerance of the Protestant ascendency that controlled affairs. Fathers John and Thomas Digges were Jesuit missionaries active "in the counties" for most of the concluding years of the last century. . . .

During the months preceding his death, Mr. Meehan made all the preliminary arrangements, but was unable to complete the edition. We deem it an honor to carry on his work.

The editor is deeply grateful to Mr. Robert H. Elias of the University of Pennsylvania, whose introduction "The First American Novel" immediately follows. This monograph could never have been, were it not for Mr. Elias' valuable discovery, and he has since proved himself most kind in providing essential suggestions and material. The results of his researches were first published in *American Literature* (vol. 12, n. 4, January 1941). We take this occasion to acknowledge the generosity of the Editorial Board of that periodical, and of its publishers, the Duke University Press, in allowing us to reprint this article as our introduction.

To Mr. Clarence S. Brigham and his staff of assistants at the American Antiquarian Society of Worcester, Massachusetts, we owe special thanks. It is their copy of *Adventures of Alonso,* a first edition, that we have reproduced in facsimile, by the painstaking efforts of the Heffernan Press of the same city.

Further acknowledgments are due to Mr. Franklin Hopper, Director of the New York Public Library, who permitted us to use the title page, which, as Mr. Elias shows, gives the vital clue to authorship, and to Mr. Edward L. Gookin, Registrar of the Harvard Library, who furnished us with the important advertisements found at the end of the Harvard copy of the novel.

This attractive volume has been made possible by the patronage of our many members and especially of our Honorary President, His Excellency, the Most Reverend Francis J. Spellman, D.D., Archbishop of New York.

THOMAS J. McMAHON

New York, March 1, 1943

Adventures of Alonso

ADVENTURES

OF

ALONSO:

CONTAINING

Some Striking Anecdotes of the present Prime Minister of Portugal. [i.e. Pombal Sebastian Jose de Carvalho e Mello, marquis de]

By a Native of *Maryland*, some Years resident in *Lisbon*.

VOL. I. and II.

By Mr Digges of Warburton in Maryland

LONDON:

Printed for J. BEW, No. 28, Paternoster-Row.

M,DCC,LXXV.

Courtesy of N. Y. Public Library

TITLE PAGE OF COPY IN THE NEW YORK PUBLIC LIBRARY, WITH THE VITAL CLUE TO AUTHORSHIP, THE PENCILED INSCRIPTION: "BY MR. DIGGES OF WARBURTON IN MARYLAND".

[ix]

THE FIRST AMERICAN NOVEL*

ROBERT H. ELIAS
University of Pennsylvania

WAS *The Power of Sympathy* (Boston, 1789) the first American novel? It may well have been the first published in this country, but it was probably not the first novel written by an American citizen. Fourteen years earlier, if circumstantial evidence can be believed, Thomas Atwood Digges, of Warburton Manor, Maryland, had had *Adventures of Alonso: Containing Some Striking Anecdotes of the Present Prime Minister of Portugal* anonymously printed by John Bew in London.

I

The principal clues leading to this discovery are to be found in two statements on the title page of the New York Public Library's copy of the book. The first statement, part of the printed title, is that *Adventures of Alonso* was "By a Native of Maryland, some Years resident in Lisbon."[1] The second, in pencil, is that it was "By Mr. Digges of Warburton in Maryland."[2] If there is any doubt of the publisher's good faith in the first instance, that doubt is somewhat dispelled by the confidence apparently responsible for the identification in the second, and conviction is strengthened by the additional disclosure that the handwriting in question not only is typically late eighteenth century, but also closely resembles Thomas Digges's own.[3] *(See page ix)*

---

*This was originally written as a magazine article in *American Literature* (vol. 12, no. 4, January 1941), concerning the authorship of *Adventures of Alonso* and should be read in the light of that purpose. It does not pretend to be the exhaustive biographical and critical study expected as an introduction to an edition of this kind.

[1] Oscar Wegelin (*Early American Fiction 1774-1830*, New York, 1913, 1925) lists the book simply as "By a Native of Maryland." It is not included in Joseph Sabin's *Bibliotheca Americana* (New York, 1868-1936), or in Lyle H. Wright's *American Fiction 1774-1850* (San Marino, Calif., 1939).

[2] Mentioned by Robert B. Heilman, *America in British Fiction 1760-1800* (Baton Rouge, La., 1937), p. 70 and n.

[3] Digges's letters are to be found mainly among the Franklin papers in the

Adventures of Alonso

Yet even without the explicit information presented by this single title page it would be possible to make some reasonable inferences, from the contents of the book itself, as to the author's life and loyalties. It appears, to begin with, that he had first-hand knowledge of Portugal and the neighboring countries. Native words enter naturally into his sentences; familiarity with the region's physical aspects, distances and topography, characterizes his descriptions; and personal acquaintance with the events and the locale colors his political as well as fictional anecdotes. Moreover, a few of the characters with active roles seem to be persons who really existed and were known by the writer. In the New York Public Library copy of *Adventures of Alonso,* for example, someone many years ago identified Capt. J— (I, 70) and Mr. H— (I, 77) as "Jarvis" and "Hake." Capt. J—, in the story, is commander of an English frigate, and Mr. H—, a friend of Alonso's father, is "an English gentleman belonging to the factory" at Lisbon, who dies before the adventures are completed. At that time, contemporary accounts show, there were living at least two Captains Jarvis of the British navy, one of whom was kind to American prisoners during the Revolution, and two Messrs. Hake of Lisbon, one of whom was director of the bank and the other of whom died in Lisbon, July 30, 1772, at the age of twenty.

Furthermore, if it is fair to look for autobiography in the biography of the hero, the contents of the book indicate that the author was a son of respected parents and a Catholic and that he was educated in England near London in order to be taught something about mercantile activity; for Alonso, at the age of fifteen, "was . . . sent to an eminent boarding school in the vicinity of the capital, accompanied with a private tutor of the Roman Catholic religion,"[4] while his father, a merchant of good standing, hoped

---

Historical Society of Pennsylvania, American Philosophical Society, and University of Pennsylvania; the Hamilton, Jefferson, Madison, Washington, and Digges-L'Enfant-Morgan papers in the Library of Congress; the Lee papers at Harvard; the Emmet and Ford collections in the New York Public Library; the Rufus King papers in the New York Historical Society; and the John Adams papers, at present sealed from the public. These, together with letters to and about him in some of the above collections, are the principal sources for information about Digges.

[4]*Adventures of Alonso* (2 vols.; London, 1775), I, 15.

that "by living some time with a people, whose grandeur and opulence depended chiefly upon their commerce . . . [Alonso] would acquire higher and juster notions of what he was intended for."[5] In addition, if Alonso's conduct can be said to represent the author's idea of heroic behavior, the attempt to smuggle diamonds out of Brazil and the endeavor to carry on contraband trade with the Spanish settlements bear the stamp of approval and intimate that, given the occasion, the author would have acted, or would act, in like manner himself.

Finally, there is the substantially more definite information to be gleaned concerning the writer's politics and nationality. Judged by the words he puts into the mouth of his protagonist, he reveals himself as either an Englishman sympathetic with the American struggle for equality or an intrasigent American. Thus Alonso takes a stand against despotic government and finds fault with Pombal, the prime minister, for having ruined Portugal's commerce through deterrent taxes, through the creation of monopolies, and through unlawful seizure of property. And thus also, as if to bring the point home to the British reader, Alonso makes remarks obviously intended for consumption in the land where the book was published.[6] After terming the English people "a good sort" and "honest and sincere," he tells a group of acquaintances that "sensible people" believe Britain "ripe for a more arbitrary government" and that "without some violent concussion in the state, to give play to the passions, and thereby restore the constitution to its first principles, the boasted freedom of England will soon be on a level with other states." Parliament is "venal," he warns, while the king's ministers place themselves above the laws.

> The pre-sentiment of the loss of their liberties . . . ought to fill the mind of every Englishman with horror—They ought to contrast opulence, independency and happiness—the appendages of freedom—to despotism—the uncertainty of property, and all that train of evils which accompany arbitrary power. This picture they ought constantly have in view, in

---

[5]*Ibid.*, I, 9.
[6]*Ibid.*, I, 122-128.

Adventures of Alonso

order to awaken their attention to their interest, prosperity, and welfare.

In sum, added to the explicit clues already cited, the internal evidence of *Adventures of Alonso* suggests that the author would in all likelihood have been a Catholic, have gone to England for his education, been interested in commerce, and of course have been before 1775 some years resident in Lisbon, where he would have made some friends. He would also, when the American conflict broke out, doubtless have opposed George III and his ministers, and might even have carried on contraband trade with the Colonies if he were not there himself fighting. If it can be shown that there was a Mr. Digges of Warburton, Maryland, who was some years resident in Lisbon before the publication of *Adventures of Alonso* and who, beyond that, fulfilled those other qualifications implied by the book, then his identification will have something solid for its foundation.

II

Without any question, Thomas Atwood Digges is the Mr. Digges of Warburton in Maryland who best embodies the characteristics of the anonymous writer. He came from an old Catholic family, orginally of Kent, and could trace his lineage back to the time of Richard I, perhaps even to Alfred the Great himself. Among his more illustrious ancestors were Thomas, the mathematician; Sir Dudley, author of *The Compleat Ambassador* and Master of Rolls under Charles I; and Edward, royal governor of Virginia in 1656. His father, William, was a good friend of George Washington's, and Washington's letters and diaries show that the two families exchanged frequent visits and were on the most intimate terms. Warburton Manor, the home of the Diggeses ever since Edward's eldest son had gained possession of it in the 1680's, now Fort Washington, was situated on the north side of Piscataway Creek and the Potomac nearly fronting Mount Vernon. Between these two estates, it is said, intercourse was maintained by a unique code of signals and by elegant barges imported from England, and Washington Irving relates that whenever William Digges received Washington he was "always . . . rowed by six negroes, arrayed in a kind of uniform of check shirts and black velvet caps."[7]

Thomas was born at Warburton some time in 1741, according to the most reasonable calculations, the second of the six sons of Ann Atwood and William Digges.[8] Family tradition has it that he and a younger brother, George, were sent to Oxford for their education, and a portrait,[9] painted reputedly by Sir Joshua Rey-

---

[7]*Life of George Washington* (5 vols.; New York: G. P. Putnam & Co., 1855-59), I, 321.

[8]The evidence is contradictory: cf. *D. A. R. Magazine*, LVII, 130-131 (March, 1923); copies of the wills of both old and young Charles Digges in Semmes Genealogical Collection, Maryland Historical Society; Jane Baldwin Cotton, *Maryland Calendar of Wills* (Baltimore, 1901-28), VIII, 267-268; MSS: Digges to Jefferson, May 30, 1818, and Jefferson to Digges, June 15, 1818 (Jefferson papers, Library of Congress); Digges to Madison, Feb. 9, 1812, and Nov. 27, 1815 (Madison papers, Library of Congress). I am indebted to Mrs. Russell Hastings of New York for additional data.

[9]Owned by Mrs. Cecil Morgan, Macon, Ga., and reproduced in *D. A. R. Magazine*, LVII, 126 (March, 1923), and in Paul Wilstach's *Potomac Landings* (Garden City, N. Y., and Toronto, 1921), p. 100.

Adventures of Alonso

nolds and showing Thomas in the wig and gown of an alleged Oxford society, is invoked as proof. Although Oxford has no record of any Maryland Diggeses' ever having studied there, it may still be true that the two boys were schooled somewhere in England, even if not at Oxford, thus continuing the parallel with Alonso.

In any case, Thomas proved himself the most adventurous member of the family and was the only one of the Messrs. Digges of Warburton Manor to have gone to Lisbon before 1775.[10] Charles and Francis had died young; Henry perished at sea; and neither George nor Joseph left America until a few years after *Adventures of Alonso* was written and published. William Digges, the father, was of course perpetually present. But Thomas, on February 23, 1767, was in New York City getting ready to go to Lisbon. On that day he wrote Francis Street, a Philadelphia merchant:

> I have . . . bespoken a passage in a Ship that will sail from this to Cadiz about this day week, and as it is not distant from Lisbon more than 30 or 40 leag^s. it will not be very inconvenient to me; as I am told there are often opportunitys both by Land & water from thence to Lisbon[.] I could have wished to have seen you at Philadelphia, as I want some account given me of the nature of the Country to which I am bound & which I may probably stand in need of, however I suppose there are many Englishmen in Cadiz, who can direct me wch way to take for the most ready conveyance to Lisbon in which place there are some Gent^n. to whom I am personally known & when I get among them I shall think myself snug enough. . . .[11]

If he acted according to plan, he must have gone on the Ship *Earl of Hertford,* which the New York newspapers show cleared the

---

[10]The account of Digges's career is based on the MSS already cited in n. 3; on MSS in the Samuel Adams, George Bancroft, and Henry Laurens papers in the New York Public Library and the Franklin papers in the Library of Congress; on the published writings, correspondence, and diaries of John Adams, Franklin, Jefferson, Rufus King, Laurens, Arthur and William Lee, Madison, Washington, and George III; on the volumes of the American Revolution's diplomatic correspondence edited by Jared Sparks and by Francis Wharton; and on B. F. Steven's *Facsimiles of Manuscripts in European Archives Relating to America 1773-1783* (London, 1889).

[11]MS, New York Public Library.

customhouse on Monday, the twenty-third, but had not yet sailed on the twenty-sixth; and if the trip took what seems to have been the usual length of time, he must have arrived at his destination by the middle of May.

References in letters later written to Benjamin Franklin demonstrate that Thomas Digges actually did go to Lisbon. He said that Lisbon was a place where "I am well known & a little respected."[12] He introduced William Burn "of the house of Messieurs Burn & sons of Lisbon" as "a particular Friend of mine" who had been helpful to Americans in Lisbon, "among whom I am a grateful example."[13] And he offered to be of assistance to John Jay and William Carmichael, who were being sent to Spain, "a Country that I know well."[14] Digges knew not only Lisbon, but, obviously, the surrounding country too.

How long he was there is not certain. If the death of Mr. H— in the novel is based on the death of young Hake, Thomas Digges was probably still in Lisbon on July 30, 1772. But he did not stay long after that, for some time in 1773 or 1774 he became a resident of London. In June, 1775, the *London Magazine* and the *London Review of English and Foreign Literature* noted the appearance of the completely anonymous *Adventures of Alonso*. And then there is no word of him until almost two years later, when letters by, to, and about him in the correspondence of men active in diplomatic circles abroad during the Revolution reveal that he, like the author of *Adventures of Alonso,* was opposed to arbitrary government and devoted to democratic principles and that, like Alonso himself, he was even a trader in contraband.

At the very outbreak of hostilities Digges made the most of opportunities to serve his country. As private agent, he furnished Arthur and William Lee with useful intelligence, fed and clothed imprisoned Americans, and shipped locks for guns and muskets to America, under cover of clearance for Spain. In 1778 he offered his services to Franklin, and on May 3, 1779, he went to Passy and swore allegiance to "the thirteen United States of

---

[12]MS, July 6, 1779, Franklin papers, Historical Society of Pennsylvania.
[13]MS, March 15, 1780, Franklin papers, Historical Society of Pennsylvania.
[14]MS, Dec. 4, 1799, Franklin papers, Historical Society of Pennsylvania.

America,"[15] thus becoming *de jure* the rebel that he had been and continued to be *de facto*. He now not only provided Franklin with the political and military news of the day and, in co-operation with William Hodgson, David Hartley, and the Rev. Mr. Wren, furnished prisoners with money, food, and clothes, as well as arranged the transfer of the sick from dank vaults to healthier quarters; but he also endeavored to keep the cartel ship afloat with exchange prisoners and to force the Admiralty to respect the agreements of English soldiers paroled by the Americans. Later, when John Adams arrived in Europe, he became the means of inserting pro-American propaganda in the British newspapers.

Throughout the period of battle and bickering Digges supported the American cause. He declared that "American Independency" was his "favourite wish";[16] he called the British blundering in provoking the war, in prosecuting it, and in blinding themselves to American sovereignty; and, occasionally, with the hope of terminating the conflict, he forwarded to Franklin peace proposals from minority members of Parliament. Moreover, his sincerity convinced men who knew him. Arthur Lee, in 1777, recommended him to Congress for an appointment; William Lee, early the next year, suggested he be named commissioner to Portugal; and Captain Conyngham praised him for his aid to Americans who had succeeded in escaping from English prisons. "Happy we to have such a man," Conyngham wrote Franklin in 1779.[17]

Yet Digges's integrity has been questioned and his right to be called an American challenged. For this a misunderstanding with Franklin is largely responsible. When Franklin asked Digges for an accounting of the prisoners' money expended during 1779 and 1780, Digges could not render it, for the prudence that had prompted him to use some two dozen pseudonyms in his correspondence[18] had impelled him to place his papers "in a safe &

---

[15] MS, Franklin papers, American Philosophical Society.
[16] MS, Digges to Franklin, Dec. 19, 1778, Franklin papers, Historical Society of Pennsylvania.
[17] Edward E. Hale and Edward E. Hale, Jr., *Franklin in France* (2 vols.; Boston, 1888), I, 347.
[18] Sometimes he signed his own name or initials, sometimes no name, but usually it was one of the following, or their initials: B. B—d, Pierre J.

distant quarter."[19] This, of course, left Franklin only unsatisfied and suspicious; consequently, when Hodgson wrote in 1781 that Digges had gone to Bristol without providing certain necessary funds and was there secretly shipping goods to Boston on a vessel supposed to be bound for New York, Franklin was convinced that "If such a Fellow is not damn'd, it is not worth while to keep a Devil";[20] and both he and Hodgson proceeded to warn everyone against Digges. By the time Digges himself heard of this, it was too late: help he had given some indiscreet prisoners had resulted in the seizure of his papers, and he was now deprived of access to the evidence that could absolve him. Moreover, subsequent events, instead of clearing Digges, actually offered Franklin additional reasons for believing Hodgson and the worst. In an attempt to ask the favor of having his property restored, Digges did the ministry the favor of carrying a communication to John Adams, then in Holland, just at the time North fell from power; and, to some, Digges thus appeared to be in the pay of the British. When a few days afterward Digges returned to London, Shelburne so garbled the report of the interview with Adams that Adams was misled into believing Digges could not be trusted. Then, finally, as if another instance were needed, Jonathan Williams wrote Franklin on June 17, 1785, that Digges was in a Dublin jail in consequence of his "Folly & Wickedness."[21] This all must have seemed but further proof of roguery at that time, and it has usually been accepted as such since.

As a matter of fact, the events from which Hodgson and Williams drew inferences only reaffirm Digges's loyalty to America, while the inferences themselves emphasize the price Digges

---

Bertrand, Alexr. Brett, P— C., Wm. Singleton Church, Jacques Vincent Drouillard, P. Drouillard, V. J. Drouillard, Pierre J. Du Vall, Wm. Ferguson, Wm. Fitzpatrick, Donald Forbes, Wm. Forbes, Allen Hamilton, Arthur Hamilton, Wm. Hamilton, Alexr. Hammilton [*sic*], Alexr. McKinlock, A. McPherson, W. P., Wm. S. Ross, Wm. Russell, Robt. Sinclair, John Thompson, I. W—.

[19]MS, Digges to Franklin, Sept. 20, 1779, Franklin papers, Historical Society of Pennsylvania.

[20]*The Writings of Benjamin Franklin,* ed. A. H. Smyth (10 vols.; New York, 1905-1907), VIII, 231-232.

[21]MS, Franklin papers, American Philosophical Society; quoted in Hale, *Franklin in France,* II, 47 n.

had to pay for it. His valuable shipments of musket locks, clothing, and sail and tent materials to America in war time, naturally, because of the tremendous risk, demanded extreme caution and methods that might well have aroused Hodgson's suspicions; and his efforts after the war to send skilled craftsmen, indentured servants, and machinery from the British Isles to the United States made him liable to a fine and imprisonment that could explain his predicament in the Dublin jail. Personal ill-will and physical punishment were what men like Digges knew they had to endure. So, probably, when Digges was in Bristol subjecting himself to Hodgson's censure, he was supplying America with useful materials; and when he was behind bars in Ireland for what Williams considered follies, he was very likely paying for his endeavors to ship men and vital machinery to Franklin's homeland.

For some years after 1785, Digges remained abroad, and continued to furnish illustrations of his allegiance to the new nation. In 1792 he was still helping Englishmen and Irishmen to emigrate, having sent a score of "very valuable artists & machine makers"[22] across the ocean in the course of the previous year. In 1793 he provided Jefferson and Thomas Pinckney with information concerning attempts to counterfeit coins for use in America. And in November and December of 1797 he assisted Rufus King in ferreting out some of the details of the Blount-Chisholm conspiracy to seize Spain's North American territories for the British. Finally, between April 10, 1798, when he shipped Washington a box of seeds and potatoes from London, and February 8, 1799, when he dined at Mount Vernon, Digges returned to Warburton Manor.

Whatever doubts existed as to his patriotism had in all likelihood been dispelled some time before. In 1794, on the basis of the bad reputation given him by Franklin and Hodgson, an attempt had been made to confiscate his estate, but, doubtless because of Washington's testimony, it had come to naught. The President

---

[22]MS, Digges to Alexander Hamilton, April 6, 1792, Hamilton papers, Library of Congress.

had lightly dismissed the quarrel between Digges and Franklin as of little consequence and declared "that the conduct of Mr. Thomas Digges toward the United States during the War . . . and since . . . has not been only friendly, but I might add zealous."[23] Certainly no doubt existed after Digges's return, for Washington had him over for dinner; Jefferson maintained a cordial correspondence with him, discussing agriculture, sheep-herding, and political chicane; and the Madisons regarded him with friendly affection. Indeed, until but a few years before his death, he was active in the political circles of Jefferson, Madison, and other leaders, stamping out the remnants of the Tory party.

His final days were unhappy ones, however, and he may have died with a grievance against the government. He was not only plunged into the misunderstanding involving L'Enfant and the construction of Fort Washington at Warburton Manor, but he was also plagued with damages to his fisheries and farm caused by the work on the fort. It was in vain that he claimed reimbursement. The officials did nothing, and the depredations continued. When, in addition, storms dilapidated his house and illness and age weakened his body, he forsook Warburton for less troubled lodgings in the city of Washington, where. it seems, he died in the middle of December, 1821. One of his nephews, John Fitzgerald, had written L'Enfant on December 6, requesting the return of an old pot that was being repaired at the shop and saying, "My Mother desires me to present her compliments & ask if you have heard how her Brother is—."[24] By the twenty-fourth, another nephew, William Dudley Digges, was able to compose a letter beginning, "Since the death of my Uncle I have good reason to believe that I am entitled to the immediate possession of the estates of Warburton and Frankland. . . ."[25] After that date there was some discussion about the disposal of the property, but the name of Thomas Atwood Digges was buried in silence, to

---

[23]*The Writings of George Washington,* ed. W. C. Ford (14 vols.; New York and London, 1891), XII, 420-422.
[24]MS, Digges-L'Enfant-Morgan papers, Library of Congress.
[25]*Ibid.*

be resurrected only by those historians who occasionally encountered it in the unfair fulminations of Franklin.

Yet this was the man who could have written *Adventures of Alonso*. His life and sentiments were identical with the author's as far as the author's life and sentiments can be detected in the book. Therefore, inasmuch as all the clues—the inferred, the inscribed, and the imprinted—lead to him, must we not conclude that he was *the* "Native of Maryland, some Years resident in London"?[26]

---

[26]This conclusion agrees with that reached in 1932 by Engene D. Finch, of Phillips Exeter Academy, who is now completing a biography of Thomas A. Digges (see *American Literature,* XI, 300, Nov., 1939). I did not discover until April 1939, that he and I were both doing the same thing, and then I learned that Dr. Finch had been working on the project since 1935. Inasmuch as my labors covered scarcely a year, I relinquished the larger subject, while he, in return, graciously consented to let me publish the facts about the authorship of *Adventures of Alonso.* [Since the original publication of this article my attention has been called to derogatory comments about a Digges in Frank MacDermot's *Theobald Wolfe Tone* (London, 1939). Although these comments may lead to a new estimate of Thomas Atwood Digges's character, they do not alter the evidence concerning his loyalty to the United States or concerning his authorship of the novel.]

III

It would be a mistake, however, as a consequence of the foregoing, to regard *Adventures of Alonso* as so autobiographical and political that it lost its right to be called a novel. It may describe real events and living persons, but in this it merely takes its place near the beginning of a great American tradition that includes such diverse examples as *Charlotte Temple* and *U. S. A.* It may talk of economic security and the dangers of despotism instead of Constancy's blessings and the pitfalls of Vice, but in this it merely acquires a distinction that sets it apart from its more sentimental contemporaries. If there is a labyrinth of political nashgab, there is also a strong thread of fiction to lead the reader through it.

Surely the narrative itself is more than a transcription of actual occurrences. Briefly stated, it is the story of a young Portuguese (Alonso) with a respectable future in business, who elopes with a married woman (Eugenia), spends all his money, and then, placing his beloved in a convent for safekeeping, sets out to regain his fortune. His schemes, which vary from an attempt to smuggle diamonds out of Brazil to trading in contraband with the Spanish settlements, provide such adventures as an escape from a Spanish sloop, a tramp by compass over the inland wastes of Panama, and enslavement to a lecherous Moor. By good fortune and coincidence, however, he reaches home unscathed, receives his father's forgiveness, and hears that Eugenia's husband is dead; but Eugenia, alas! despairing of her lover's return, has become a nun; and, by the time Alonso reaches the convent, she has become a corpse. So, after her funeral, Alonso returns home to comfort his father in his last days, to inherit great wealth at the old man's death, and, made wiser by "misfortune and error," to endeavor to tread in the good merchant's footsteps.

It is perhaps a tribute to the author's semirealistic treatment that the English critics disagreed as to how the book should be classified. The *London Magazine* entered it as "Miscellaneous,"[27]

---

[27] XLIV, 316 (June, 1775).

but called some of the events "too extraordinary to be true."[28] The *London Review* simply listed it under "Miscellaneous" and made no comment.[29] The *Critical Review: or, Annals of Literature*,[30] the *Gentleman's Magazine*,[31] and the *Monthly Review*[32] placed it in the "Novels" category, while the *Westminster Magazine; or, The Pantheon of Taste* considered it "Extravagant, but amusing"[33] and the *Town and Country Magazine; or, Universal Repository of Knowledge, Instruction and Entertainment* compromised with "A political romance, may be pronounced truly *romantic!*"[34]

The actual criticism that was attempted, however, exhibited a somewhat greater degree of unanimity. Although the *London Magazine* found it worth while to reprint some of "the most striking anecdotes" concerning the Portuguese prime minister's arbitrary regime as letters-to-the-editor,[35] the political discursions were precisely what the *Monthly Review* thought "dull and tedious. It is one of those performances, which . . . will be read without emotion, and forgotten as soon as it is laid aside." And the *Critical Review,* while admitting that the "adventures of the hero" were "amusing" and that the conclusion was "effected by a circumstance wholly unexpected," declared, "The writer of this book amuses himself with too much political matter, (especially as it relates chiefly to a foreign kingdom,) to render his book a favourite with the readers of novels." Then it added, rather whimsically:

> The author generally writes in a tolerable style, though we have noted the peculiarity of some of his phrases. "They immediately began to set about getting ready," is one which we are confident the author will alter in the second edition. We shall therefore not produce any other instance of negli-

---

[28]XLV, 46 (Jan., 1776).
[29]I, 476 (June, 1775), 576 (Recapitulatory Catalogue).
[30]XL, 163-164 (Aug., 1775).
[31]XLV, 393 (Aug., 1775).
[32]LIII, 274 (Sept., 1775).
[33]III, [602] (Sept., 1775).
[34]VII, 492 (Sept., 1775).
[35]XLV, 16, 46 (Jan., 1776), 86-87, 87-88 (Feb.), from *Adventures of Alonso,* I, 70-74, 59-63, 114-119, respectively.

gence, but, to adopt his own phraseology, *begin to set about concluding* this article.

It is highly doubtful that the gentlemen of the *Critical Review* seriously believed there would be a second edition, and no such edition has been discovered, but there was, some time in 1775, a second issue, with a changed title page. As a matter of fact, it would not be necessary to find both issues to suspect that two existed. The copy in the New York Public Library—or, better yet, the similar but perfect copy at Yale—and the magazine notices would be sufficient. The Yale copy is in its pristine state— original boards, uncut pages, with end papers and fly leaves intact —and consists of two volumes numbered separately but bound together; judging from the likeness of the paper of text, fly leaves, and end papers, the volumes were bound together in the printer's shop when published.[36]

The title page for Volume I of this issue reads:

ADVENTURES/OF/ALONSO:/Some STRIKING ANECDOTES of the prefent PRIME MINISTER OF POR-/TUGAL./ (rule) / By a Native of *Maryland,* fome Years / refident in *Lifbon.* / rule) / VOL. I. and II. / LONDON : / Printed for J.BEW, No. 28, Paternofter-Row./(row of twenty-four tiny circles) / M,DCC,LXXV.

Where a title page for Volume II should be, though, there is only a stub, which forms part of the signature. That one title page was meant to serve for both volumes of this two-in-one edition is clear from the wording "Vol. I. and II." A title page for the second volume would certainly have been superfluous. Yet the presence of the stub in its place, in the New York Public Library copy as well as in the Yale copy, indicates that there had probably once been a title page there that had had to be cut out. In that

---

[36]The N. Y. P. L. copy is identical except for imperfections: it lacks the half-title in Vol. I and is bound in two volumes, contemporary boards and leather spine. As the fly leaves are of different paper from the rest of the pages, the printer was probably not also the binder. The title page of Yale's copy bears the inscription, "H: Hill 1775/from the Author," which does not resemble Digges's writing, but does resemble what is apparently the owner's "H: H:/1775" on the inside front cover. For aid in collating these two copies I am indebted to Mr. Gilbert Troxell, of the Yale Library, and Mr. Gerald D. McDonald, of the New York Public Library.

Adventures of Alonso

case, there must have been another title page for the first volume too, for, if the present one is the original, why should one for Volume II have been included at all?

Careful examination of both the New York Public Library and Yale copies justifies the inference that the title page is a cancel. For one thing, the watermark is unique, unlike that on any of the other pages of the book. The New York Public Library copy bears the mark of an Indian with upraised tomahawk, his arm stretched at an angle, while the handle of the weapon is vertical. The Yale copy has that of an Indian head and "Pro Patria." Although elsewhere in both copies a Greek warrior may be found with a spear poised at the same angle as the arm that holds it, there are no real Indians to be espied! Another thing, in the Yale copy may be discerned a stub to which the title page is pasted. Despite the fact that the stitches run through the page proper rather than the stub, it is no less a cancel, for it was, after all, designed for the one-volume form and would naturally have been tipped in before the final sewing and binding. Thus it would seem that both Yale and New York Public Library copies are instances of a second or later issue and that there was a previous issue containing a different title page for the first volume and also a title page for the second volume.

The magazines that mentioned the book in their columns help in some measure to confirm this conclusion. In the first place, they always listed *Adventures of Alonso* as in two volumes. And in the second place, they never referred to its being "By a Native of Maryland, some Years resident in Lisbon."[37] Since the Yale and New York Public Library copies betray signs of changes and since the reviewers probably saw the first issue that was published, it is to be supposed that the first issue was in two volumes, each of which had a title page that lacked the informative by-line. If the publisher or author had wanted to alter the title later, it would

---

[37] *"Alonso"* sometimes spelled with "s," sometimes "z"; but magazines often used these letters interchangeably when the sound represented by "s" was voiced; so no other issues are indicated thereby. Differences that occur in listing the book as 8vo. and 12mo. can be traced to the habit of describing books sometimes according to the folding of the sheets and other times according to their size.

have been economical to print only one new page and snip the superfluous old one, while to bind both volumes in one gave the work a more substantial appearance than it could have had in the form of two separate thin volumes.

Precisely what the motives for the change were is uncertain, but that there actually was a change is, fortunately, not a matter of mere speculation, for copies of the suspected first issue are to be found at Harvard, the British Museum, American Antiquarian Society, and Library Company of Philadelphia.[38] They all have title pages for each volume, which may be seen to differ from the Yale and New York Public Library copies as expected:

ADVENTURES/OF/ALONSO:/CONTAINING/Some STRIKING ANECDOTES of the preſent PRIME MINISTER of POR-/TUGAL./(rule)/VOL. I./(rule)/LONDON:/Printed for J. BEW, No. 28, Paternoſter-Row./(row of twenty-four tiny circles)/M,DCC,LXXV.

ADVENTURES/OF/ALONSO:/CONTAINING/Some STRIKING ANECDOTES of the preſent PRIME MINISTER of POR-/TUGAL./VOL. II./LONDON :/Printed for J. BEW, No. 28, Paternoſter-Row./(row of twenty-four tiny circles)/M,DCC,LXXV.

The Harvard and American Antiquarian Society copies, the two that have the oldest bindings, are each in two volumes separately bound,[39] while the Harvard and Library Company copies have something the other copies lack—advertisements at the end of the second volume. The collation is as follows:

Volume One

Pp. 148, consisting of half-title: "ADVENTURES / OF / ALONSO." (verso blank), pp. [1, 2]; title page as above (verso blank), pp. [3, 4]; text, pp. [5], 6-148; "The END of the FIRST VOLUME.", at bottom of p. 148. Signatures: [A]², B-K⁸. Running heads throughout text: "The AD-

---

[38]For information concerning the American Antiquarian Society's copy, I am indebted to Mr. R. W. G. Vail; for information concerning the British Museum's, to Mr. W. A. Marsden, Keeper of the Printed Books. All other copies I have examined myself.

[39]The Harvard copy was evidently bound after 1777, for the owner's name and date ("18 Decemb^r 1777") on the title pages have been cut into by whoever trimmed the pages. The American Antiquarian Society copy is in its original binding.

VENTURES OF ALONSO." ("The ADVENTURES, &c.", p. 148.)

Volume Two

Pp. 144, consisting of half-title as in Vol I (verso blank), pp. [1, 2]; title page as above (verso blank), pp. [3, 4]; text, [5], 6-129; "The END.", at bottom of p. 129; p. [130], blank; advertisements: "BOOKS, &c. printed for J. BEW ...," pp. [131], 132-144. Signatures: A-I^8. Running heads as in Vol. I, throughout text but not advertisements.

Binding

According to the magazines, there were two states: sewn at 4*s*. and bound at 5*s*. or 6*s*. The A. A. S. copy is in its original full leather binding, with red leather labels on spine; it has one fly leaf in the back of both volumes and a stub where one was originally in the front; but precisely when this copy was bound is uncertain. If the Yale copy represents the binding used at the time of not only the second but also the first issue, then what binding there is should be marble paper boards. This copy has a fly leaf front and back and the same paper throughout.

Measurements

The uncut Yale copy measures 10.5 x 17.0 cm. The edges of the pages are flush with the covers.

Whether or not the presence of the advertisements in the Harvard and Library Company copies and their absence from the British Museum and American Antiquarian Society copies indicate another issue is difficult to assert, for the identity of the binders is in doubt and, consequently, the absence of the advertisements may be due to the binder's or owner's whim. On the other hand, the Yale and New York Public Library copies also lack the advertisements, and from the Yale copy it can be seen that these final pages were never included in this issue at all, the first page (p. 129) of the signature of which they form a part (the I-signature) having been pasted onto the preceding page. So perhaps the advertisements do become a "point." If so, the copies with them would be the first issue, while the copies having unchanged title pages but lacking the advertisements would be the second, and the copies with the changed title page would be the third. *(See ads at end of this volume)*

The matter is somewhat confused by another "point." On page 120 of the second volume of the Harvard and American Antiquarian Society copies, the final period in the heading "CHAP. XXV." has slipped up a half-line. Whether this error is one that occurred or one that was corrected during printing cannot be determined from the text, which is everywhere else identical in all six copies—except, of course, for the advertisements—but it nevertheless indicates two states of the text, with resulting bibliographical complications. Thus, for example, even if the misplaced period should be a characteristic of the earliest sheets, it might still appear in a copy with the altered title page, inasmuch as the sheets of the text do not show signs of more than one printing. Assuming that the issue with the changed title page never contained the advertisements, there are then six possible variations: there are the copies having the original title pages, with and without the advertisements, with and without the misplaced period; and the copies having the changed title page, with and without the misplaced period.

No description of this book would be complete without mention of the German translation, which was published in Leipzig in 1787 by Schwickert, under the title, *Alonzo's Abenteuer* (in two parts, 154 pp., 8vo. "10 gr.").[40] "Welch ein Nonsense!" cried the *Allgemeine Literatur-Zeitung*.[41] "Eines von den Englischen Alltags-Producten—denn auch dort giebt es Papierverderber, wie bey uns!—das sicherlich keine Verdeutschung verdient hätte," they declared. Alonso was "ein Nichtswürdiger," and the discussions of politics, economics, and history were branded as "die einfältigsten Gespräche." If this review is indicative, *Alonso's* German reception was marked by very limited enthusiasm. Nevertheless, *Adventures of Alonso* was apparently the first novel by a citizen of the United States, and, not only that, it was the first American novel to be translated. In terms of priority, its value can scarcely be denied.

---

[40]Title spelled *"Alonzos Abendtheuer"* in *Allgemeine Literatur-Zeitung*, No. 298, p. 686 (Dec. 13, 1787), and *"Alonzo's Abentheur"* in *Gesamtkatalog der Preussischen Bibliotheken* (Berlin, 1932), II, 3.

[41]Pp. 686-687. The book is reviewed under the heading, "Schöne Wissenschaften."

ADVENTURES

OF

ALONSO.

ADVENTURES

OF

ALONSO:

CONTAINING

Some STRIKING ANECDOTES of the present PRIME MINISTER of PORTUGAL.

VOL. I.

LONDON:

Printed for J. BEW, No. 28, Paternoster-Row.

M,DCC,LXXV.

ADVENTURES
OF
ALONSO.

CHAP. I.

ALVARES was a merchant in one of the principal towns in Portugal, situated upon the sea coast; and though the prejudices of the people of that country unhappily incline them to look with contempt on those who embrace that sphere of life, yet the riches which he had acquired, his benevolence and charities, the goodness of his heart, and withal,

withal, a great simplicity of manners, had not only engaged the good-will and affections, but the general respect of the province he lived in.

ALVARES had an only son whom he was determined to bring up to business, in spite of the entreaties of his mother, whose vanity led her to endeavour to have him brought up to the law: but the old man was inflexible; he well knew, that to arrive at preferment in his country, the slippery road his son would have to tread, and that the mazes and duplicity of an arbitrary court, the uncertainty of favour, and the slavish dependance upon a minister, would not only render his fortune precarious; but must, as he advanced in power, fetter those principles

ples of justice and equity, which in every character, but more especially in such as ought to be confidered as the arbitrators of the rights of their fellow-creatures, fhould be held facred and inviolate. Befides, Alvares had three daughters, whom he would be the better able to fettle advantageoufly in life, by bringing up his fon as a merchant: for, as his bufinefs alone, if managed with good fenfe and attention, was equal to a rich inheritance, he would have it more in his power to provide refpectable hufbands for his daughters, by the fortunes he would be enabled to give them.

FORMERLY the common method of providing for young women of family of reputable parents, was by putting them

them into nunneries, where they were maintained at an easy expence; but since the law made by the present minister, which in some measure compensates for his political errors and oppressions, prohibiting the entrance of either sex into convents, without the express leave of the king, rendered that impossible; he was obliged to adopt some other mode of provision; and none appeared to him more eligible than the spirit of that law which had in view the increase of inhabitants.

ALVARES's connections in trade were mostly with the English; and as he found that language essentially requisite in his business, he resolved to send his son into that country: besides, he was persuaded

persuaded that education there was far superior to what was to be met with in Portugal, and he determined to spare no expence in that article. He judged, too, that by living some time with a people, whose grandeur and opulence depended chiefly upon their commerce, he would acquire higher and juster notions of what he was intended for, and would be the means of erasing from his mind the unfavourable impressions of his mother.

ALONSO (for that was the young man's name), having attained his fifteenth year, Alvares thought it time to put his designs into execution; for he was apprehensive, that if he sent him at an earlier age, he would lose that *amor patria* so natural to mankind; he therefore

fore took an opportunity one morning of entering upon the subject with his wife, whose expostulations he knew would not be wanting upon this occasion, and that every engine would be put in force to frustrate his plan. Antonia, (so she was called) no less surprised than mortified, used every endeavour and intreaty to dissuade her husband from his resolution; but as neither her prayers nor arguments could prevail, she had recourse to her confessor and the clergy, whom she easily engaged on her side, by representing the danger of her son's happiness in a future state, by being sent among a nation of heretics.

However, their reasons were as fruitless as those of Antonia's. Alvares's knowledge

knowledge of the world, and his acquaintance and connection with people of most nations, had opened and unchained his mind from the narrow prejudices of his countrymen: all, therefore, that they could obtain, was to get his promise, that Alonso should be placed in such hands as would watch over his religious tenets, and inculcate those mysteries which all good Catholics consider as essential to their salvation.

This point being settled, he resolved that his son should take his passage in a vessel that was then going for London. Having, therefore, equipped him for the voyage, and the ship being ready to sail, Alonso, after the tender embraces of his mother and his family, was accompanied on board by his father.

It was then that the steadiness and inflexibility of Alvares was put to the severest trial: for his affections were strong, and he loved Alonso. "My son, said he, you must be sensible how much I consider this voyage as advantageous to your future welfare, by suffering you to part from me; and I hope that your conduct will justify the measures I have taken for your happiness. You are going into a distant country, but you will meet with many of your father's friends. I have recommended you to their kindness and care, but I hope your own merit will be the best recommendation to their favour. You know the plan I have

have formed for you; its completion depends much upon yourself. Apply, therefore, with diligence and earneſtneſs to your ſtudies, and convince your parents of your duty and affection, by the ſhortneſs of your abſence; for though I would by no means have your education and the acquirement of knowledge reſtricted as to time, yet its duration muſt depend much upon the uſe you make of it."----The young man wept----Alvares embraced him, and they parted.

CHAP.

CHAP. II.

ALVARES had but juſt left the ſhip, when a fine breeze ſpringing up, ſhe immediately ſet ſail.---The novelty of the ſcene and the ſea-ſickneſs, ſoon diſengaged the mind of Alonſo from the diſtreſs that the ſeparation from his parents had occaſioned.---In three weeks he arrived at London. The captain, to whoſe care he was intruſted, took the firſt opportunity of accompanying him to the correſpondent of Alvares, whoſe houſe he was to conſider as his home.

ALONSO

ALONSO was received with all the kindnefs that was due from a man whofe friendfhip for his father was cenrented by a long and advantageous connection in trade. After fome weeks' recreation and amufement, Mr. Stephenfon, (for that was the gentleman's name) thought it proper to put Alvares's plan into execution. Alonfo was therefore fent to an eminent boarding-fchool in the vicinity of the capital, accompanied with a private tutor of the Roman Catholic religion; a man, however, of a liberal and enlarged mind, and well adapted to the employment he was engaged for.

WE will pafs over the hiftory of this part of his life as too juvenile to be interefting---fuffice it to fay, that, as he was

was a youth of strong natural sense, and of a quick apprehension---of an engaging aspect and genteel deportment, he made a rapid progress in the attainment of those branches of learning and education which are considered either as beneficial or graceful.---It may not perhaps be amiss to remark, that of all the different studies which he was employed in, none engaged his attention so much as History and Geography.

ALONSO had now completed his twentieth year; and as Alvares was persuaded, from the flattering accounts he so often received of his accomplishments, that his residence in England had answered the ends he proposed, he thought it was time to send for him home;

home;---however, in this he confulted his friend, and was determined to be guided by his advice. Mr. Stephenfon told him, that though he had finifhed his academic education, he thought it would be very proper to let him remain in his houfe for fix or feven months with his tutor, in order to render his addrefs eafy in the commerce of the world, and to give him fome knowledge of mankind.

Alvares readily fubfcribed to this opinion, and Alonfo was happy in partaking of the pleafures of fociety for the remainder of his ftay.

At the expiration of that time, he embarked for Portugal: he would willingly have continued fome months longer, and

wrote

wrote to his father for that purpofe, but the declining health of his mother---her anxiety to fee him, and the neceffity Alvares thought there was to introduce him into bufinefs, and the knowledge of his affairs in cafe of any accident to himfelf, were reafons that rendered it imprudent to comply with his requeft.

It is needlefs to mention the joy the old man and Antonia felt on the arrival of their fon---every branch of his parentage joined in their congratulations, and Alonfo was for fome days almoft fmothered with embraces.

Alvares the more he examined and attended to his fon, the more he was pleafed---and exulted in the education
he

he had given him---Even Antonia joined in the applause of his measures; for though she was not a woman to form a right judgment of other accomplishments, she could not but allow that his appearance surpassed her most sanguine expectations---------however, not many months elapsed, before an event fell out that at once destroyed all their happiness.

Among the ladies who visited Antonia and her daughters, was Donna Eugenia de Miranda, a person of great beauty in the town of -------------. Alonso became deeply enamoured of her; and as she was the intimate and friend of his eldest sister, he had frequent opportunities of seeing and entertaining her with his passion, notwithstanding the jealousy and watchfulness

ness of her husband; for Donna Eugenia was married; but this was one of those ill-assorted matches, where youth and beauty were sacrificed to riches and old age---Don Pedro her husband was upwards of threescore.

The advantages of Alonso's person have been already mentioned; and as the education he had received gave him great superiority over the youth of his own country, he did not find it an arduous task, in a climate where the passions between the two sexes are so easily inflamed, to inspire Eugenia with the kindest sentiments towards him.---Business now was no longer regarded; and the schemes the good Alvares had formed for the happiness of his son, gave way to the

the charms and allurements of Eugenia. However, that he might have a more unbounded enjoyment allowed of than stolen interviews, he determined to endeavour to persuade her to forsake Don Pedro, and fly with him into Spain.

THE affections of Eugenia were too deeply engaged to withstand his entreaties; it was therefore agreed that they should go privately to Lisbon, and that Eugenia should there be equipped in men's apparel, and from thence travel as Alonso's brother. In the mean time, as it was necessary to look a little towards futurity, Alonso had the address to raise a considerable sum of money upon his father's credit:---Eugenia too was equally provident, and did not forget her jewels and trinkets of value.

CHAP. III.

OUR two lovers got undifcovered to Lifbon, where they remained no longer than was neceffary to complete Eugenia for her intended difguife.

As foon as that was accomplifhed, Alonfo ordered mules to be hired in the Province of Alemtejo, and taking the advantage of a fine evening, croffed the Tagus with his miftrefs, and immediately proceeded on their journey through bye roads to Badajoz, the firft frontier town in Spain, where to their great joy they arrived without being known.

IT was now for the firſt time they thought themſelves ſecure in each other's embraces; for what with the reſtleſs jealouſy of an incenſed huſband, and the fond anxiety of indulgent parents, they were certain no expence or diligence would be wanting to find them out.--- Being therefore free from apprehenſion, and their purſes well furniſhed with money, they gave the reins to Pleaſure; for their paſſions were too violent to let them moralize on their ruinous conduct.

AFTER ſolacing themſelves ſome days in Badajoz, they ſet out for Madrid.--- The badneſs of the roads---the uneaſineſs of the calaſhes---the tireſome ding-dong pace of the mules, with the continued tinkling

tinkling of their bells, and above all, the forlorn accommodation of their inns, render travelling in Spain fit only for Lovers or Philosophers; so that our adventurers arrived at the capital without the usual complaints of the journey.---Their first step was to provide themselves with a proper apartment, and then to be fitted with such cloaths as were most in fashion, that they might appear in public without being particularised as strangers---Eugenia, however, in spite of her sword, and other manly accoutrements, did not yet find herself mistress of that confidence so necessary in her situation to prevent a suspicion of her sex.

THEY

THEY had not been long in Madrid before the King signified his intentions of reviewing the regiment of horse-guards, and appointed a day for that purpose. As Alonso had always intelligence of the amusements of the town, he was resolved not to let slip an opportunity of being present at a sight which seldom fails to engage the general attention; accordingly the two cavaliers were punctual to the hour of rendezvous.

ALONSO was not a military man, and his companion less so; it is therefore not surprising if they took but little notice of the exercise or evolutions: besides their minds were too much engrossed with the pageantry of the court, and of the spectators themselves, to attend to any thing besides---but the regiment being ordered to make a charge, they halted at the end of their career with their front close to where they stood.---What was the horror and confusion of Eugenia, when the first object she cast her eyes upon, was her husband Don Pedro observing her at the head of his squadron, with a wild and distracted look!---his countenance threatened vengeance alternately on both---Eugenia was so agitated that she was ready to sink down; and Alonso was struck with such amazement and wonder, that he had hardly the power of assisting her: fortunately for both, the regiment was ordered to go through some other manœuvre, which removed from their sight the most terrifying object they had ever yet beheld;

so

so that gathering together their scattered spirits, they hurried through the crowd, and made the best of their way to their lodgings.

As soon as they got home they bundled up in haste what was valuable, and changing their cloaths, bade an immediate adieu to Madrid.---They travelled the remaining part of that day on foot; and the better to elude the search of Don Pedro, they once more changed their apparel with two common labouring men, whom they observed at some distance from the road, at work in a vineyard.

HAVING got to a village about four leagues from Madrid, towards the dusk of the evening, and worn out with fatigue from the agitation of mind and the diſtance they had walked, they reſolved to go no further that night.---- They had now leiſure to reflect upon the ſtrange adventure which had befaln them, and to form ſome plan that might ſecure them from falling into the hands of Don Pedro.----It was now upwards of a month ſince they had left ----------, their native place; and Alonſo, deſirous of keeping their abode a ſecret, had kept up no correſpondence with his friends---- they were therefore loſt in conjectures how Don Pedro came to be at the head of a ſquadron in the Spaniſh guards, when it was but ſo lately they had left him as a captain of cavalry in Portugal.

AFTER.

After ruminating on what was best to be done in their present circumstances, it was thought most adviseable to get into France as soon as possible. For this purpose, early in the morning, Alonso purchased a small ordinary mule, for he was afraid that a good one might appear as too great a contrast with the garb they were in, and alarm the suspicions of their hosts. Having likewise bought a pair of alforges *, and a borracho †, which they filled with wine and provisions, they set out on their journey, cotoying the high road to Bayonne. Alonso walked by the side of Eugenia, who rode on the little mule, and at night they took up their lodgings in a small town,

* A pair of cantines made of coarse wool.
† A leather skin to hold wine.

where he thought they might safely make a purchase of another beast and a change of apparel. In this manner they travelled towards France, taking up their quarters constantly at some distance from the high-way, in order to be secure from pursuit.

At the end of twelve days they found themselves at the foot of the Pyrenees, and in three more, they had the happiness to arrive at St. Jean de Lus.

CHAP,

CHAP. IV.

OUR travellers at once found themselves in safety and in paradise, compared to the country they had left. Whoever has made that journey, will allow the justness of the comparison.

This change of scene happened very opportunely to Alonso; for a gloomy thought would now and then steal across his breast, and imbitter the gaiety of his disposition. The frowns of a father, whose care and indulgence he had so ill requited; the anxious tenderness of a mother, almost overcome with disease, and

and the affections of his sisters whom he fondly loved, would stare him at times in the face.---These gloomy reflections, the newness of the objects, and the vivacity of the people they had got amongst, soon dispelled from his mind.---As for Eugenia, secure in the attachment of Alonso, she never once regretted the change she had made.

They found so pleasant a contrast between French Hotels and Spanish Posadas, that they were in no hurry to leave St. Jean de Lus;---however, after some days repose, and repairing their wardrobe with such dresses as were proper for travelling in, according to the fashions of France, Alonso fixed upon Marseilles as their place of abode.---He was inclined to take

take up his residence in that city, in preference to any other in that part of the kingdom from its size and populousness, from its great trade to most parts of the world, and from the facility with which he could convey himself to any other country.

ACCORDINGLY he hired a chaise for the journey, and taking in their rout such places as he thought were worth seeing, or would afford them entertainment, they arrived in safety at Marseilles.---They had not been long there, before they found their finances nearly exhausted; recourse was therefore to be had to Eugenia's jewels, which were sold for a sum of money, which was not only sufficient for their present exigencies, but with tolerable

rable management would even have allowed them to live sometime with dissipation.---But œconomy had but a small share in Alonso's character; and their expences made such hasty strides to distress, that they were soon reduced to the *pavé*; ---like too many young travellers, they fell a prey to those harpies, who in all large towns take advantage of the extravagance of youth.

In this dilemma, what was to be done? ---Various schemes were thought on; and circumstanced as they were, it was necessary to fix upon some one or other before they were absolutely reduced to want.

As Alonso was one day ruminating in this mood on the quay of Marseilles, he heard

heard by chance of a ship that was bound for Cadiz.---It immediately occurred to him that he had an old school-fellow who had been sent over to England upon much the same plan as he had been by Alvares, and was now settled in one of the most substantial houses of business in that city.

Alonso had always lived in the strictest amity with Pacheco, (for that was his name), and he did not doubt but when he made known to him his distress, that he would not only be relieved, but that some method would be found out which, with the exertion of his abilities, would secure them from future want.

Of the different projects that run at that time in his head, none appeared to him so advantageous as to get out to the Spanish colonies in America, which he was persuaded from the influence of Pacheco he would accomplish: besides, his curiosity for travelling would be gratified, and to return home in his present circumstances was not to be thought of.

Full of his intended schemes, and elevated with the thoughts of being able to extricate himself from his present difficulties, he hastened home to Eugenia ---He found her pensive and melancholly, but the unusual chearfulness of his countenance bespeaking some lucky change in their affairs, her features immediately took another turn.

Alonso

Alonso communicated to her his project, and expatiated with so much confidence on its success, that they were soon of one mind.

The first thing therefore to be done, was to find out the Captain of the vessel, and agree for their passage.---This point being settled, and the ship being ready to sail, they turned every thing they could spare into money, and went immediately on board.

Eugenia was by this time so accustomed to the disguise she had assumed, that she was no ways apprehensive of a discovery of her sex in the common intercourse of society.---But the scene was now changed, and they were going to a country where they would be within the reach of Don Pedro.---Their precautions, however, succeeded---Eugenia kept constantly in bed; and the weather was so favourable during the voyage, that she hardly paid the common tribute to the sea. In five days they arrived at Cadiz.

AFTER satisfying the Captain, they took advantage of the first boat to carry them a-shore, and retired to a posada in the most sequestered part of the town.. ---As soon as they had taken some refreshment, Alonso desired the landlord to recommend them to such an apartment as suited their circumstances to hire; for the inns in Spain, though the worst, are notwithstanding the dearest in Europe---
besides

besides they could not escape being known in a house of public resort.

When they were settled in their lodgings, Alonso began to make enquiries for his friend, whom to his great joy he found was in Cadiz, and considered as one of the richest merchants in the city.

After reasoning some time on the best way of making himself known to him, he wrote him the following lines:

" If Don Pacheco entertains the sen-
" timents of his earlier years, and is
" desirous of relieving the distresses of a
" friend, he will call at ———————, in
" the street of ———————." Having dispatched

patched this note, he waited the refult with anxious fufpence.

Don Pacheco on receiving it, haftened immediately to the place of rendezvous.---What was his furprife, when he met with Alonfo!---the tears ftarted into his eyes with joy, in meeting with the friend and companion of his youth.

After the firft embraces and the mutual affurances of efteem and regard, Pacheco enquired for Donna Eugenia---Alonfo confounded and furprized, hefitated what to fay---Come, my friend, fays Pacheco------lay afide your difguife---I am informed of your adventure, and you may truft to my difcretion in whatever relates to your intereft.

Alonso

Alonso finding it in vain to diffemble, introduced him to Eugenia, who confused at the knowledge Pacheco had learnt of her story, betrayed at once all the manliness she had acquired.

As soon as the compliments were over, Alonso impatient to know how his friend had come to be acquainted with his adventures, urged him to relate every particular he knew on that head.

Whereupon Pacheco told him, "That a ship having arrived at Cadiz, from ------, (the native place of Alonso) soon after he had absented himself, and the cargo being configned to their house, he had not so soon forgot their old fellowship,

ship, as not to enquire after him.---The captain, continued Pacheco, told me of your amour with this lady; that you had gone off together, and had so well concerted your disguise, that notwithstanding all the search that was made after you, they had not been able to trace the rout you had taken.---At first *you* were not suspected; and if it had not been for an old woman, who it seems was the confidante of your amour, they would have remained longer in their ignorance---Alvares was so enraged, and attributing the death of your mother"---
" The death of my mother! exclaimed Alonso---is she then dead?" " What, did you not know it?" answered Pacheco. ---" Alas! no; replied Alonso---but I pray you go on; hide nothing from me!
---What

—What said you of my father?" " Alvares, resumed Pacheco, attributing his loss (though I understand that your mother had been long in an ill state of health) to your flight, and the consequences it had occasioned, declared in the first transports of his anger, that he would never see you more." Here Alonso fetched a deep sigh, and Eugenia was so much affected, that Pacheco was unwilling to proceed. " I beseech of you, said Alonso, relate to us the consequences you hinted at; whatever they were, we must know them one day or other; and your friendship will at least be a balm to our afflictions :" after much entreaty, Pacheco went on.

"Don Pedro, furious and diftracted on miffing his lady, immediately fixed upon Don Gufman, a cadet in his regiment, as the author of this injury; for it feems Donna Eugenia was to have been married to this gentleman before the offers of Don Pedro were accepted of by her friends as a more advantageous match. Being confirmed in this opinion from the coolnefs and indifference of Donna Eugenia, and free from any other fufpicions, he inftantly went in queft of Don Gufman, and meeting with him in the ftreet, drew on him, and in a peremptory voice bade him defend himfelf: Gufman fell; Don Pedro made his efcape into Spain, and I underftand is now a captain in the King's guards."

Here

Here astonishment, grief, terror, and dejection agitated alternately the minds of Alonso and Eugenia.

As soon as Pacheco observed the emotions began to subside, which this recital had occasioned, he renewed his protestations of amity and service.—Alonso embraced him: " My friend, said he, it is but just that I should feel that misery which I have been the cause of to others.---O ill-fated passion! (did he exclaim), what a train of evils hast thou occasioned! the murder of Gusman! the exile of Don Pedro! and the misery of their families will be endless cause of remorse---and oh! my unhappy parents! my mother! whose last moments I have hurried with sorrow to the grave! my
father

father too! whose indulgent kindness"---Here tears express'd the anguish of his heart; Eugenia was entranced in woe, and Pacheco in silence respected the sorrows of his friend.

CHAP.

CHAP. V.

WHEN they were once more a little composed, Pacheco, who was waiting for an opportunity to engage Alonso in conversation, express'd his surprise that he had been so long ignorant of the events he had related; " But I must confess, Madam, said he, (addressing himself to Donna Eugenia) this is no great sign of my gallantry; for I have only to turn my eyes on your person to be convinced, that a man who enjoys the pleasure of your society, must be indifferent to ought besides; but pray, Alonso, tell me how I came to have the happiness of meeting with you at Cadiz?"

Alonso then informed him of every circumstance that had befallen them since their departure from ‒‒‒‒‒‒‒‒. Pacheco could not avoid dwelling upon the strange rencounter with Don Pedro. "It has so much the air of romance, said he, that I should certainly have considered it in that light, if I had not been satisfied of the truth of it from your own mouth; but to come more immediately to what now concerns you, continued Pacheco,--- the resolution you took to come here, I consider as the best mark you could have given me of your friendship; and your confidence shall not be disappointed--- In the first place, your exigencies require some supply; (and pressing his purse upon him) I beg of you, make use of this for the present---I am rich, and

and will anticipate your wants; in the mean time, let me entreat of you to accept of an apartment in my house, and consider it as your home---there can be only one objection to it, Madam, (addressing himself to Donna Eugenia) I am married; and you might not chuse to expose yourself to the scrutinizing eyes of your own sex; but even if your disguise should be discovered, I will venture to answer for the prudence and secrecy of my wife." Eugenia thanked him in the best terms she could think of, but begged to decline his offer; in her present turn of mind, she wished to be retired---Alonso was likewise of the same sentiments, and he thought it would be running too great a risque of a discovery, as they could not avoid company, and

perhaps,

perhaps, falling in with some one or other who might know them. "I will press you no farther on this subject, said Pacheco; let us consider then in what else I can serve you—some plan or other must be fallen upon, for to return to ———, at present, you will allow it is quite out of the question." "Certainly; answered Alonso. I have entertained myself, continued he, with the thoughts of getting out through your means to the Spanish settlements in America.— What think you of the scheme?" "I am afraid it is impossible, replied Pacheco; you must at least be first master of our language, in order to pass for a Spaniard; but that might be got the better of by application, before any ship goes to that part of the world.—I am

apprehensive

apprehenfive too for Donna Eugenia---I fuppofe you would not willingly leave her behind; and even if fhe were inclined to follow you, I forefee a great many difficulties; however, I will think of it, and confult with my friends." Alonfo was a good deal difpirited at the fmall profpect he had of fuccefs: " If, faid he, our India fhip went regularly as it ufed to do, I would go to that country; for I have feveral relations there in very refpectable fituations in life; and I am fure they would receive me with kindnefs, and that fome road fhould be chalked out whereby I fhould make my way good."

" In that cafe, faid Pacheco, I have news to tell you, which perhaps will be

very

very agreeable: The laſt account I received from Portugal mentioned, that they were getting ready the Goa ſhip with great expedition, and that it was expected it would ſail in the courſe of a few weeks." " I am rejoiced at what you tell me, replied Alonſo.---Can you deviſe no method by which we can get ſecretly to Liſbon?" " There is an Engliſh frigate juſt now in our harbour, ſaid Pacheco, that is bound for that port; if you chuſe it, I will ſpeak to the conſul of that nation, with whom I am intimately acquainted, to procure you a paſſage." " By all means, returned Alonſo with eagerneſs; I aſk but this further inſtance of your friendſhip." " Then I will immediately ſet about it,
answered

answered Pacheco; in the morning we will meet again.

As soon as they were left alone, Alonso began to pass in review the various events of the day; a silent tear would now and then steal down his cheeks, claiming the sympathy of Eugenia: she again catching the sorrowful state of his mind, would be so sunk in dejection and grief, as to require all his tenderness and love to alleviate. The night afforded them but little rest; and Alonso impatient to know the success of the application of his friend, arose almost with the sun; however, he had not been long up, before Pacheco arrived. " I am come, said he, to give you joy; but it is with an aching heart--- the man of war sails this evening, and you

you will be welcome guests.---On leaving you I went immediately to the conful's, and told him my errand in the prefence of the captain, who happened fortunately to be in company; I informed him that I came to afk his intereft to procure a paffage in the English frigate to Lifbon for two of my friends, Portuguefe gentlemen, and brothers :---the captain was fo obliging as to fay, that I needed not have made ufe of the conful's intereft; that my own was fufficient.---His name is J----, a man well known and refpected in this part of the world, and who will treat you with great kindnefs." " Heavens! exclaimed Alonfo, what fhould we have done without your friendfhip?—I am quite happy, my dear Pacheco, at what you tell me—I have now no doubt
of

of our getting to Lisbon in time for the India ship—This is all I desire; for I have there a friend whose confidence I can rely upon, and whose assistance will be sufficient to put my plan into execution." "Since we must part so soon then, said Pacheco, I am glad at least to find you satisfied with your prospect; but I must insist upon your accepting of this further supply—Come, I will have no excuse—you know, I run no risk—your father is rich, and this storm will one of these days blow over." "Well, be it so then, answered Alonso; I find it is in vain to resist the delicacy of your friendship." "I must now leave you for the present, said Pacheco; besides you have no time to lose—I will call on you in the afternoon, and accompany you on board—

Go and prepare your companion for the voyage—tell her she must put on her boldest looks."

As soon as he was gone, Alonso returned to Eugenia, and informed her of all that had passed.—They then immediately began to set about getting ready; and the hurry and agitation it occasioned, contributed to drown the recollection of what had been the cause of so much sorrow.

In the evening, Pacheco was punctual to his promise—he accompanied them on board—recommended them to the Captain, and with a tender and affectionate embrace, gave the last testimony of the value and sincerity of his friendship.

CHAP.

CHAP. VI.

ALONSO was now as impatient to arrive in his own country as he had formerly been to get out of it—and he was so agitated between the hope and fear of getting there in time, that every change of wind raised or depressed his spirits.—As for Eugenia, her only consolation was the love of Alonso; and her happiness and misery rose in proportion to his.—In the mean time, they had all the reason in the world to be satisfied with their treatment: both the Captain and the Officers behaved to them throughout the voyage with the humanity and politeness of gentlemen.—Eugenia however,

ever, thought it moſt prudent to decline their convivial pleaſures, and never failed pleading the indiſpoſition occaſioned by that kind of travelling as an excuſe for confining herſelf to her cabin.—But it was not ſo with Alonſo—he entered freely into their mirth and good humour —he was perfectly maſter of the Engliſh language; and the frankneſs and openneſs of his manners—his good ſenſe and an uncommon fund of knowledge for a young man at his time of life, contributed not a little to eraſe the unfavourable opinion they entertained of his countrymen.

One day that the converſation turned upon the good and bad qualities of different nations, Alonſo was aſked if aſſaſſination.

nation was as common in Portugal as it is in general underſtood to be. He anſwered, " That it was not; that it began to loſe ground, and that he believed it was owing to a greater depravity of manners."
—This appeared to them ſo great a paradox that he was deſired to explain himſelf. Alonſo, the better to be underſtood, and to vindicate his countrymen from the reflections which this cuſtom has occaſioned, ſaid, " it was neceſſary to enter into the out-lines of the hiſtory of Portugal."

" Moſt nations (continued he) trace their anceſtors from remoteſt time.—Jubal the ſon of Japhet, they pretend was the firſt who peopled our country—— however, without entering into diſquiſitions

tions which are only an additional mark of the vanity of mankind, I will confine myself merely to what may be ascertained with some degree of truth——The Greeks, Phœnicians, and Carthaginians, are the first people spoke of as the inhabitants of Portugal; and the various antiquities which are to be met with, corroborate History in this particular:—after them came the Romans, who remained in possession of it till the decline of their empire; when the Goths, Huns and Vandals made those famous revolutions in Europe.—Whatever then were the customs and manners to this period, they were such as were authorized by the most enlightened people at that time in the world.

"The

"The northern nations had not that continued poffeffion of Portugal, which they had of their other conquefts; for they were interrupted by the Moors, who in their turn again were difpoffeffed of it; fo that their cuftoms and manners had not time to take root; and as a proof of it, duelling is to this day little practifed among us, which is evidently a Gothic inftitution.

"It follows then, that the power which individuals affume among us to do juftice to themfelves, is derived from the firft inhabitants of Portugal, the Greeks and Romans; and has been handed down to their pofterity, notwithftanding the different revolutions that have happened.

"It

"It is no doubt happier for a people to remit all their animosities into the hands of others, than to decide them themselves; but as neither morals nor legislation have yet arrived to that perfection, is it not absurd, as with you, for a man to put himself on the footing with one who has violated every principle of honor and equity, and not only expose his life, but often fall a victim to the villain who deserves to lose it?—These are the arguments which we use.—However, what has been the great cause of assassination among us, is jealousy; —but now the intercourse and communication is grown so great, that a man sees it would be an endless task to punish the infidelities of the other sex— We therefore begin to imitate the manners

ners of our neighbours, and are satisfied with making reprisals on each other—You have all been in Spain; and I am persuaded you must have observed with surprize the familiarity in which men and women live in general with each other, though they are still considered by those who have not been among them as the same jealous kind of people they were about an hundred years ago.—They copied from the French—the French taught the Italians, and we shall soon be equal to either."

Most of the company were very well pleased with the conclusion of this argument, and were elated at the thoughts of solacing themselves with the black-eyed

eyed Lisbonians, without the apprehensions of a Stocada *.

ALONSO in the mean time retired to Eugenia, no ways desirous that she should be discovered on board an English man of war.

* The stab of a poniard.

CHAP.

CHAP. VII.

IT was now between four and five days since they had left Cadiz; and as the wind had been moſtly favorable, they were expecting every hour to diſcover the coaſt of Portugal.

Alonso was walking on the deck, when the man at the maſt-head, cried out, " The rock of Liſbon."—As they drew near, the firſt object of habitation that preſented itſelf to their ſight, was a ſmall convent made of cork, on the ſummit of the rock.—The officers began to rally him on the ſcore of religion, and aſked if he could come off with as good a grace a grace on that fubject, as he had on the other.

ALONSO, who was always ready to laugh at the follies and abfurdities of mankind of whatever nation, entered freely into their mirth, and told the following ftory of the fuperftition of his countrymen:

"NOT long ago, in the town in which I was born, (one of the moft confiderable in the kingdom,) I was witnefs to one of the moft ridiculous fcenes my eyes ever beheld.—Several people had been bit by mad dogs, and the unhappy fufferers were fent about three or four leagues diftant to an hermitage dedicated to Noftra Senhora de Vitelina, to offer

fer up their prayers for a cure; as she had the fame of restoring her votaries who had fallen under that calamity, to health.—However, the poor wretches died in spite of the interceffion of her Saintship: and as several others had been bit, it was suggested to one of the principal inhabitants, that there was in the family of a certain nobleman of high rank in Lisbon, a small iron, which had been made a present of many years ago by a Pope to one of his Ancestors, who was at that time ambassador at Rome. This iron had been consecrated by his Holiness, and was held as an infallible preventative to the bite of a mad dog, to those who were burnt with it on the fleshy part of their hand.—A messenger was thereupon immediately dispatched to

Lisbon

Lisbon for this iron, in behalf of the inhabitants of the town of———.

" Its arrival was ushered in with the ringing of bells—a charcoal fire was brought out into the market-place; and the whole inhabitants of town and country, from the bishop to the peasant, and from old age to infancy, went through this blistering ceremony, and retain the mark to this day."—The officers could not help admiring this instance of the imbecility of human nature—But, *à propos*, says one of them, now that we are upon the subject of religion—what say you to the inquisition? allow that that tribunal will reflect an eternal disgrace on your countrymen.—" Say rather, on human kind, replied Alonso.——Remember

member the penal laws in your own country, and the reigns of your Henry the Eighth and Queen Mary—there have at leaſt as many been burnt in England, as have ſuffered by the inquiſition.

"In ſhort, the truth is, no nation has been exempt from the tyranny of ſuperſtition; and the cloud which darkened England, and moſt parts of Europe, is not yet diſpelled in Portugal.—Our witches and ſorcerers, continued Alonſo, are now ſent as impoſtors to the houſe of correction, and the inquiſition is conſidered as an engine of ſtate."

"The crown, then, ſaid one of the gentlemen, will become more arbitrary; and the people as they get out of the hands of the priests, will fall under the rod of the minister."

" 'Tis true, return'd Alonso; and experience but too well justifies what you have advanced—few states have felt more severely the despotism of a minister than our own under the present government."—And yet, replied Capt. J——, the Count de Oyvras, (now Marquis de Pombal,) is considered as a great man in many parts of Europe.—" That is more than he is by his own countrymen, answered Alonso; and however they may be behind hand with other nations in the arts and sciences, and commerce of living; they are not so blind, but they can easily discover when the interest of the state is sacrificed to the advantage of of individuals, or suffers by a ruinous policy.

" We are more burdened at this present time, continued he, than at any former period; for besides the established revenues of past reigns, the king now receives from a late tax the whole riches of his subjects once in ten years; our commerce languishes, and is almost ruined by the monopolizing companies of the Brazil trade; the laws are trampled upon, and even private property is not secure against his venality; the army is like a body without a soul; in short, he has exhibited such instances of rigour and cruelty, that he is the dread of the whole nation.—Every domestic confidence is destroyed by the emissaries he is known to employ.—Perhaps, when his avarice is satiated, and he is arrived at the summit of power, he may, like Augustus, do good to mankind; but believe me, at present there is no order, no rank in society, but what detests him; and surely if he was a great man, he would at least have some party to espouse his cause.—I mean not, however, to depreciate what there is valuable in his character.—The measures he has pursued with the church, were dictated by the soundest policy; and it must be allowed, it required some exertion of power to go through with them.—They cannot fail promoting the increase of population; and it is to be hoped, that future reigns, unfettered from the chains of the priests, will restore vigour to the laws."

WE

"We are much obliged to you, said one of the company, for giving us this epitome of your prime minister; but as one is naturally led to ask questions about a man, whose administration has been so much the subject of conversation in England—pray what family is he of?—how came he first into the cabinet?"

"As to his family, answered Alonso, his ancestors where what we call Homems Branco, (white men;) in short, his father was a provincial gentleman in low circumstances in the north of Portugal—he served during his younger years in the army, beginning, as was the custom of those days, with a musket—he arrived to the rank of lieutenant, but was afterwards dismissed the service as a bad officer.

cer.—He then came to Lisbon to sollicit some place in the civil department; and as he had received a liberal education, he found means to get employment in one of the public offices—he afterwards had the addreſs to recommend himself to the people who were then in power, and was appointed succeſſively as Envoy to the Courts of London, Paris, the Hague, and Vienna. At this laſt, he was married to a German of diſtinction; by which means he ſtrengthened his intereſt at home; for the then Queen of Portugal was of the Houſe of Auſtria, and he managed to get ſo much into the good graces of her Majeſty, that at his return he had the art to ſupplant the Secretary, through whoſe protection I have underſtood he had been raiſed."

By

By this time they had entered the Tagus—The weather was serene and mild, and tho' the evening began to approach, the sun had not got below the horizon—Every thing contributed to the grandeur and magnificence of the prospect—the breadth of the river—the stillness of the water—the sporting of fish, and the beauty and variety of the country struck their senses with admiration.—Eugenia was upon deck, and joined in the general applause.—At night they cast anchor in the harbour; and our adventurers, after many protestations of gratitude and regard, took advantage of the boat to go ashore.

CHAP. VIII.

AS soon as they were landed, Alonso went in search of a porter to take charge of their trunk, and proceeded to look out for a lodging in the most sequestered parts of the city. As he was perfectly acquainted with the geography of Lisbon, it was not long before he found an apartment suitable to their purpose.

It was now that Alonso stood in need of all his caution to keep himself unknown; for he had every thing to apprehend from the resentment of the family of Don Pedro, and the friends of the deceased Don Gusman, who would naturally consider him as the author of their misfortunes.

THE

THE first enquiries he made, were to know the forwardness of the Goa ship; and finding that it would soon be ready for its intended voyage, he addressed himself to Mr. H――, (an English gentleman belonging to the factory, a friend of his father's, with whom he was intimately acquainted,) for advice and assistance in the accomplishment of this scheme.

THE method Alonso took to procure an interview with this gentleman, was to request of him to call at his lodgings at a certain time; that he would excuse any further explanation, than that he would meet with one, to whose person and family he was no stranger, and who stood in need of his confidence and friendship.

Mr.

Mr. H—— did not fail to repair to the place of rendezvous at the appointed hour—How great was his surprise at the sight of Alonso!—He embraced him with kindness. " But how is it possible, he exclaimed, that you dare shew yourself in this place ?" " Mr. H——, answered Alonso, you are the only one I have entrusted with the secret; and it is on your kindness and friendship I depend, to extricate myself out of the difficulties I am in." He then gave him a detail of the various scenes he had gone through, since he left ——, and of his resolution to go to the Indies.

Mr. H——, after hesitating a little, said, he saw a better prospect for him in the Brazils; that the fleet to those parts

parts was ready to sail, and that he did not doubt but he would be able to get him into some employment in that part of the world, where a more extensive line would be opened to him than the Indies. Alonso overjoyed, closed in immediately with the proposal. The next day Mr. H—— returned, and informed him, he had procured him a place of between three and four hundred pounds a year, and that he must get himself ready to embark. It was then that Alonso formed a resolution which required all his efforts to execute. "Mr. H——, said he, I have but one favour more to ask of you, and which I know your influence can procure—use your interest to get me two years advance:—this request appears strange to you—excuse
giving

giving my reasons for the present; but depend upon it, they will soon justify me in your own mind."

Alonso delivered himself with such earnestness and expression, that Mr. H— declined urging any questions on this head, and promised his endeavours to serve him.—As he was a man of great weight from his extensive dealings, and of so amiable and worthy a character, that both natives and foreigners revered him, he did not find it very difficult to succeed in this farther application for his friend. The next morning he returned with the money. Alonso embraced him—" You shall now be a witness, said he, of the use I make of this sum;" and taking him by the hand, led him into the apartment of Eugenia. " I pre-

"I present to you, said Alonso, my benefactor and friend; one who considers our conduct rather as the effect of intemperate youth than premeditated vice."— Eugenia confused at so unexpected a visit, was immediately covered with blushes. Alonso then, with a faultering voice, and the tears starting into his eyes, asked her if she was convinced of his love. The frame of Eugenia shook at the strangeness of the question, and the agitation she saw him in. She could hardly articulate an answer:—at last, with a trembling accent, she said, "How could I ever doubt it?" "Alas! resumed Alonso, we must part." "Part!" exclaimed Eugenia. "But to meet again," added Alonso. He then informed her of the obligations he had to Mr. H—, of the imprudence and impossibility there was of her accompanying him, and the necessity he was under of going immediately on board. " Ah ! Alonso, I see through the rest—and must it then be so ?—Oh, Heavens ! will you leave me ?—What ! torn from the object of my love—an outcast from my friends, abandoned by the world—will you thus forsake me ?" " Oh, Eugenia ! returned Alonso, rend not thus my heart—when time has calmed the agitation of your mind, you will approve of the measures I have taken for your happiness.—This sum is sufficient to maintain you in a retirement not only with decency and ease, but in safety from the taunts and the malice of the world ; and I swear to you by all I hold dear, by the constancy and

and ardour of my love, that I will preferve for you an inviolable attachment; and if in the future courfe of events our paffion can be united with the fanction of the laws, I will embrace the opportunity with joy." A mournful filence enfued; and Eugenia, pale, dejected, and overcome with grief, caft a look of the fofteft languifhment on Alonfo. Mr. H—— felt for their diftrefs; but as he could not but inwardly applaud the refolution of his friend, and apprehenfive that it might give ground from the fcene of tendernefs, he enlarged upon the expediency and advantage of his going abroad.

" It is impoffible, Madam, continued he, that you can remain long together

in this country without being found out;
and if that should be the case, I need
not describe the unhappy consequences
of a discovery both to yourself and
Alonso.---Don Pedro is in Spain, and
Gusman in the grave, but you know
they have left friends and relations behind them.---Suppose yourselves, however, free from private vengeance, yet
the execution of the laws would involve
you in ruin; and though the clemency
of the king might mitigate their rigour,
yet the greatest indulgence you could
expect, would be imprisonment to yourself, and exile to Alonso.---Pardon me
this freedom of expression; but an ill-
timed delicacy might be the ruin of you
both: Consider on the other hand, that
Alonso's absence secures safety to you,

and

and promotes his own welfare; and where could he go to so much advantage as to the Brazils?—he is already in possession of an employment, from the emoluments of which, he is able to establish you in ease and independency." "Alas!" said Eugenia, and must Alonso toil two long years to promote my ease? Is it on these conditions I am to live in independency?—rather let him keep the money, and endeavour to find out some way that I may accompany him."

"Madam, replied Mr. H——, I admire the force and the delicacy of your love; but Alonso will have no need to slave in that country, to make himself amends for the disinterested mark he has given you of his attachment:—There are

are many avenues to wealth, and the abilities of Alonſo leaves no room to doubt of his ſucceſs."

"As to your accompanying him, it is quite out of the queſtion—I could give you numberleſs reaſons againſt it, —but believe me, you would be diſcovered; and the knowledge of the diſguiſe would not only prove fatal to yourſelves, but be attended with diſagreeable conſequences to me; and ſuch has been the ſecrecy I have been obliged to make uſe of in this affair, that Alonſo for the future is not to be known by his own name. Come, Madam, continued Mr. H——, take courage;—look forward with the hopes of happy days—your affairs are not ſo deſperate

sperate as you imagine—remember Don Pedro is old, and you will have frequent opportunities of hearing from Alonso."

Eugenia was a little calmed by these representations; and Alonso judging it the critical moment to put his resolution in force, a carriage was immediately got ready, and Mr. H—— accompanied them to the convent.

The abbess was a woman of great sense and feeling; and being accustomed to see distress and affliction take refuge within their walls, received them with sympathy and kindness.

Whilst the two lovers were drowned in tears and embraces, Mr. H―― took her to one fide, and informed her of fuch particulars as he thought neceffary, refpecting her new gueft.—At laft the mournful fcene of feparation took place; and Alonfo filent and melancholy retired with his friend.

CHAP.

CHAP. IX.

ALONSO returned to his lodgings immersed in grief; and putting together the few necessaries he had left, proceeded immediately on board. Mr. H—— accompanied him. "My friend, (said he), how can I ever requite your goodness, and the service you have done me? Yet I beg of you, give me this further instance of your friendship—Acquaint my father with what you have seen; and tell him, that I beseech his forgiveness and love."—" I will, (answered Mr. H——); and I have no doubt of his returning affection."—" I pray you, too, (added Alonso) let Pacheco know

this part of my hiſtory."—Mr. H——
promiſed he would.——They then embraced, and parted.

As ſoon as he found himſelf alone, he
retired to his cabin, and throwing himſelf on the bed, gave full vent to his
afflictions.

The firſt object that in idea preſented itſelf to his mind, was the unhappy Eugenia—a prey to anguiſh—comfortleſs and
repining among ſtrangers!—Then ſtart-
ing up with phrenzy, curſed his fatal
reſolution, and wiſhed himſelf aſhore—
Don Pedro, then, and the friends of
Don Guſman, would occur to his re-
membrance, and moderate his fury—
the idea, too, of an offended, indulgent

gent father, whose frowns he dreaded more than the vengeance of his enemies, would stare him in the face, and convince him it was best to be where he was.—At last, overpowered with the fatigue and agitation of his mind, sleep welcomed him to repose.

In the mean time, the ship proceeded on her voyage with a prosperous gale; and before he awoke, had lost sight of land.

What first disturbed his rest, was something of a small size, and very hard, that he found himself lying upon—he perceived it was something in his coat pocket, which had got under him, and putting in his hand to take it out, he found it was a purfe——he was hardly yet a-wake, to know where he was——at laft, recovering from his flumbers, and tracing the various fcenes he had lately gone through, he was foon convinced that Mr. H—— was the author of this friendly piece of fervice.

As he had left all the money he had received for the fupport of Eugenia, without ever taking thought about himfelf, this generofity of his friend was very well timed.

AFTER taking fome refrefhment, he defired to know what paffengers were on board; for as yet he had made no enquiries of that kind.——He was informed, that there was a Francifcan
friar

friar—a Brazil merchant—an officer of the army, and a young civilian, who was returning from college to his own country. Alonso was very well pleased with this intelligence; for though he knew his countrymen, in general, had confined notions, yet the different professions of his fellow-passengers, he was persuaded, must have enabled them to acquire a greater share of learning, and knowledge of the world, than was to be met with in people of more ordinary stations in life.——He was resolved, therefore, to make one with them at dinner, and to endeavour to dissipate, in conversation, the gloom which hung upon his mind.

As soon as the captain had introduced him to his other guests, the cordelier, whose countenance bespoke the most good humour, immediately began the conversation;—" Gentlemen (says he), I give you joy on the acquisition of our comrade. — Sir, (continues the priest), addressing himself to Alonso, I see you have been one of the votaries to love— Your air and manner bespeak it, and I don't doubt but you have touched the heart of many a fair lady—I see the adventures of this young gentleman will afford us great entertainment."— " My good father, (replied Alonso), if you will make us confidantes of yours, we shall need no other pastime to the end of the voyage." — The company smiled,

smiled, and approved of the reply.—
" Why, it is true, (resumed the friar) that I can speak, without boasting, of some atchievements that way; and you know, major, (addressing himself to the officer) that the ladies don't always confine their favours to smart cocked hats."
—" Gentlemen, (continued the priest) I am a Brazilian by birth, and belong to the convent of Capuchins, in the Rio de Janeiro—Our superior found it necessary to send somebody over to court, on the business of the Order, and I was pitched upon for that embassy.

" On my arrival at Lisbon, I presented myself, with letters of recommendation, to the archbishop of Evora, through whose interest with Paulo de Carvalho (brother

(brother to the count de Oyeras,) I was given to underſtand I was to depend upon ſucceſs.—The archbiſhop received me with a great deal of cordiality, and promiſed his good offices in favour of our Order.—In effect, he ſpoke to Paulo de Carvalho, and preſented me to him.

"His Excellency told me, that my buſineſs ſhould be done.—However, I did not preſume that his words would be immediately made good; and laid my account with a good deal of attendance.—In the mean time, I congratulated myſelf on being known to the brother of the prime miniſter; and as the reception I had met with entitled me to take frequent opportunities of paying

paying my court to him, I did not find it difficult to commence an acquaintance with his favourite valet.—After our intimacy was pretty far advanced, he made me the confidante of his master's amours.—This was just what I aimed at.——I found likewise, to my great joy, that an old friar of our Order, was confessor to his mistress.—I therefore lost no time in getting acquainted with him; and as he thought himself a party concerned in the success, he espoused our cause with great warmth, and introduced me to Donna Mariana de Mendonia, the lady in question: I told my story with so good a grace, that what with that, and a small present I made her duenna, to bribe her mistress's favour, I got frequent interviews. In short, I played

my

my cards fo well, that Donna Mariana chofe to fpend her retired hours in my company; and I foon found her intereft of more weight than the archbifhop's; for I not only fucceeded in my own bufinefs, but have been the means of preferment to this gentleman."

" 'Tis true, (faid the major); and if it had not been my good fortune to get accidentally acquainted with his reverence, at the minifter's levee, I fuppofe I fhould ftill have been dancing attendance in the anti-chamber."—" Padre, (continues this gentleman) to judge of your fuccefs in your own country, from this inftance of your addrefs in Portugal, you muft have acquired fo many laurels, that I would willingly ferve my noviciate

ate under you, on our arrival."—" Sir, (anfwered the friar, pretending to affume a grave air), I find you have miftaken the purity of my intentions—don't you fee that my connections with Donna Mariana, were only to ferve our holy Order, and our mother church, on which depends the falvation of mankind?— What! did you think me fo carnally difpofed, as to enjoy her with a vicious appetite?"—My dear father, (refumed the officer), I don't difpute the purity of your motives; but I dare fay you did think much of Paradife at the time." The company laughed; and the jolly cordelier said fmilingly, " I fee I have been ferving a Samaritan and a finner."

CHAP.

CHAP. X.

DURING this converſation, the merchant and the young civilian had remained ſilent, teſtifying only by their geſtures, the different effect it had on them.— Alonſo deſirous to be better acquainted with their characters, and to gather ſome information upon a ſubject he was perſuaded the former was well converſant in; addreſſed himſelf to him in this manner. " Sir, (ſaid he) what an happineſs it is for our country to be poſſeſſed of ſo vaſt a continent in America!— Our commerce and riches in that part of the world, not only ſecure us from contempt; but give us weight among

among other nations.—For we muſt allow that Portugal is in itſelf but a mere ſpot."

" Sir, replied the man of buſineſs, if it is from the trade and riches of the Brazils alone we derive conſideration; we ſhall ſoon fall, I am afraid, in the opinion of mankind." " How ſo, aſked Alonſo?"—"Why, (reſumed the merchant) till the preſent miniſter's time, the trade to the Brazils was open to all his majeſty's ſubjects; and the community at large derived advantage from it; but the eſtabliſhment of the companies, with ſuch excluſive privileges, has proved not only ruinous, by annihilating that ſpirit of enterprize and induſtry which reſults from the proſpect of gain, and is the ſupport of thouſands, but confines the wealth acquired by the trade of that part of the world

world to a few, which before was generally diffused throughout the kingdom.

"I can assure you that our exports to the Brazils are so much decreased, that those countries which supplied us with their manufactures, must in time be insensibly affected by it. And as the returns are only in proportion to the exports, there must be a great diminution of the revenues of the king, and of the number and property of the inhabitants. This is so much the case, that my errand to Lisbon was, principally to represent the bad effects which have been felt from this ruinous policy; and to beg in behalf of the merchants and others, a restoration of the former freedom of trade. But I have not been so successful as

our

our friend the friar here. — The Count de Oyeras has no miſtreſs, and beſides he is too fond of money.—Indeed I fee'd his ſecretaries and ſervants, but I had not wherewithal to bribe the maſter; for I need not tell you the advantages which reſult to his excellency, from the eſtabliſhment of the companies.— Unfortunately his politics and the intereſt of the ſtate, are too often at variance; otherwiſe his private emoluments would not be ſo much attended to."

"Oh! it would be endleſs, (ſaid the civilian) to mention the inſtances of his avarice and ſelfiſhneſs; however, I cannot help taking notice of one, which falls more immediately under the cognizance of my profeſſion, and which probably

probably you are unacquainted with. There is a perquisite of about two hundred milreis*, that belongs to the principal secretary of state, for every new law that is made. There have been more 'enacted during his administration, than from the time of the establishment of the Braganza family to the time of his coming into office; and it is plain it could be with no other view, than private interest: for there never was a period that the laws were so little attended to. And such is the despotism of the man, that though from the constitution of the monarchy, out-judges† ought to be appointed every three years, on which the property and security of

* Between fifty and sixty pounds.
† Juiz de Foras in Portugal.

the subject so much depend, yet he reserves the time in his own breast, and keeps the vacancies unfilled up; thereby rendering the most established law in our government, arbitrary and precarious; that the people may be accustomed to no other authority, but the will of the king or his minister."

" What then! (says the major) I see that your profession holds him in the same degree of estimation as ours!—Well, there will be the greater jubilee when he makes his exit."

" Gentlemen, (said Alonso) this man whom you exclaim so much against, is however considered in Europe, as one of the greatest ministers of the age; for my own part, I am so far from that opinion, that I cannot help joining with the general voice of my countrymen. Foreigners do not consider the uncontrouled power he exercises; and that the inactivity and inattention of the king allows him to do just what he pleases.—Place any man but of moderate abilities, and a tolerable share of courage at the helm, with the authority he enjoys, and I am confident, that was he but a friend to mankind, he would not only acquire a greater name, but would be a blessing to his country."

This proposition was readily assented to; " But since, (says the merchant) that we have reasoned so freely upon his bad qualities, it is but just to remark instances

ces wherein his policy has proved beneficial. It muſt be granted then, that his conduct with regard to the Engliſh has been maſterly; and that inſtead of eight hundred thouſand pounds, formerly the balance of trade in their favour with us, it is now reduced to one fourth of that ſum, ſo that we receive the difference in the manufactures of other nations, at a much eaſier rate, than from them."

"It is only time, (anſwered Alonſo) that can determine the advantages of this policy, and perhaps the period is not far off. According to the treaties between the two kingdoms, England has an excluſive right to the furniſhing us with their manufactures; and in conſequence of this preference, they

they are bound to protect us from the attempts of our enemies. Now the breach of these treaties has raised the resentment of the English, and perhaps, when our enemies think fit to be troublesome, they may consider it as not worth their while to grant us assistance.—Nay, they may even argue that they will receive greater advantages by Portugal falling into the hands of the Spaniards;— that conniving at this addition of strength, would detach them from their connections with France, and induce them to make a more beneficial treaty of commerce with them, than they could do with us.----However I will readily allow, that if England considers it as her interest to support our independency, notwithstanding these infractions, then our

our minister has acted the part of a good politician."

During these profound arguments the friar kept nodding from his chair, and played time with his nose to the discourse of our reasoners.---- At last, silence taking place, he suddenly cried out, Gentlemen, a truce for one moment.---- I challenge any of you to a party at backgammon.---- The officer said he was his man.; so the tables were called for.

CHAP.

CHAP. XI.

ALONSO no sooner found himself at liberty, than he retired to his cabin, in order to indulge that melancholy from which he had so lately emerged.---- The transition was so quick, that it seemed as if his mind had borne with impatience any other sentiment. However he was no longer agitated with that violence of passion which had almost subdued his reason, and brought him to the brink of despair. Eugenia was the first object of contemplation, and a sudden tear would accompany the soft emotions of his soul, at the remembrance of one whom he held so dear. Then the ills their

their amour had been the cause of, would present themselves to view. These again would make way for more pleasing sensations—the approbation of his conduct in placing her in ease and safety in retirement, and the distant but pleasing hopes of events favourable to their love. The resentment and anger too of his father, he flattered himself, would be appeased by the representations of his friend, and contribute to reconcile him to the situation he was in. With these sentiments he went to bed, and did not awake till the next day, that the captain came and told him, That they were sailing with God and a fair wind; and if he took such long doses, they would be at the end of their voyage before he got out of his cot. Come, here are the other

other gentlemen, continued he, who have been enquiring after you since daybreak.

Alonso, who found himself quite refreshed, and in better spirits than he had been for some time past, hastened on his cloaths, and immediately joined the company.—" Cavalheiro, (says the friar) I have beaten these four gentlemen all round, and I only want you to add to my triumph—but we will not begin yet.—Come, captain, let us have something to eat;—Hold, I will treat you this morning myself.—Boy, bring me that round small box that is in my cabin.—Here, gentlemen, is a present of Donna Mariana's---cakes and sweet-meats made with her own hands.---Come, fall to."

to."---The company did not need much pressing; and the officer desired to drink to the health of his patroness---" Father, (continued he) when I return to Portugal, I hope you will make me your ambassador to Donna Mariana, that I may have an opportunity of acknowledging the favours, which, through your means, I owe her."---" Ah! Lorenzo, (he exclaimed) if thy misfortunes had not happened quite so soon"---" Lorenzo! (answered the friar) who is Lorenzo? What has he to do in the present case?" ---" A young man, a brother officer of mine, (replied the major) who was lately banished to Angola, which you know is the most wretched and unhealthy settlement we possess on the coast of Africa."---" And how came he to be banished?"

nished?" (asked the priest) " For the same reason (answered the major) that you or any of us would have been—for speaking too freely of the minister---Some injustice had been done him in the regiment, and he gave his tongue too much liberty in accusing his excellency as the author of it.---All the interest that could be made in his favour, was not sufficient to appease the marquis's *courroux*; and I was lamenting that his disgrace happened before I was acquainted with you, that I might have saved him from destruction."---" I am sorry for it; (returned the friar) I dare say I should have been of use to him." " I doubt of that, father, (said the man of business,) our minister has been always found implacable in these cases, and of his life as a foldier in the artillery, was difcharged as unfit for fervice. The king remained in arrears to him fix years pay; and, befides, he claimed the value of a mule, which had been preffed from him during the war, for his majefty's fervice.—He fet forth his claims in a petition to the king, which he prefented himfelf.—After waiting fome days in fruitlefs attendance, he prefented another, which the king likewife received, and gave to one of his fuit.---However, as this met with the fame fate as the firft, he determined to prefent a third; but the king recollecting the man's face again, pufhed it on one fide, and faid to him, "Fellow, why do you plague me thus with your petitions?"---The old foldier was obliged to retire, but fullen and thoughtful, thus he reasoned with himself.---" I have served the king the best part of my life --- I am now old, and he owes me money---yet he not only refuses to pay me, but treats me with contempt---I will have satisfaction."

Accordingly he provided himself with a long stout stick, with which he was resolved to give his majesty a drubbing the next morning as he went a-hunting;---he therefore planted himself, very composedly, at the park gate; and just as his majesty passed through, he fell most heartily upon him; and if he had not been immediately seized, he would probably have brought the king to the ground.---The attendants in their fury would instantly have dispatched him,

him, if they had not been prevented by the king, who called out to them to spare his life. He was ordered into strict custody; and, soon after, all his friends and relations, and those with whom he had any intimacy or acquaintance, were sent to prison, in order to find out who it was that had instigated him to so rash an action;---but all their enquiries proved fruitless, and it did not appear that he had any accomplices, but had acted merely from a principle of taking satisfaction for the injustice the king had done him.---What became of the poor fellow afterwards, God knows;---but the army owe him, at least, this piece of service, that sometime afterward their arrears were paid."

CHAP.

CHAP. XII.

THE Company thanked the major for his anecdote; and as they had by this time finished their repast, and the sweet-meats and cordials (Portugueze fare) being removed, the friar, who did not like long arguments, took the advantage of a pause, and called for the tables.—" Now Cavalheiro (says he, addressing himself to Alonso) you are going to encounter the first player in the Brazils; so placing the men, and rattling the dice, they immediately set to.—The friar lost the two or three first hits in tolerable good humour; and would only now and then exclaim at the lucky throws of of his adverfary: but Alonfo's advantage continuing, he began to grow uneafy.— At laft not being able to get a fingle game, he very calmly put the box upon the table, and looking ftedfaftly on Alonfo, " Pray, Sir, (fays he) where did you learn to play at back-gammon?"—" In England, (replied Alonfo.") ---- " In England! (cried the friar) What among hereties.! —— Among people under the dominion of the devil! ---- Truly I am not furprifed. at your beating me. But pray, what carried you to that country? I hope you was not long in it." " Several years, (anfwered Alonfo.) I was educated there." ---- " What! you educated there! the young man is loft! ruined! undone! Your parents furely could never be good Catholics. --- Well, what

what a plentiful harveſt Satan will have to reap in England!----Yet theſe Engliſh were formerly a nation of ſaints. Alas! what a pity it is that the good St. Mary, that queen of bleſſed memory, was ſucceeded by ſuch a woman as Elizabeth!----What martyrs there muſt have fallen in that reign!" "O truly a great many martyrs (replied Alonſo); do you know Father, that one Rapin, whom they conſider as their beſt hiſtorian, ſays, that in the reign you allude to, out of nine thouſand four hundred prieſts, who were at that time Roman Catholics, only one hundred and eighty of them choſe to quit their benefices, to preſerve their religion? All the reſt turned Proteſtants. My dear father, (continued Alonſo) theſe Engliſh are notwithſtand-
ing

ing a good sort of people. "What! and have neither the mass nor the cross among them! A very good kind of people truly! but does not our holy father the pope send missionaries to convert them? Methinks I could suffer martyrdom in so good a cause." "O yes, (replied Alonso), and be crucified in their bagnios."— "In their bagnios! (returned the friar), pray how is that?" "A very pleasant kind of martyrdom, (said Alonso) and what the disciples of St. Francis are very fond of. Imagine yourself in a handsome room, elegantly furnished —wax lights—a good supper—fine wine, and a Donna Mariana to partake of it.— Now father, say ingenuously would you think much of paradise in the agonies of crucifixion?"—The company laughed, and the padre shaking his head—" I see (said he) that he is a lost sheep."

" Raillery however aside, (says the civilian) I am glad to find myself with one who has been so long in a country that makes such a distinguished figure at present in the world.—From this little anecdote you have mentioned of their bagnios, I suppose they are not that brutal kind of people they are represented."—" By no means, (replied Alonso), their manners to be sure are not so gentle or officious as ours, but it must be allowed they are more honest and sincere.—I have heard it said indeed, by foreigners, who have been long among them, that since the last peace, they have been making great strides towards the

the politesse of their neighbours.—However there are sensible people who condemn that outward grimace, which prevails at present through the lower ranks. They say these manners are unnatural to their constitution, and look upon it as a sign that they are ripe for a more arbitrary government."—It is certain, (replied the civilian) that despotism and exterior politeness originated together with the Romans."—" For my own part, (said Alonso) if I might venture an opinion on this subject, I should be inclined to compare the English liberties to those of the Romans under Augustus; and I am persuaded that without some violent concussion in the state, to give play to the passions, and thereby restore the constitution to its first principles, the
boasted

boasted freedom of England will soon be on a level with other states." "And yet, said the lawyer, to judge from the accounts we have in the gazettes, of what passes in that country, it would seem as if the king sometimes had hardly the power to keep himself upon the throne."

"These clamours which you hear of, are nothing at all (returned Alonso); and the king knows too well his own strength, to be apprehensive about them. In short, their parliament is so venal, that a majority is always devoted to the crown; and though it does not seem to be the intentions of the present monarch, to place himself above the laws, yet his ministers will sometimes act as if it was. On these occasions,

the

the people will be noisy; but what avails it? Their representatives are the first to betray them.—You will naturally say—Why don't the electors chuse honester men? and that the whole mass of people must be corrupt. I will allow, that there is something in this; but then you must know, that there are a great many boroughs at present in England, that are fallen to such poverty and wretchedness, as to be inhabited only by miserable fishermen; at the same time, that many of the most opulent and flourishing towns in the kingdom have not that privilege of representation. —It therefore cannot be justly said, that the morals of the people are in general corrupt, as long as this inconvenience exists; but if it is not reme-
died

died, and there should come a prince inclined to exercise the authority over his subjects which he found himself possessed of, they would then either become violent, outrageous, and reform the constitution, or be forced to submit to the yoke." " The pre-sentiment of the loss of their liberties, (continued Alonso) ought to fill the mind of every Englishman with horror——— They ought to contrast opulence, independency and happiness—the appendages of freedom—to despotism—the uncertainty of property, and all that train of evils which accompany arbitrary power. This picture they ought constantly to have in view, in order to awaken their attention to their interest, prosperity, and welfare."

" I must

"I MUST confefs (fays the civilian,) that you appear to me an extraordinary inftance of the force of education.—— Why, you fpeak with the enthufiafm of a Roman, and have quite forgot that you are only a Portuguefe."

CHAP.

CHAP. XIII.

IT would be endlefs to recount the various converfe and paftime during the remainder of the voyage; fuffice it to fay, that Alonfo's travels and philofophy were a great fund of entertainment to his fellow-paffengers.

THE friar, indeed, would fometimes think that his tenets were not quite orthodox; and he was confirmed in this opinion, from an argument that one day very accidentally arofe, in fpeaking of the former happinefs of the world. Alonfo faid he was of opinion, that there was more general happinefs in our days,

days, than in those of any other period. The civilian himself seemed startled at this proposition; and though he generally coincided with him in most points, he differed from him in this.—" Pray let us hear (said he) how you make out this doctrine." " I am persuaded (resumed Alonso) that this way of thinking is greatly owing to an ignorance of the state of society, in the different ages of the world; let us, therefore, take a cursory view of antient and modern times, and then determine how far the golden days of antiquity are preferable to our own.

The Assyrians, Medes, and Persians, are the first large assemblages of mankind, who present themselves to our view.—The Egyptians, too, were famed
in

in those days for their power, riches, and learning; yet these people were all comprehended in part of Asia, and a small part of Africa; and as the governments of the East, have, in all ages, been founded on extreme despotism, it will be hard for us to allow any tolerable share of happiness to men who were continually subject to the tyranny and caprice of their governors. As to the Grecians, who are the next in progression, though their arts and learning are accounted, to this day, the noblest monuments of human wisdom; yet the possessions of these venerable ancients, were, excepting some few colonies, confined to part of Turkey in Europe, the islands of the Morea and Archipelago, and a small skirt on the coast of Asia:

Afia: and when once Alexander came to usurp the sovereign command over them, and conquered the Persians, the former had forfeited all pretensions to the virtues of their ancestors; and the latter continued to be governed by the same arbitrary principles, to which they had ever been accustomed.—The Romans and Carthaginians were then the only people who enjoyed freedom; but they were at that time too inconsiderable to be ranked among the large societies of men.—These two republics encreased in power and rivalship, till the latter was entirely overthrown; and during the interval of contention, while the Carthaginians were in the zenith of their glory, their government was so arbitrary and severe to the people under their subjection, that the history of their power is not that of the happiness of men*. It was not so, indeed, with the Romans.——In their advancement to greatness, they were famed for their simplicity, integrity, magnanimity, and disinterestedness; and governed with mildness and justice their extensive conquests. In the end, they became the arbiters of kings and states; and the energy of their government diffused happiness, for a time, to the universe.

* The Carthaginians, in order to render the Sardinians and Corsicans more dependent, prohibited them, on pain of death, from planting, sowing, or any thing of the like kind. Livy, Book VII.

It

It is, then, under the Romans, that we muſt fix upon ſome period, as the happieſt of antiquity. Suppoſe that of Auguſtus. It is true, that at that time, the republic had aſſumed a more arbitrary appearance; however, the Romans ſtill retained a great love of freedom, and enjoyed it both in their manners, and in their government; and, as it was at that time they were at the heighth of their power, none other, I think, can be ſo properly pitched upon. —The Romans were then in poſſeſſion of Italy, Spain, France, part of Germany, Britain, Turkey in Europe, a conſiderable part of Aſia, Egypt, and the moſt fertile parts of Africa, and all the iflands of the Mediterranean, Morea, and Archipelago.—A vaft empire!

"Let us now compare thofe days with our own; for to the decline of the empire and its total overthrow by the northern nations, none other can come in queftion.

"In the firft place then, we will allow, that their perfons and properties, at the time we are fpeaking of, were fecured by the vigour of the laws, but thofe of the conquered nations were held in continual uncertainty; and how fmall a portion the Romans bore to the people whom they had fubdued, is eafily feen by comparing the limits of Italy
(allowing

(allowing the utmoſt latitudes not only to its inhabitants, but to thoſe of their municipal towns) to their extenſive conqueſts.---And it will be readily granted, that many governors of provinces were guilty of the moſt flagrant injuſtice, and by the treaſures they had amaſſed, ſcreened themſelves from the puniſhment they deſerved.

" As to their manners at this period, they were ſociable and eaſy—that rough but honeſt fierceneſs had gradually worn off from a continual intercourſe with foreign nations; from a ſeries of proſpeperity, which had introduced eaſe, affluence and luxury, and from the accumulated

mulated learning, arts, and sciences of the Grecians and other nations.

"Now, with respect to our own times---The present civilized state of the world comprehends Europe in a more exalted state than ever was known. It is true, that that part of the Roman empire in Asia and Africa was happier, and more flourishing than it is at present;--- but so great a part of Europe which was at that time immersed in barbarism, and where government, arts, and sciences, now flourish, fully compensate for.

"BESIDES, consider the present state of America;---the English colonies alone, on that continent, afford a prospect of rivalling the greatest empires of antiquity.

"At what period of time shall we find such numerous bodies of men, as at present, governed independently by their own laws? and though the governments that actually exist, do not in general tend to produce those great examples of patriotism and heroic virtue as are to be met with among the Greeks and Romans, I will venture to affirm, that there is a more extensive philanthropy, and an easier commerce among mankind than ever was known."

Here Alonso stopt.----The friar began to yawn.----" Sir, (says he), to be sure you

you have made all you have been saying very plain; but it is all Hebrew to me.---I thought it was as I said;---Your Englifh education has made you an heretic---You reafon too much to be a good catholick."------The others feemed inclined to be of his way of thinking; and even the civilian, though he could not confute what Alonfo had advanced, thought it the fafeft doctrine to continue in the old track---that the world is growing worfe and worfe.

C H A P.

CHAP. XIV.

IT was now about six weeks since they had left Lisbon; and as the constancy of the trade winds enabled them to determine, with tolerable precision, the time of their arrival, they expected every hour to come within sight of land. In a day or two afterwards, they discovered the coast of Brazils, and were not long before they cast anchor in the Rio de Janiero.

Alonso had so conducted himself during the voyage, that he had entirely gained the affections of his fellow passengers;

fengers; for though he was greatly their fuperior in point of abilities, yet he was far from that arrogance and prefumption fo common to his countrymen; and as they were moft of them natives of that part of the world, they did not fail to fhew him the kindeft inftances of their fervice.

THE firft enquiries he made, as foon as he got a-fhore, were to know if any conveyance offered of writing to Europe; for neither abfence nor the diftance he found himfelf from Eugenia, had leffened his attachment and love.---To his great joy he found there was a fhip almoft ready to fail; he, therefore, did not let pafs that opportunity

of

Of ALONSO.

of informing her of his arrival, and inclosed it in a letter to his friend Mr. H——. As soon as he found himself a little settled, he began to cultivate, thro' the means of his cabin friends, a more general acquaintance. He found the inhabitants of that part of the world more hospitable than those of his own country; and as they were more affluent and rich, they could, with the greater ease, exercise their beneficence. The count de B—— was at that time captain-general—a man so universally beloved, that the people, in general, would have sacrificed their lives to serve him; for he was not like the common run of governors in that part of the world.— He respected the interests of his sovereign;

reign;—but, as an individual, he was just, humane, liberal, of great affability, and was satisfied with the emoluments annexed to his rank, without aiming at acquisitions which must have been disgraced with tyranny and extortion.

Alonso was so fortunate as to get into the good graces of the count de B——; and as he found himself continually gaining ground, he did not doubt but that his excellency would, in time, give him such an instance of his protection and patronage, as would be greatly to his interest and advantage.—It was not long before his expectations were gratified.—He was appointed to an employment

ployment in the diamond mines, which promised the most flattering prospect; for, independant of a large addition of salary, there occurred such opportunities of gain, that those who had the address to profit by them, never failed to acquire a great and rapid fortune.—It is true, that this method of jumping, at once, into affluence, will not stand the test of much casuistry; however, custom has rendered it so far justifiable, that it is taken for granted, that those who meet with such large temptations, will try every expedient to elude the vigilance of the laws, established for the security of that valuable branch of the revenue.

Alonso

Alonso congratulated himself on the career he had got into, and already began to tower with the hopes of his future grandeur :—but what contributed much to moderate his joy, was, that he had not received any accounts of Eugenia, or his friend Mr. ———, though he had been much longer in the country than was neceſſary for that purpoſe—he began therefore to doubt of the ſafety of the common method of conveyance, and was apprehenſive that his letters might have fallen a ſacrifice to the ſuſpicions of the miniſter.—What confirmed him in this idea was, that the ſhip he wrote by had arrived in ſafety in Liſbon ;—however, it was ſome conſolation to him, ſuppoſing that

to

to be the case, that he had not exposed himself to his resentment or ill will.

In the mean time he determined to proceed more cautiously for the future; and, accordingly, he procured the confidence of a gentleman who was going to Portugal, and who promised to deliver his letters with his own hands.—In these he acquainted Eugenia and his friend, of every circumstance that had befallen him of any note since his arrival, and pointed out to them the method it was necessary they should observe, to secure him the conveyance of their answers.

As soon as he had got every thing ready

ready for the long journey he was going to undertake, he set out for the mines.—He had not less than twelve hundred miles to travel, and that in a country where the rude hand of Nature is almost unimproved.—However, his constitution was proof against all the hardships and inconveniencies he met with,—and he had the pleasure to find himself at his journey's end without any accident.

The END of the FIRST VOLUME.

ADVENTURES

OF

ALONSO.

ADVENTURES

OF

ALONSO.

CONTAINING

Some STRIKING ANECDOTES of the present PRIME MINISTER of POR-TUGAL.

VOL. II.

LONDON:
Printed for J. BEW, No. 28, Paternoster-Row.
M,DCC,LXXV.

ADVENTURES
OF
ALONSO.

CHAP. XV.

IT is necessary to observe, that all diamonds of a certain size, belong to the king; and those of an inferior one, are the property of the person who has that contract from the crown. Negroes are employed in working in the mines, and they are doubly watched, and examined, both by the officers of the king, and thofe appointed by the contractor: however, it will fometimes happen, that they find means to conceal ftones of great value, notwithftanding all their precautions. Thefe flaves have the indulgence of feveral hours, on holidays, to cultivate a fmall piece of ground, which is allotted to each of them for their fupport; and this they generally improve, fo as not only to afford them fuftenance, but feveral articles for fale, fuch as fowls, vegetables, and fruits.—Thefe they go to market with, and frequently to people's houfes to difpofe of.

As

Of ALONSO.

As Alonſo was much liked, and had got a great name for goodneſs and generoſity; a negroe came to him one morning, with the pretext of offering him ſome oranges. " Signior, (ſays the black), I believe you to be a true man, and I am going to truſt you in preference to any other, with what is much for your intereſt, and I hope too, my own. I have here three diamonds, which I have found means to conceal. Look at them,—they are larger than have been found for many years.—Theſe may be the means of making your fortune, but they never can mine. Therefore take them, and I ſhall be quite ſatisfied with whatever acknowledgement you may think proper to make me.—

Alonſo was not at all diſpleaſed with this exordium, and he ſaw, with one glance, that the offer was a very tempting bait. He therefore took out between two and three ounces of gold duſt, and gave it to the ſlave, who was very happy with the exchange.

As ſoon as he was alone, he examined, with more minuteneſs, the acquiſition he had made.—The loweſt value he put upon them was fifty thouſand pounds ſterling, and he had no doubt of diſpoſing of them for that ſum, provided he could get ſafely to Europe.—But there lay the difficulty.—He found it too romantic, and even impracticable to attempt his eſcape to the Spaniſh ſettlements.

ments.—The distance they were at, and the woods, savages, and wild beasts were unsurmountable obstacles; and to return by the way he came, he would be exposed to almost an inevitable discovery; for the road is so strictly guarded, and all those who come from the mines are so narrowly examined at each stage, by the officers appointed for that purpose, that it is next to impossible to elude their search.

In these circumstances, the diamonds were almost as useless to him, as if they had remained in the earth; and yet so great a prize deserved some risk.—Numberless schemes and plans came into his head, but they appeared so futile, and he he found so many obstacles on all sides, that at times he would give up the thoughts of attempting any.—One day however, as he was ruminating on this subject, an idea struck him, which afforded him great hope of success—It was to hollow a piece of a common branch of a tree, and put the diamonds into it; and as the people of that country are in general addicted to smoaking, he purposed to make use of this stick to light his segar with, at the different stages on the road, where they are searched; and throw it negligently on one side, and when they set off again, to take it up, as if by chance, and light it again, in order to last him to the next place of rendezvous.

AFTER

After canvassing this project maturely in his mind, he resolved to put it into execution.

The count de B—— was at that time preparing to return home, as a new governor was appointed to succeed him. Alonso therefore determined to endeavour to get to the Rio de Janeiro before his departure, and to accompany his excellency to Portugal, in case he eluded the search he was going to be exposed to.— However he did not give out that he intended returning to his own country, for this would have raised a great suspicion against him; but only that he was going to pay his respects to his excellency, and to request his patronage in the

the advancement of his interests at home.——This seemed very plausible; because it was well known, that it was owing to the protection of the count de B——, that he enjoyed the employment he was then in possession of.

The superintendant of the mines readily granted him leave of absence; and he was even glad of so good an opportunity of paying his court, through Alonso's means, to the governor.

It is needless to mention the anxiety and uneasiness of a man who had so great an interest at stake.——The first day's journey, was, in particular, distressing.——However, as his stratagem was

was not found out, he began to be a little more confident; and from day to day, his hopes were so buoyed up with the succefs he met with, that he did not doubt but he should impose on the eyes of all these Argos's.

He had now travelled near twelve hundred miles, and was within sixty of the capital, when he met with an officer, who was more circumspect and minute than is customary, towards the end of the journey. Alonso, on these occasions, always shewed the greatest alacrity and readiness, in going through the common method of examination; and was particularly officious, in satisfying those who were more scrupulous than others

others in their search.—It was this officiousness that ruined him; for it increased the suspicions of the officer, and made him more mistrustful than he otherwise would have been.—All his attention was directed towards Alonso; and observing him, as he was going away, to take up his stick, to light his segar with, he desired to look at it.—Alonso presented it with a forced laugh. —But, what were his feelings! when the officer, on breaking it, discovered a treasure of such value! It was in vain to equivocate.—He was sent to prison; and in an instant, all his airy hopes and prospects of grandeur were contrasted with despair.

CHAP.

CHAP. XVI.

AFTER he had lain some days in confinement; and that he had returned to such a temper of mind, as to be able to reason a little with himself on what was best to be done in this calamitous situation, he resolved to write to the Count de B——, to lay before him the whole transaction, and to implore his wonted goodness and mercy.

But

But the officer who had made the difcovery, took care to prevent the count de B——, from a knowledge of what had happened; becaufe, in that cafe, he would not be able to take advantage of his acquifition; for he no fooner found himfelf mafter of fo great a treafure, than he began to devife means to efcape.—He therefore gave ftrict orders, that Alonfo fhould not only be deprived of pen, ink, and paper, but of every means of communication.

Alonso became fuch a prey to melancholy and dejection, that it was with difficulty he bore up againft the evils with which he found himfelf on all fides furrounded. One day, that he was
revolv-

revolving in his mind, in this piteous mood, the different events which had befallen him; tracing up the cauſe of his preſent deplorable ſituation, to his firſt miſconduct in life, the jailor came in abruptly, and told him to take courage, for that he brought good news.—
" What is that?" ſays Alonſo, impatiently. " Why, (continued the jailor), the officer who ſent you to priſon, is not to be met with.—It is ſuppoſed he is gone off with his booty.——The count de C——, our new governor, is arrived.—His predeceſſor is gone; and as nothing can be proved againſt you, I don't think there is much need for fear."

Alonso, who would gladly have thought himself even with fortune, on condition of his liberty, was overjoyed at what he heard; but as foon as the firſt tranſports were over, he recollected that the count de C—— was a man remarkable for his cruel and tyrannical difpofition; and that probably he would not hefitate to impofe the moſt rigorous fentence upon him.——He, therefore, from that moment, was determined to try every method to make his efcape, which he entertained great hopes of effecting, from the prefent difpofition of the jailor: for this purpofe, he readily joined with him in opinion, that his confinement was no longer to be looked upon in a ferious light; as the only
perfon

person who could appear against him, was not to be found.—He took care not to mention the new Governor's character, because that might have induced him to guard him with more precaution than he otherwise would do.

The readiest way that occurred to Alonso, to obtain his liberty, was, to endeavour to bribe the keeper.——He had gold dust about him, to the value of about one hundred and fifty pounds; and he was persuaded that the tenth part of it would be a sufficient temptation to secure his connivance.

Addressing himself, therefore, to the jailor, " I have not, to be sure, the leaſt reaſon, (ſays he) to make myſelf uneaſy; for, independent of theſe favourable circumſtances, you know, it is the cuſtom with new governors, to ſhew acts of indulgence on their arrival; and as nothing can be proved againſt me, I ſhall certainly be included.—The only thing that mortifies me, is, that I muſt yet remain ſome days longer in priſon. —But, now that I think of it, I don't ſee why you could not releaſe me without this delay—I don't mean that you ſhould juſt open the priſon doors to me; becauſe that would look too much like aſſuming an improper authority, in depriving his excellency of marks of grace; but that you ſhould contrive matters ſo, as to facilitate my eſcape."—"But what do you

you propose doing, (asked the jailor), when you are at liberty ?"—" To make the best of my way to some of the Spanish settlements, (replied Alonso), and here is the means of expedition, (taking out a small paper of of gold dust).—We will divide it together.—One half will be sufficient for my purpose."——This argument had the desired effect; for the jailor, that very night, put it in his power to recover his freedom.

Alonso no sooner found himself at liberty, than he was restored to new life and vigour; but as he did not think himself safe, as long as he was
within

within reach of the Count de C——, he made what hafte he could to Nova Colonna, where he arrived after incredible fatigue, and met, once more, to his great joy, with an afylum in the Spanifh dominions.

CHAP.

CHAP. XVII.

FOR the first few days he was so elated, in having got free from the unlucky scrape he had fallen into, that his mind was not troubled with many disagreeable reflexions; but he was no sooner reconciled to safety, than he found the situation he was in comfortless and irksome. He was now farther

removed than ever from his friends.—
It was in vain to expect to hear from
them, and in his prefent circumftances,
he was refolved to be filent.

In the mean time, it was neceffary
to endeavour to ftrike into fome line,
as would at leaft enable him to live.—
It is true, he was not in immediate
want, as he had gold duft remaining
to the value of about one hundred and
twenty pounds; but unlefs that he
could improve his fituation, that fum
would be foon exhaufted.

Chance, or rather a feries of fixed,
but unforefeen events, which had fo
often

often directed his course, once more presented itself to his relief.

An English vessel was about that time stranded on the coast, and the captain and the crew who were saved, took refuge in Nova Colonna.

The English manners were more natural to Alonso, than those of his own country, so that he soon formed an intimate acquaintance with the captain: He was a sensible, intelligent man. One day that they were conversing together, he mentioned the great advantage that was to be reaped by carrying on a contraband trade with the Spanish settlements;

ments; and that if he had but about one hundred and fifty pounds more than he was master of, he did not doubt but that he should soon be able to acquire a fortune.

Alonso asked him how he would proceed, supposing he had the sum he wanted.—He said he would buy a sloop with part of it, and the remainder he would lay out in merchandize purchased at the English colonies, which he would barter for dollars; and he had no doubt but that the men who were with him, would willingly engage in the enterprize, provided they had the assurance of large wages.

Alonso

Alonso thought this scheme bore a promising appearance—" I have, (said he) about the sum you mention, and if you like it, we will join fortunes together." "With all my heart, (returned the captain)." The proposal was joyfully accepted of, and they immediately set about purchasing a small vessel.—The men entered readily into the plan, and the better to secure their fidelity, they thought it adviseable to advance each of them a months wages, whichthey were to lay out in merchandize.

As soon as all was ready, they set sail for Jamaica, in order to lay out their

their overplus in such goods as were best suited to the Spanish markets.

When they had taken in their cargo, their first voyage was directed to the island of Cuba.

Here they traded with so much success, as to get between three and four hundred per cent. clear gain.—From thence they sailed to one of the Caribbee Islands, to lay out their money in fresh goods; for though Jamaica was more convenient for them, they were obliged to steer their course so as best to elude the Spanish guarda costas.—After they had purchased a fresh cargo,

cargo, they returned again to Cuba; but from the same prudential motives, to a different part to where they had been the time before. They had the good fortune to make as beneficial a voyage as the laſt; ſo that as their capital was greatly increaſed, they determined to make for Port-Royal, and there purchaſe a larger veſſel, in order to carry on a more extenſive trade.— Here they arrived in ſafety, and met with a ſhip ſuited to their purpoſe.— They then augmented their complement to thirty men; and provided great guns and fire arms, in order to reſiſt the Spaniſh cruizers, in caſe they

had

had the misfortune to fall in with them.

Alonso now once more faw his profpects bear a flattering appearance, and he began to entertain the moſt fanguine hopes of getting the better of his misfortunes.—He even did not doubt but that he ſhould have little caufe to repent the lofs of his diamonds; for he was certain that a few more fuccefsful voyages would put him in poffeffion of a fplendid fortune.

The impoffibility, however, he was in of hearing from his friends, was a

great

great subject of grief to him, in his prosperous situation.

As soon as their vessel was ready for sea, and that they had laid in as much merchandize as they were able to purchase, they steered towards Porto Bello. It was about that time of the year that the money was expected there from the silver mines, so that they entertained the most flattering hopes of the success of that voyage. They were not disappointed, and they met with so great a vent for their cargo, that Alonso accounted himself worth upwards of four thousand pounds. Happy would he have
thought

thought himſelf, had he retired at this period.——But tempted by the avidity of gain, and the ſuccefs they had hitherto met with, they not only continued their trade, but ventured upon more dangerous voyages. — This proved their ruin. — Off the coaſt of Carthagena they had the misfortune to fall in with a Spaniſh ſloop of war. All their efforts to eſcape were in vain.—She gained ground continually upon them. ——— It was, therefore, determined to ſtake their fortunes upon their courage, and defend themſelves to the laſt extremity.

WITH

With this resolution they began the engagement with great fury. The captain was killed almost at the first onset, by a ball which took off part of his side; however, Alonso immediately took upon himself the command, and continued the fight with obstinacy for near three hours.— Many lost their lives on both sides; —but as the Spaniard was far superior to them both in guns and men, they were nearly over-powered, and would inevitably have fallen into their hands, if they had not run their vessel ashore, and left her a prey to the enemy.

CHAP. XVIII

THEY were so closely pursued that they had but just time to strike into the woods to save themselves from being made prisoners.

As soon as they found themselves in safety, they took a short turn round the coast, in order to observe the conduct of the Spaniards without being disco-

discovered. It was not long before they had the disconsolate sight to behold their ship crowded with the enemy, and busy in unloading the cargo, and conveying it to their own. When this was done, they set fire to her; and Alonso and his companions, in a few hours, saw her sink into the sea.

This was not, however, a time for fruitless lamentation — they found themselves alone—defenceless—without sustenance—far from any human habitation, and in a country where they durst not make themselves known. —Besides, out of two-and-thirty when they

they first began the engagement, their number was reduced to seventeen, and several of these were wounded.

The Spaniards had, by this time, got at some distance from the shore — the first thing, therefore, to be done was to see whether any provision could be met with that might have escaped the flames; and, to their great joy, they had not searched long before they had the good fortune to fall upon a considerable quantity of biscuit and some beef; but no liquor, nor arms of any kind was to be found.

In spite of all their care and attention

tention to thofe who were wounded, two of them unfortunately died, and they were obliged to remain near three weeks on that part of the coaft, to wait the recovery of the others.— During that time they lived fparingly upon their bifcuit and beef; but to make amends, they were well fupplied with the fruit they met with in the woods.

As foon as they found themfelves well enough to encounter with fatigue, they determined to endeavour to travel acrofs the ifthmus to Panama, which, from that part of the country they were in, they judged would not be above one hundred

hundred and twenty miles;—here they had no doubt of meeting with some ſhip bound for Europe; and they could with ſafety give out, that they had been wrecked on the oppoſite ſide of the coaſt; for they were perſuaded, that at ſuch a diſtance from where their veſſel had fallen into the hands of the Spaniſh ſloop, they would not know any thing of the matter.

It muſt be remembered, that it is not in America, particularly in that part of it, as in Europe, where there is ſo great a facility of communication.

ALONSO

Alonso had fortunately a small compass at his watch chain, which enabled him to direct their rout; so that, tying up in their handkerchiefs the remains of their provision, and being armed with stout clubs, pointed at one end, and seasoned a little in the fire, they set out upon their journey.

The most formidable enemy they had to apprehend, were the wild beasts. And tygers, wolves and monkies, they met with in abundance.— However, as they kept as close together as the country would admit of, they durst not attack them in the day-time, and at night they were intimidated with large fires.

It is incredible the hardships and fatigue they underwent; and what with the closeness of the woods, and the rocks and precipices they had to climb, they made so little progress, that they were, at times, almost disheartened——At last, to their great joy, on the eve of the fifteenth day, they came within sight of the South Sea, and, soon afterwards, arrived at Panama.

They presented themselves to the governor, half famished; and looked
more

more like spectres than men; for, besides the fatigue they had undergone, the provisions they had set out with were soon exhausted, and they had been obliged to subsist upon such fruits and berries as they could meet with.

Alonso related to him the history of their distress; and he was a man of so much goodness and humanity, that he immediately ordered a plentiful meal to be prepared for them,

The Spaniards could not sufficiently admire the idea of travelling through

a wild and uninhabited country with
a watch compass.

They crossed themselves repeatedly
with surprize.—They well knew the
use of it at sea, but this was the first
time they ever heard of steering on
shore.

It was a very great happiness for
them to be received with so much hospitality and kindness; for they were
not likely to meet with a passage so
soon as they expected, for Europe.—
The treasure from the mines they
were informed would not arrive in less
than two months, and no ship would
sail

fail for Old Spain, before the galleons that were to convey it.

They were told, however, that if they chose in the mean time to employ themselves in the coasting trade, they need not remain idle.—This they in general were glad to accept of, and soon after most of them separated.

As for Alonso, he determined to wait quietly at Panama, till an opportunity offered of conveying him to Europe; and to engage in no further enterprize in that part of the world.—Every scheme he had entered into had been attended with ill fortune—Besides,

sides, he was desirous to return to his own country.—He did not know, and it was not unlikely, but some favourable event might have cast up since he left it.—Don Pedro was old;—He might be dead, and in that case he flattered himself with the hopes of being united to Eugenia.—His father too was advanced in years, and if he had not yet paid the tribute to nature, he was persuaded, after so long an absence he would receive him with parental arms.

CHAP.

CHAP XIX.

HE had not been long in Panama before a ſhip put in from ſtreſs of weather, that was bound from Mexico to Cadiz.—This Alonſo conſidered as a moſt fortunate circumſtance, and he immediately agreed with the captain for his paſſage.

IN order to defray the expences of
the

the voyage, and to furnish himself with the necessary articles of apparel, he disposed of his watch and some trinkets, the sole remains of the wreck of his fortunes.

THESE kind of things bear such high prices in that part of the world, that he found himself in possession, after allowing for the deduction of all charges to their arrival in Old Spain, of about thirty pounds sterling. With this sum he could be able to look about him a little in Cadiz, till he received news from home, which would determine his future plan.

He

He hardly had time to equip himself before he was hurried on board, that they might take advantage of the wind, which had turned in their favour.

There were paſſengers beſides himſelf; the governor of Guadalajara, two officers, and a merchant belonging to Cadiz; with the latter Alonſo immediately commenced acquaintance.—" I preſume, ſir, (ſays he) that a fellow citizen of yours—a gentleman of great worth and property, my friend, is not unknown to you;— Don Pacheco, I mean."—" Don Pacheco! (cry'd the merchant,)—he is my

my brother-in-law—married to my sister."—" Is it possible! (exclaimed Alonso)"—"Most certain, (replied the merchant,)—And are you a friend of his?"——" I have that happiness, (said Alonso)—we were school-fellows in England, where our regard for each other first took root; and when I was in Cadiz some years ago, he gave me such proofs of his friendship, as can never be erased from my mind."
" What you tell me, (answered the merchant) gives me very great pleasure;—I am exceeding glad to meet with the friend of one for whom I have so great a regard.—But is there nothing extraordinary in finding you

you in this part of the world."—" I confefs it, (returned Alonfo)—Don Pacheco will inform you of my hiftory to the time of my leaving Cadiz;—have patience until we arrive there, and you fhall know the fequel."

" Be it fo (replied the merchant,) in the mean time give me leave to make you better known to our fellow-paffengers, my particular friends. Gentlemen, (fays Don Pablo, for that was his name,) I have the pleafure to meet with, in the perfon of this cavalheiro, the early companion and friend of my brother-in-law,—they were

were educated together in England." Alonso was saluted with great civility; and this introduction, at once paved the way to intimacy and goodwill.—" Sir, (says the governor, who was a man of great knowledge, and had seen most of the courts of Europe,) I cannot help admiring the strange revolutions that happen in the world, from the circumstance which Don Pablo mentions of you and his brother-in-law, being educated in England; little did our ancestors think in the days of Charles the fifth, that their offspring would, of all countries, be sent there for instruction.

I RE-

Of ALONSO.

I REMEMBER to have read, that at that time the Spanish was the fashionable language of Europe; and, indeed, it could not well be otherwise, considering the great power of our monarchs at that period.—The French afterwards had their turn, but I am afraid these Inglezes are now going to turn both out of doors."—" That will depend much upon you, gentlemen, (replied Alonso, addressing himself to the governor and the officers), for according to your argument, language always is the attendant on power."

" O! I understand you (says the gover-

governor).—You mean, we must fight better.—The conclusion is rather severe, but I must confess it is just.— Well, I hope we shall make as good use of our swords as our neighbours, when it comes again to the trial; at least, our king was taking the right way for that purpose, when I left Spain.—He was then putting the army on a more respectable footing than it had been for many former reigns; and our soldiers, by this time, I suppose, have got quite the Prussian air. Pray, how goes the military on in your country?—Before I came into this part of the world, I was in garrison on the frontiers towards Portugal;

gal; and I remember, you were then bufied in exercifing and difcipling your troops.—But, I forget that you are not a military man.—This is an uninterefting fubject." "I beg your pardon, Sir, (anfwered Alonfo)—I don't know whether I can fatisfy you in thefe particulars, as I was not brought up in that line of life; but I cannot hold the fubject in the light you mention.—An army is the right hand of moft ftates; and, of courfe, an object of interefting difcuffion."—" Well, pray then, (refumed the governor) can you tell me if the pay of the military is augmented in Portugal; for without that, I have ever been

been of opinion, it was all loft labour."—" It was not, (replied Alonso) when I left the country."——
" Then this great minifter of yours, has done nothing at all.—Your service has no bottom; and it is downright tyranny to pretend to enforce difcipline, when the officers are ftarving.—A captain, if I miftake not, has only two guineas and a half a month."——" No more," (replied Alonfo).—" So that your officers are ftill of the loweft ranks of people."—
" They are, (anfwered Alonfo) and muft continue fo; for none of tolerable families will enter into a profeffion that does not afford them bread."
—" Cer-

—" Certainly, (returned the governor).—It would seem, then, (he continued) that the Marquis de Pombal never meant to have an army; or at least, if he did, it does him very little credit.—And yet I have been told, that his flatterers have grouped that, as a compliment, into an historical picture of his administration." " Adulation and interest, you know, Sir, (said Alonso) generally go together. —His excellency has been used to gross food, and does not content himself with a spare diet."----" But pray, (continued Alonso) what are the advantages that your service has to boast of in the present reign? For though

though I am no military man, I like to hear of great or good things."

" Why, in the firſt place, (anſwered the governor) our pay is ſufficient, through all the different ranks, for a gentleman to live upon.----The men are likewiſe allowed ample ſubſiſtence.----They are regularly and comfortably cloathed; and have ſuch good quarters, that every common ſoldier has a bed to himſelf.---Beſides this, each man is now entitled to his diſcharge, after ſerving five years; but if he chooſes to continue five more, he has an addition of rank; and at the expiration of every five years,

years, he may either have his discharge, or go on with succeffive gratifications, till he has ferved thirty years, when he retires, with the rank and pay of enfign for life. So that I doubt whether any fervice in Europe can boaft of fo happy an eftablifhment; and foldiers, who in all other countries look upon their profeffion as martyrdom and flavery, muft confider it in ours, as the road to refpect, independency, and eafe.

CHAP.

CHAP. XX.

ALONZO could not but congratulate himself on the happy change of his situation, compared with the dangers, difficulties, and distresses, he had so lately encountered;—he found himself on board a good ship—sailing homeward, with a fair wind, and in such company as dissipated the remains of his vexation and chagrin.

ONE

Of ALONSO.

One day that the conversation turned upon the vast dominions belonging to Spain in America, Alonso said, he could help frequently remarking the great debility of their government in that part of the world, and that it appeared surprising to him, that the English, with whom they had been so frequently at war, allowed them to remain with such extensive and unguarded conquests. They must certainly (continued he) fall a prey to the first enterprising enemy.

"There is a good deal of truth in your observation (answered the governor)—but the English have too much

much sense to envy us possessions that have been the ruin of our country;—besides, they receive more advantage by their being in our hands, than if they were in their own."——"Pray how do you make that out?" (asked Alonso)—"Very easily," replied the governor.

"In the first place, our colonies, next to the expulsion of the Moors, have been the chief cause of the depopulation of Old Spain; and as long as this cause exists, it will become more and more a desert; so that far from allowing of emigration, the king, in my opinion, would do well to to recal home all his American subjects.—Now, were our colonies in the hands of the English, it is likely they would still be more drained of inhabitants, from the greater difference that there is betwixt their climate and the warm continent of America, than there is betwixt ours.

"In the next place, they enjoy all the advantages of trade, without the inconveniencies; for they supply us with manufactures which must employ thousands of their people, whilst the boasted riches of our mines afford labour but to few, and that of the most unhealthy kind. In short, the vast treasure

treasure which is sent annually to Old Spain, goes mostly to them and other nations of Europe;—a very small proportion of it remains to us.—But this gentleman (addressing himself to Don Pablo) can give more light upon the subject. Pray, (says he) what do you think may be the yearly amount of the exportations to our colonies?" —" They were computed to be about two millions two hundred thousand pounds, in the year 1740, (replied Don Pablo), and I imagine they are much the same at this day.—Out of this sum the manufacturers of Old Spain were not supposed to amount to more than two hundred thousand pounds.

You

You see then, (continued the governor) that we are working merely for the aggrandizement of others. The council of Francis the First, king of France, has often been accused of blindness, for having slighted the offers of Columbus as chimerical;—but, I believe, they did, by chance, a very wise thing. Spain has acted like that mad king, who prayed that all he touched might be turned into gold, and was afterwards obliged to return to the gods to beg that they would put an end to his misery."

After some pause, the conversation took a more sprightly turn; and

as they were approaching the latitude of Europe, the officers, who were young men, began to lay their plans of amufement, and the pleafures they fhould enjoy on their arrival. " But (fays one of them)—allow that our long cloaks and flouched hats were very convenient, and I could almoft have wifhed Squilaci had been hanged for attempting the reformation, I am not ufed to make love in a French drefs."—" Pray, fir, (fays the other addreffing himfelf to Alonfo,) as you have been in Spain fince we were, can you tell us how this was brought about?"——" Yes ;—I happened to be at Madrid foon after, (re-
-plied

plied Alonso). The king, whom you know likes to carry things with a high hand, took it into his head to oblige his subjects to dress like other nations.—However, it was supposed, that his secretary, Squilaci, had advised him to it.——This was an odious measure to a people who have a natural aversion to changes, and who were long habituated to their customs. It proved the ruin of Squilaci, in spite of the favour and protection of his majesty.; for the orders were no sooner given out, than the inhabitants, with one accord, rose and surrounded the palace, erected a gallows, and made strict search for Squilaci,

laci, whom they would certainly have hung up;——fortunately he made his escape, and got off to Naples, his own country. The people, in the mean time, exasperated that he was not to be found, grew more outrageous, so that the king, apprehensive of bad consequences, appeared to them in the balcony of his palace, and with difficulty persuaded them to retire; not however, without first promising that Squilaci should never more be admitted into his councils.

" THE count d'Aranda, one of the most popular noblemen, was appointed to succeed him; and as his majesty does
not

not readily lay afide what he takes in hand, he infifted upon the count's going through with this meafure.—— However, he left the management of it to himfelf.

"The count accordingly called together all the heads of the different profeffions—tradefmen and mechanics in Madrid, and told them, that his majefty wifhed to fee his fubjects drefs like the reft of the world; and that as he was perfuaded it only depended upon their example, he hoped they would chearfully comply with what the king had fo much at heart.

"This

" This addrefs had the defired effect; and they were so pleafed with the manner of bringing about the reform, that one and all cried out, Viva el Rey, Viva el Conde d'Aranda; and the fame people who not long before were ready to set fire to the palace for attempting this innovation, received it with acclamations and joy.———A remarkable inftance (faid the governor) what the *manner* of doing a thing will accomplifh."

WHILE they were thus paffing time in the cabin, they were fuddenly alarmed with the pulling of ropes———the unfurling of fails———the

the noife, the cries, and the running to and fro of the men.

THEY hurried upon deck to fee what was the occafion of all this difturbance.——A Moorifh xebeck was giving chafe to their veffel. The captain advifed them, if they prized their liberty, to arm and prepare for a vigorous defence; for, in fpite of all the fail he could crowd, the enemy would foon be along fide of them.

THE idea of flavery infpired them with the moft defperate courage; and breaking open the ftore cheft in a moment, they inftantly armed themfelves with piftols and cutlaffes. As the xebeck drew near, they obferved fhe carried fixteen guns, and was crowded with men.

Soon after the engagement began, the firft efforts of the enemy to board them were baffled, and feveral loft their lives in the fea; however, as this is the conftant practice of fighting with the Moors, they were not difcouraged at the firft attempt.— They immediately made a fecond, in which, after an obftinate conteft, they got forty of their men on board. It was now nothing but a fcene of carnage and confufion.—However, notwithftanding withstanding the superiority of numbers, they made such destruction among them, that they would probably have mastered those they had on board, if, in the heat of action, the xebeck had not poured in a fresh supply. —With these it was in vain to contend; for out of five-and-thirty hands which they mustered at the beginning of the engagement, only nineteen appeared in a condition of defence.—All the rest were either killed or wounded, and among the latter were the governor, one of the officers, and Alonso.—The captain, therefore, to save those who who were still left, ordered the colours to be ftruck, and immediately furrendered.

A loud huzza was the pæan of triumph, and, in an inftant, they were hurried on board the enemy's fhip, and loaded with irons.—Thofe who were wounded, they ordered to be taken care of, not from any principle of humanity or tendernefs; for the Moors are, of all people, the moft mercilefs and cruel; but from the hopes of ranfom, or, at leaft, the benefit of felling them, in cafe they were not able to purchafe their liberty.

Soon after manning their prize with

with their own hands, they steered
for Barbary, and in a few days arrived
at Sallee.

CHAP.

CHAP. XXI.

OF all the misfortunes that had happened to Alonso, none could be compared to the misery of his present situation.----Wounded----a captive, and in slavery, among the most execrable of the human race. "Surely, would he exclaim, Providence has inflicted upon me this calamity, as a punishment for my sins!"

Soon

Soon after their arrival, in the division of the spoils, he fell to the share of Ibrahim, nephew to the captain.---He was a young man of five-and-twenty, but had the moroseness of old age.

At first, he treated Alonso with some kind of goodness, and took care to have his wounds properly dressed and cured; for he was in hopes of obtaining a large ransom, and rated his freedom, as of a man of the first consequence; but as Alonso could not reconcile himself to the thoughts of applying to his father for relief, and much less, to procure his liberty

at

at so great an expence, he slighted the proposals of his master.

Ibrahim, inraged at his disappointment, condemned him to the most ignominious employments; however, as he was soon afterwards to go to sea, and afraid to trust him, in his absence, to the intrigues of his women, he was resolved to dispose of him: for this purpose, he sent to Aldalid, a rich man in the neighbourhood, informing him, that he had a slave to dispose of----young, comely, and handsome; and gave him the first offer.

Aldalid was one of those characters

ters which are to be met with in that country, who, being palled with the enjoyment of women, fought for pleasure in the abandoned proſtitution of his own ſex.

As ſoon as he ſaw Alonſo, he agreed with Ibrahim on his own terms.

It was very agreeable to Alonſo, to find he had got a new maſter; for he was perſuaded he could not make a change for the worſe.---Every thing tended to confirm him in this opinion; for he was no ſooner in the poſſeſſion of Aldalid, than his chains were taken off, and his only employment was in watering the garden, and
gather-

gathering the fruits and flowers for his master.---Besides, dresses were provided for him, which seemed as much designed for ornament as for use. Alonso, in the mean time, had formed an intimacy with an old Spanish slave, with whom he had frequent opportunities of conversing.---" What a savage Ibrahim is, (says he to him, one day that they were together) compared to our master !---It is, at least, some consolation for the loss of liberty, to fall into such good hands. Aldalid does not even appear to have the jealousy of his countrymen." " Jealous ! replied Pedro, (for that was his name) No; what should he be jealous for ?" " O ! I do not doubt (continued Alonso)

lonſo) but that he takes ſuch precautions with his women, as to put them out of reach."----" Women! (ſays Pedro, laughing)----why, what do you think he gave you theſe fine flowing robes for?"---" Ah! I underſtand you, (returned Alonſo)---what! does he mean me, then, as an object for his luſt?"----" Certainly, (anſwered Pedro) and you are not the firſt of your country, who have complied with his deſires.----Why, he looks upon you as an eaſy conqueſt.----He once met with an Engliſhman, indeed, who was ſo refractory, that he was glad to get rid of him.---Beſides, as he had trepanned him, he was afraid, leſt it ſhould be known to the
empe-

emperor; for the English and they are always good friends."

"I promise you, (says Alonso) that he will find me as refractory as the Englishman.---But tell me, Pedro, is there no means of escape!"---"None, (says Pedro) that I have been able to devise, or I would not have been here so long.----Besides, these high walls that surround us, which you see are impossible to scale, those who are destined for his pleasures are so closely watched, that it would be instant death to those who had the care of them, in case they escaped; and you are at this moment so narrowly observed, that our conversaversation will be mentioned to Aldalid."

Alonso now found himself more distressed than ever; and wished, a thousand times, he had fallen a victim in the defence of his liberty. " Ibrahim, (would he say) was mercenary and cruel; but then I was not exposed to dishonour.—Aldalid is rich and luxurious; and would prefer the gratification of his appetites, to a large ransom."

On whatever side he turned himself, the most disagreeable reflections presented themselves to his mind.— This point, however, he was determined

mined upon—to refist the importunities of Aldalid, at the rifk of his life.

Alonso had fcarce finifhed this foliloquy, before he was fummoned to appear.—The flave who was the meffenger of this order, endeavoured by every art to infinuate himfelf into his favour.

"Happy young man, (faid he) from this day you are going to command in thefe walls.—You are the favourite of Aldalid.—Remember, in thofe moments which will give you fuch an empire over his heart, that I was the meffenger of your good fortune." Alonfo, with difficulty, forbore fhewing his refentment; but
pre-

pretending not to underſtand his meaning, he ſaid, "He was very fortunate, that his ſervices had ſo ſoon engaged the attention of his maſter."

ALDALID, as ſoon as he appeared, deſired him to be ſeated and partake of a repaſt he had ordered to be prepared. Alonſo was helped to what was moſt delicate; and the geſtures, looks, and manners of Aldalid, plainly indicated his intentions.

As ſoon as they were alone, he proceeded to careſſes; but Alonſo, diſguſted with his familiarities, treated him with contempt and diſdain. Aldalid, however, was not to be ſo eaſily

easily repulsed.—" Come, (said he) lay aside these airs, and comply with my desires.—If I did not love you, I would not be trifled with. I chuse rather to gratify my passions with good-will, than by force; but if that is necessary, you must be sensible it is in vain to resist."—This he delivered with a kind of emphasis; but immediately changing his tone, he resumed his fondness, and was proceeding to the most disgusting indecencies, when Alonso, pushing him aside with violence, desired him, with a peremptory voice, to desist; that he would sooner part with his life, than be subservient to his lust.

ALDALID,

ALDALID, enraged, called furiously for his slaves.—"Vile christian! (he exclaimed) thou shalt live, and shall satisfy my desires!——Here, slaves, secure him."——Alonso, in a moment, was surrounded; but drawing instantly a poniard from his breast, he laid the first who approached him dead at his feet.—Then, flying furiously upon Aldalid, threatened him with immediate destruction.—The rest, terrified and dismayed, gave the alarm with their cries; and in a moment the house was filled with the neighbourhood, and those who were passing by.

As it is death, by the laws of the Moors, for a slave to threaten the life of his master; Alonso, who was found with one hand fastened to the breast of Aldalid, and in the other, a poniard, was immediately seized and bound, in order to be carried before the Cadi, that sentence might be inflicted upon him.

Among those who had rushed in, to see what was the occasion of the tumult, was a christian renegade.— At the sight of Alonso, he started back with surprize; but immediately addressing himself to him in Portuguese.—" Am I mistaken, or not?
(said

(said he) Do you recollect me?"
" Methinks I have seen your face,
(returned Alonso).---Ah! I remember.---You are the officer who took
the diamonds from me."------" The
same, (replied the renegade) and I
will repay your loss with usury.---It
is no time now, to discourse on this
subject.------We must hasten to the
judge.------The dress and attitude I
found Aldalid in, are an incontestible
proof of his attempts. I will declare it
to the Cadi; and not only your life,
but your liberty, will be secured."

'As soon as they appeared before
the judge, Aldalid declared, that he
had

had been put in danger of his life by Alonso, who had killed one of his slaves; and that he was come to demand immediate justice.

Alonso then made his defence, and appealed to those who were present, to witness the situation in which Aldalid was found; but as the Moors bear a general odium to all Christians, and see with reluctance the administration of justice to their advantage, none would bear testimony in his favour.—Alonso was just going to be condemned; when the renegade advancing towards the judge, desired to be heard.

He

He then declared, upon the alcoran, that he was one of the firſt who got into the apartments of Aldalid, at the beginning of the fray; and made his evidence appear ſo clear, in favour of Alonſo, that he was acquitted, and reſtored to freedom.

Alonso once more exulted in the recovery of his liberty; but could not help admiring the ſtrangeneſs of the events which had befallen him.— at the ſame time, the renegade, taking him by the arm, deſired him to accompany him to his houſe, and conſider it as his aſylum, and his home.

CHAP.

CHAP. XXII.

AS soon as they had got to an inward apartment, the renegade, addressing himself to Alonso, said, "I will now satisfy your curiosity; for I am persuaded you are impatient to be informed how I came to be in this situation. Know then, that soon after I had sent you to prison, I set about contriving in what manner I could

could appropriate to my own benefit, the treasure that had fallen into my hands; for I need not tell you, that conscience is little consulted, where such advantages are to be made, at the king's expence.

"I HEARD that a merchantman was going to Lisbon at the same time, with the man of war that was to convey home the count de B———; I therefore gave strict charge to the keeper, that on no condition, you should be indulged with pen, ink, and paper, or any other means of communication, that I might the easier get off, before his excellency could have

have any intelligence of the matter. And as the count de C——, the new governor, could have no proof againſt you, in caſe I made my eſcape, I was in no pain for your ſafety. The plan I had formed, anſwered my moſt ſanguine expectations.—I got to Rio de Janiero the evening before the veſſel ſailed, and ſecured my paſſage, with the help of a good bribe to the captain. As our ſhip could not keep company with the man of war, ſhe ſoon out-ſailed us; and we had no ſooner got off the coaſt of Africa, before we fell in with a zebeck, belonging to this port, of twenty guns, and a hundred and fifty men.—It was in vain

vain to make any refiftance; fo we immediately furrendered. I was fo chagrined at my misfortunes, that, in a fit of defpair, I threw the diamonds into the fea.—I repented, indeed, afterwards, that I had not concealed them as you had done.—Moft likely, they would never have been difcovered.

" As there was no probability of paying my ranfom, I was expofed to public fale.

" The mafter who fell to my lot was rich, old, and a great bigot to his religion;—his name was Hali. I was

better

better treated than I had reaſon to expect, and I had the addreſs to ſecure the confidence and kindneſs of Hali, by diſtant hints of becoming a muſſulman. In the mean time he died, and left his wife all he was worth. I had been deeply enamoured of Sulina in his life time, and ſhe contrived to give me proofs that my paſſion was not unacceptable. When ſhe was freed from her connections with Hali, ſhe propoſed to me marriage. It was neceſſary to change my religion, and this made me heſitate complying for ſome time.—At laſt love got the better of my ſcruples.— I turned Turk—became her huſband, and

and I am now endeavouring to perfuade her to quit this country, and retire with me to fome part of Europe. Thefe are the particulars I have to inform you of relative to my adventures.——I need not mention to you how defirous I am to be acquainted by what ftrange fatality you come to be in this place."

Alonso was juft going to begin, when, "Hold, (fays the renegade)— I have yet given you but little proof of my hofpitality.——Let us firft take fome refrefhment." The beft fare that the houfe afforded was ferved up; and, during this interval of feftivity,
they

they could not help admiring the strange revolutions of fortune.

As soon as the repast was over, Alonso began to relate the most interesting particulars of his life, from his first setting sail for England, to the adventure that had befallen him with Aldalid.

"I must confess, (says the renegade, when he had done,) that before I heard your history, I considered my own as unparalleled.---But come, let us now resolve upon what is best to be done in your present circumstances. It is by no means adviseable to remain

main here—you would, perhaps, become a sacrifice to the malice of these people;——even I myself will stand in need of all my address to guard against their revenge. I imagine your utmost ambition, at present, would be to find yourself safe in Cadiz."——
" Certainly, (answered Alonzo)——I could there, with facility, learn news from home; and if Pacheco is living, you know how much he is my friend."

" Well then, (returned the renegade), there is just now an English vessel in our harbour bound for Gibraltar;——It is upon the point of sailing.

sailing.———I would have you take your passage in it; you would then soon be in the neighbourhood of Cadiz."———" This is most joyful news, (replied Alonso) let us hasten to secure the opportunity." They immediately went in search of the captain.——He was on board, and had just given orders to take up the anchor—They were not long of agreeing, and the renegade, who knew the circumstances of Alonso, prevailed on him to accept of a sum of money, that was not sufficient to defray the expence of the voyage, but would prevent him, for some time, from falling into distress.

ALONSO

Alonso insisted on his promising to give him the first accounts of his arrival in Europe, that he might have an opportunity of acknowledging this kindness.—Matters being thus settled, they embraced each other, and parted with mutual protestations of friendship and regard.

CHAP. XXIII

ALONSO now, once more, found himself upon an element that had twice proved destructive to his happiness;—but Neptune was propitious and kind,—in two days they arrived at Gibraltar.

The first thing he did, was to provide himself with an European dress;
for

for hitherto he had remained in the robes of Aldalid.—He then hired a couple of mules, and immediately set out for Cadiz; for his mind was too anxious and uneasy to learn news of his friends to let him remain in suspence.

It was not long before he had the satisfaction to find himself in the very same posado he had been in with Eugenia, when they arrived from Marseilles;—"Here would he say, did we take the first refreshment after the fatigue of the voyage;" and a pleasing kind of melancholy took possession of his soul.

The first enquiries he made were to know if Don Pacheco was alive, and in town; and being informed in the affirmative, he was determined that very evening to make himself known to him.

Accordingly, as soon as the dusk began to set in, he went to his house.——The servant who appeared, desired to know his commands——"Tell your master (says Alonso) that an old friend waits his leisure."—— The servant shewed him into an apartment, and went to deliver his message.——Don Pacheco was not long of making his appearance; but far from expecting such an interview, and not recollecting Alonso, he saluted him with ceremony,---"Surely (says Alonso), you have forgot me!"---"O Heavens! (cried Pacheco) embracing him with ardour, is it you?---how glad I am to see you!---but how, in the name of God, came you here?---When did you obtain your freedom?"---"My freedom, (said Alonso) with surprize!---What, are you informed then of my having been a slave?---Thus it was, I remember, when we last met; you astonished me with the knowledge of my adventures.——Ah! now I recollect;

it is Don Pablo, my fellow-paſſenger, who muſt have acquainted you.—— Where is he? I am glad to find he is free." "In town, (anſwered Pacheco), and you ſhall ſee him preſently." " But tell me now, my friend, (ſays Alonſo,) can you give me no news of my family?—Know you how my father does?" "Well—replied Pacheco, and I am perſuaded he is at this moment waiting with impatience the reſult of the ſearch he has ordered to be made for you.—What joy will it be to the old man to find you again! You muſt know, that ſoon after the arrival of my brother-in-law, and that I was convinced it was you who had

ſuffered

fuffered captivity with him, I immediately wrote to your father.

"I TOLD him, that however difaftrous your fituation might be, I was perfuaded it would be fome confolation to him to hear that you were ftill alive; and that I did not doubt but that, on making proper enquiry, he would be able to learn in whofe hands you had fallen;—that done, the reft depended upon himfelf; and that I was perfuaded he would readily pay whatever ranfom might be demanded for your liberty.

"I WILL fhew you his anfwer when
we

we are a little more at leisure; suffice it to say, in the mean time, that I can assure you, from the manner in which he expresses himself, that you are dearer to him than ever.

"How happy you have made me, (exclaimed Alonso)—but there is something yet wanting to compleat my joy." "I understand you, (says Pacheco) Eugenia: she is well."

"And in the retirement I left her? (asked Alonso with impatience.) "She is, (returned Pacheco) and Don Pedro is dead." "O Heavens! (cried Alonso, in rapture,)—What a prospect

prospect of felicity opens to my mind!"

"Hold, my friend, (said Pacheco) —moderate your transports;—all is not as you imagine. Eugenia, it is true, is well, and in the retirement you left her:—but she never can be yours." "Ah! what is this you tell me? Speak:—— explain yourself, (continued Alonso, with wildness and anxiety.)" "She is lost to the world, (said Pacheco.)" "Oh, my friend, (resumed the other,) you have overturned all my hopes of happiness.——But for this, no mortal would I have envied." "Come, Alonso, (replied Pacheco)

checo) calm thefe agitations, I be-
feech you. Accept, with refignation,
what is not to be avoided; and I am
perfuaded in your tranquil moments,
you will even approve of her conduct."

"O NEVER! never! (cried Alonfo)
—See you not how happy we might
have been?

"THESE events I had treafured up in
my breaft, as my greateft confolation.
— And, alas! What do they now
avail?" " Confider, (faid Pacheco)
the many years you have been abfent,
and that, as none of your friends had
for

for so long a time heard of your being alive, it was natural for her to conclude, either that some calamitous disaster had befallen you; or that, if you were still existing, absence and new objects had effaced her from your mind.---Remember too that your passion was criminal,---and that when she found herself not only far from the object of her love, but in a retirement that presented nothing to her mind, but the mysteries of religion, and precepts of purity and holiness, is it to be wondered that she should reflect on her conduct with remorse? But still this conflict between her love and what she considered as an atonement

ment for her infidelity, was not got over without a struggle;—two years she waited after the death of Don Pedro, to see whether any tidings could be heard of you.——At last her hopes and expectations were worn out; she made interest to take the veil; and by sacrificing the enjoyments and the society of the world to penitence and devotion, she has or ought to convince you of the delicacy of her love."

Here Alonso fetched a deep sigh— "I confess (said he) the truth of what you say; but time only can effect my cure."

CHAP.

CHAP. XXIV.

AFTER some little pause, a servant came to tell his master, that Don Pablo was enquiring for him.—" Ah! my brother-in-law, (said Pacheco).—He comes opportunely.—You must see him."

THE sight of Don Pablo awakened Alonso out of the reverie he had got into;

into; and they embraced each other with transport.

" Brother, (says Don Pacheco) entertain our friend here, with an account of your flavery, and deliverance, while I go and give orders for fupper.——Remember, Alonfo, you are my gueft in Cadiz."

" My hiftory will not tire you (fays Don Pablo, addreffing himfelf to Alonfo).——If it is not interefting, at leaft you will not find it long.

" Immediately on our arrival, you know we all feparated. I became

came the property of Aizul, the second officer of the zebeck; a man, whose manners were softened by the intercourse and acquaintance he had had with Europeans.—Formerly, he had been a slave himself, in the island of Malta. However, he was extremely avaricious; and having been given to understand, that I was a merchant of great wealth, he rated my ransom at an immoderate price. I had a great desire to return to my own country; but I was unwilling to pay so dearly for it. I therefore advised him candidly, that if he would not abate of his demands, to lose no time in appointing me to such employments, as he thought would be moſt to his advantage; for that I was reſolved to continue in ſlavery, rather than purchaſe my freedom on thoſe terms. Alzul was inflexible; but however, he did not treat me with that rigor I expected. In the mean time, our court concluded a peace with the emperor of Morocco; and as one of the conditions was the liberty of all ſlaves who were Spaniſh ſubjects, I was reſtored to freedom, to the no ſmall mortification of Alzul. —However, as I had met with more humanity, than is commonly experienced from Moors to their captives, I made him an acknowledgment for his

his good ufage; and he promifed me to behave with kindnefs to any European that might fall into his hands. Soon after, I embarked on board a King's veffel, appointed to convey us to this port; where, after twelve years abfence, I had the happinefs of embracing my friends.

" As for our fellow-paffengers, the governor, and the two officers, I learnt that they had agreed for their ranfoms, and had failed for Carthagena, before the peace was concluded."

PACHECO entered, juft as Don Pablo had finifhed.——" I perceive, (said he) by your silence, that you have told your story.—Well, Alonso, how do you like the adventures of my brother?" " I think Alzul was well served, (he replied)."—" Cavalheiro, (resumed Don Pablo) my brother has informed me of your history, to the time you left Lisbon. —Remember your promise, at our first interview.—I will answer for Pacheco, that he is as desirous as myself, to know the sequel." " You have just got the start of me; I was going to make the same request, (said Pacheco)."

ALONSO,

Alonso, without more entreaty, immediately complied, and related every particular he thought was interesting. It is impoffible to defcribe the aftonifhment and furprize they expreffed at fuch extraordinary events.—" For my part, (faid Pacheco) I think they ought not to be hid from the world."

In the mean time, fupper was ferved up; and as the wife and the family of Pacheco were on a vifit in the country, they were unreftrained in their convivial mirth. Alonfo, however, in fpite of their homage to Bacchus, and the good humour of his friends, would often call to mind the fatal refolution of Eugenia, and dwell on the idea, with defpondency bordering on defpair.

As foon as Don Pablo had retired; " I beg of you, (faid Alonfo) inform me of fome particulars, I had not time to enquire into, before your brother came in.—What know you of Mr. H——." " After the firft letter he wrote to me, (replied Pacheco) mentioning your departure for the Brazils, we kept up a correfpondence together; and he it was, who acquainted me of what I told you, refpecting Eugenia.—It grieves me to tell

tell you he is no more!—About six months paſt, he died."—" Alas! and have I loſt too ſo good a friend! (exclaimed Alonſo)."——" Remember, your father is living, (anſwered Pacheco.—Come, let us put an end to this mournful ſubject.—It is now late.——You have undergone much fatigue; and you ſtand in need of repoſe."

CHAP. XXV.

WHILE the mind is burthened with diſtreſs, it is in vain to seek for tranquillity or eaſe. So it was with Alonſo. Time had not yet worn out the impreſſions of grief.—Splendour and luxury were conſpicuous throughout his apartment; but all could not invite him to reſt.

EARLY

Early in the morning, he arose, and went privately in quest of a calash, to convey him to Portugal; for he knew that would be the only method to elude the importunities of his friend; and he was impatient to embrace his father.

Pacheco, at his return, upbraided him for being so much in haste—— "What will Alvarez (said he) think of my hospitality, when you will stay but one night under my roof?" " My dear Pacheco, (replied Alonso) it will recommend me the more to his favour to part thus early from so good a friend." Just at that time the
chaise

chaise arrived. " I see then my entreaties are in vain, (returned Pacheco.) Well, take this along with you; ---it is the letter I received from your father." Soon after they took an affectionate farewell, and Alonso set out for ———.

He had hardly got upon the road, than, taking out the letter, he read as follows :

ALVA-

ALVAREZ to PACHECO.

" *Friend of my heart,*

" I don't know how to express my gratitude and acknowledgements for the news you have given me of Alonso.

" Would to God it depended only as you say, upon pains or expence, to find him out.

" Old age is drawing fast upon me, and my declining years are attended with infirmity. I loved Alonso, and his errors have been long since
blotted

blotted from my memory. Judge then of the obligations I shall owe you, if Providence, through your means, restores to me a son, who was the idol and delight of my heart."

Alonso bedewed it with tears---" Alas! my good father, would he say, thou shalt find me not unworthy of thy affection."

After a tedious journey he arrived at last at ——. Night had set in, and he got out of the chaise at the entrance into the town, that he might not be discovered. He went directly to his fathers; but in order to avoid disturbance,

turbance, he defired to fpeak with an old flave belonging to the family. Jofeph, for that was his name, immediately appeared. Alonfo took him on one fide. " How does Alvares? (fays he)." My mafter (anfwered Jofeph) is better than ufual;—the hopes of feeing his fon has given him greater fpirits;—but from whom do you make this enquiry? I am come from Africa, (returned Alonfo) and bring him good news." " Ah! let me look at you, (fays Jofeph)---methinks I fhould remember that voice.---It is him! It is him himfelf!" he exclaimed with ecftacy, and it was in vain to prevent his tranfports. In an inftant instant the house was in an uproar, and a confused kind of joy brought Alvarez to the door.——— Alonso threw himself at his feet.— " Behold, Sir, a son, (said he) who hopes for pardon from an indulgent father." " What! are you then Alonso, (cried the old man)---It is---'tis he! Rise, come into my arms---Let me embrace my long lost child. O Heavens! thus on my bended knees, with gratitude, accept my thanks."

A TUMULT of passion deprived them of utterance.—At last, the first transports over, Alonso enquired for his sisters. " Your two eldest are married, ed, (anfwered Alvares) and live at a diftance.—The youngeft is with me."—At this inftant, Maria came in, and joined in the general joy.

For fome time, there was nothing but feftivity and mirth; and the old man was never more pleafed, than in hearing the adventures of his fon.

After the novelty of his return had fubfided, he defired leave to go to Lifbon. " I fee, (faid Alvares) you are impatient to pafs a melancholy hour, at the grate with Eugenia.—Go; but remember, I fhall feel your abfence with regret."

On his arrival at the capital, he went directly to the convent.—As he approached the walls, he was so overcome with dejection and languor, that he had hardly the power to proceed. He went first to the church. The solemnity of the music struck him with awe. Alas! they were chanting the funeral service for Eugenia; and he arrived but in time to pay the last sad obsequies to her memory. * * * * * * * *
* * * * * * * * * *
* * * * * *

Soon after, he returned to ———, and became the comfort of his father.

ALVA-

Alvares is now dead. Alonso inherits great wealth; and, warned by misfortune and error, endeavours to tread in his footsteps.

THE END.

ADVERTISEMENTS FOUND ONLY IN THE COPIES OF
ADVENTURES OF ALONSO NOW IN THE LIBRARY
COMPANY OF PHILADEPHIA AND IN THE HARVARD
LIBRARY

Courtesy of the Harvard Library

BOOKS, &c. printed for J. BEW, at No. 28, Paternoster-Row; and sold by all the other Booksellers in Great Britain and Ireland.

I.

In a Pocket Volume, Price 2s. 6d. half bound, or 3s. whole bound,

THE AMBULATOR; or, The Stranger's Companion in a Tour round London, within the Circuit of 25 Miles;

Describing whatever is remarkable either for Grandeur, Elegancy, Use, or Curiosity, and comprehending Catalogues of the Pictures by eminent Artists.

To which is prefixed, A concise Description of London, Southwark, and Westminster, shewing their Antiquity, remarkable Buildings, Extent, &c. &c. &c. Not only of Use to Strangers, but the Inhabitants of this Capital. Collected by a Gentleman for his private Amusement.

"Whoever is desirous of being furnished with an account of the metropolis, and the most remarkable places within the extent of 25 miles round it, may meet with an useful and entertaining companion in the Ambulator. Besides the description being clear and copious, a short historical account of the places is frequently added."

See Critical Review, Sept. 1774.

II.

Handsomely printed in Two Volumes, Octavo, Price 11s. bound,

AMERICAN HUSBANDRY: Containing an Account of the Soil, Climate, Productions and Agriculture of the British Colonies in North America, and the West Indies. With Observations on the Advantages and Disadvantages of settling in them, compared with Great Britain and Ireland. By an American.

III.

To Schoolmasters, Parents, and Guardians, and all Persons desirous of being possessed of a valuable and cheap Dictionary, neatly printed in Octavo, Price 6s. bound, dedicated to the Prince of Wales, and Bishop of Osnaburg. Recommended by several Clergymen and Masters of Academies in town and country; and containing near Ten Sheets more than any other Dictionary of the same Kind and Price,

A COMPLETE and UNIVERSAL ENGLISH DICTIONARY, on a New Plan. Comprizing the Language, its Pronunciation, the Difference between Words esteemed Synonimous; an Epitome of the Geography and History of England, with various other Improvements.

By the Rev. JAMES BARCLAY, Curate of Edmonton, in Middlesex, and many years Master of an Academy in Goodman's-Fields, and at Tottenham; and Others.

IV. Neatly

IV.

Neatly printed on a fine Writing Paper, in Two Volumes Duodecimo, Price 5s. sewed, or 6s. bound,

LIBERAL OPINIONS upon ANIMALS, MAN and PROVIDENCE. In which are introduced Anecdotes of a Gentleman, and an Epistle from an unfortunate Lady to her Family. Addressed to the Right Hon. Lady Ch******th.
By COURTNEY MELMOTH,
Author of the Tears of Genius, &c.

From gay to grave, from lively to severe. Pope.

For a Character and copious Extracts from these entertaining Volumes, see the London Review for February, and Monthly Review for March 1775.

V.

Neatly printed in Two Volumes, in Twelves, Price 5s. sewed, or 6s. bound,

THE SCHOOL for DAUGHTERS; or, The History of Miss Charlotte Sidney. In a Series of Original Letters between Persons in Genteel Life.

VI.

Neatly printed in Two Volumes, Duodecimo, Price 4s. sewed, or 5s. bound,

THE PALACE of SILENCE. A Philosophic Tale. Translated from the French by a Lady.

VII. Hand-

VII.

Handsomely printed on a fine Writing-Paper, in Duodecimo, Price 3s. sewed in Marble Paper, or 3s. 6d. bound,

THE WHITE BULL. An Oriental History: Translated from an Original Syrian MS. communicated by Mr. Voltaire. With Notes and a Preface, in which several Bloody Transactions are brought to light. Also a choice Precedent in Crown Law.

VIII.

In Two Volumes each, printed in Duodecimo, Price 5s. sewed, or 6s. bound,

THE SCHOOL for HUSBANDS. Written by a Lady.

" The story is lively, natural, and affecting; well told, and free from those frequent episodes which are so often introduced in works of this kind, and which are too much for even the Patience of a Reviewer, &c. &c."

See Monthly Review, April 1774.

IX.

Neatly printed in Duodecimo, Price 2s. 6d. sewed, and 3s. bound, the Second Edition,

SOPHRONIA: Or, LETTERS TO THE LADIES.

X. The

X.

The Second Edition, in Quarto, Price One Guinea in Boards, Volume the First of

THE HISTORY of ENGLISH POETRY, from the Close of the Eleventh to the Commencement of the Eighteenth Century.

To which are prefixed two Dissertations:
1. On the Origin of Romantic Fiction in Europe.
2. On the Introduction of Learning into England.

By THOMAS WARTON, B. D.

Late Professor of Poetry, now Fellow of Trinity College, Oxford, and of the Society of Antiquaries.

☞ The Second Volume is in the Press, and will be published next winter.

XI.

A very proper Present for Young Gentlemen and Ladies, Price 1s.

THE SENTIMENTAL MYSTERY; or, Mystical Amusement, for the Instruction of Youth in Virtue and Good Manners. Being a choice Collection of Sentences on Cards, Moral and Entertaining, from the best Authors.

By C. MARSHALL, Schoolmaster.

Doubtless, those persons aim aright,
Who mix instruction with delight.

Each sentence contains some useful and important lesson, which youth (in amusing themselves with cards) will insensibly learn, and which parents and teachers would do well occasionally to

explain

explain and discourse on to them. Proverbs, and pithy or pointed sentences, being short and striking, are easily remembered, and are often of good use as a rule of action, and an ornament of discourse or writing.

XII.

[Found among Papers belonging to a noble Lord lately deceased] Price 1s.

THE MIRROR of HUMAN NATURE. Wherein are exhibited Analytical Definitions of the Natural and Moral Faculties, Affections and Passions, whence all Actions originate. With Maxims for the Regulation thereof.

To which is subjoined,

A Systematical View of Human Knowledge.

NOSCE TEIPSUM.

"This little Tract is said to be compiled from some papers received by the Editor in a correspondence with which he was honoured by a noble Lord, lately deceased. What noble Lord the Editor means, he does not explicitly inform us; but he gives us a very plain intimation, when he tells us, "That it is no small pleasure to him thus publicly to testify, in honour of his noble *patron,* the late Earl of Chesterfield, that he *preferred* the beauties and embellishments of the mind to all personal endowments and graces whatsoever.". It is true, no certain conclusion can be drawn from this oblique insinuation, yet is equally true, that there is nothing unworthy of the pen of Lord Chesterfield in this production. The Author has accurately

accurately investigated and defined all the faculties, affections, and passions of the human soul, and given us a very clear and distinct view of our intellectual system."

See *Critical Review, Jan.* 1775.

XIII.

Price 1s. 6d.

THE PATRIOT KING; or, IRISH CHIEF. A Tragedy. Performed at the Theatre in Smock-Alley, Dublin, with great applause.
By FRANCIS DOBBS.

XIV.

Price 1s.

EXPERIMENTS, RESEARCHES, and OBSERVATIONS on the VITROUS SPAR, or SPARRY FLUOR: Being a complete Supplement to the Discoveries made by the learned Mr. SCHEELE, of the Royal Academy of Stockholm; with the Addition of various Experiments and Observations, which never occurred to Mr. Scheele.

By that ingenious Chymist, and Alchymist, at Paris,
M. BOULLANGER, R. S. S.

Translated into English from the Author's Manuscript,
By Mr. PH. D. G. M. D.

XV. Price

XV.

Price only One Shilling.

The VOICE of FATE to the CURIOUS:

Let those who'd into future fortune look,
Consult not gypsies—but Arcandam's book.

ARCANDAM's ASTROLOGY; or, BOOK of DESTINY. Shewing the Method of calculating every Person's Nativity,—and thence their good or bad Fortune, lucky and unlucky Days, Marriage, Wealth, Death, &c. &c. Fairly deduced from the Influences of the Planets and Stars. With an Addition of Physiognomy and Palmistry. Also, the Signification of Moles, and the Interpretation of Dreams. Illustrated and adorned with elegant Cuts of the Twelve Signs of the Zodiac, and Representations of the various Forms in which the Stars they consist of are disposed; likewise a Delineation shewing the ominous Lines in the Hand.

Translated from the French of

J. F. NEVEAU, Astrologer,

Many years confined in the Bastile for foretelling the Death of the Dauphin of France, Father of the present King.

XVI.

In Two Volumes each, printed in Duodecimo,
Price 5s. sewed, or 6s. bound,

THE FORTUNE-TELLER. Being a faithful Display of the Magic Arts practised in and about this Metropolis.

If the world will, why let it be deceived.

"These little Volumes are distinguished by a vein of good sense and morality which runs through the whole performance, and renders it far from being wanting in entertainment or improvement, &c. &c."

See *Monthly Review, April* 1774.

XVII.

The Second Edition, Price 1s.

THE PHYSICIANS, a Satire; with other Poems. To which is added, a Specimen of an Enquiry concerning the Mind.

XVIII.

Price 1s.

THE ACADEMIC SPORTSMAN; or, A Winter's Day. A Poem.

By the Rev. GERALD FITZGERALD,
Fellow of Trinity College, Dublin.

XIX.

In Two Volumes, Duodecimo, Price 5s. sewed, or 6s. bound,

THE LIBERTINE HUSBAND RECLAIMED, and VIRTUOUS LOVE REWARDED.

XX.

Handsomely printed in Octavo, Price 4s. bound,

NATURE STUDIED, with a View to Preserve and Restore Health: Containing, 1. An Explanation of the Animal Oeconomy. 2. The Nature and Cause of Diseases, and their Cure. 3. The Uncertainty, and pernicious Effects of Physic. 4. The insufficiency of Theory in the Cure of Diseases. 5. Nature proved to be the best Physician. 6. How to continue and restore Health by simple and easy Methods. With an Account of a most powerful and safe Deobstruent Medicine, of great Service in many Diseases, particularly in Asthmas, Consumptions, King's-Evil, Scurvy, Palsy, Gout, Fevers, and in all Nervous Cases.

By WILLIAM SMITH, M. D.

Where may be had, by the same Author,

1. A Dissertation on the Nerves; 8vo. Price 6s. bound.

2. A System of Physic; 4to. Price 14s. in boards, or 16s. bound.

3. The Student's Vade Mecum; 8vo. Price 4s. bound.

4. The History of England; 2 Vols 8vo. Price 12s. bound.

5. The Nature of Government; 2 Vols 8vo. Price 12s. bound.

XXI. In

XXI.

In Two Volumes, Twelves, Price 5s. in Boards, and 6s. bound,

THE LIFE of the late EARL of CHESTERFIELD; or, The Man of the World. Including his Lordship's principal Speeches in Parliament; his most admired Essays in the Paper called THE WORLD; his Poems; and the Substance of the System of Education delivered in a Series of Letters to his Son.

XXII.

Price 1s. 6d. in Quarto,

Dedicated to Mrs. Eugenia Stanhope,

FREE and IMPARTIAL REMARKS on the LETTERS written by the late PHILIP DORMER STANHOPE, Earl of Chesterfield, to his Son, PHILIP STANHOPE, Esq.

By a MAN of the WORLD.

"Most of these remarks are shrewd and pertinent, and attack these Letters in all parts where they are the least vulnerable, particularly with respect to the duplicity which his Lordship recommends to his Son upon all occasions; the mean opinion he entertains of female mental accomplishments, and his Lordship's advice in regard to gallantry, where he persuades his Son to point his battery against the married part of the sex."

Town and Country Magazine.

XXIII. Neatly

XXIII.

Neatly printed in Two Volumes Small Octavo, Price bound 6s. a New Edition (being the Third), with large Improvements and Additions; and embellished with an elegant Engraving, by Walker, of the celebrated Mr. Sterne,

YORICK's SENTIMENTAL JOURNEY Continued. Volumes III. and IV.

XXIV.

Neatly printed in Two Volumes Twelves, and embellished with Two Elegant Frontispieces, engraved by Collyer, Price 6s. bound,

THE FATAL EFFECTS of INCONSTANCY. A NOVEL.

" The fatal Effects of Criminal Indulgences are here displayed in a striking and exemplary Light."

Monthly Review for Sept. 1774.

XXV.

Price 1s. 6d. sewed in Marble Paper, or 2s. neatly bound in Red, the Third Edition, with considerable Additions, of

THE TABLET of MEMORY: Shewing every Memorable Event in History, from the earliest Period to the Year 1774, classed under distinct Heads, with their Dates; comprehending an Epitome of English History; with an exact Chronology of Painters and eminent Men. To which are added several valuable Lists.

Containing,

Containing, more particularly, accidents, incidents, and remarkable events. War, peace, battles, sea-fights, sieges, &c. Laws, courts of juftice, oaths, &c. Difcoveries and fettling of countries. Inventions and ufeful difcoveries in arts. Earthquakes, famines, inundations, ftorms, tempefts, frofts, accidental fires, &c. Englifh fovereigns, with their fucceffions, and the events happening to each king, &c. The genealogy of George III. from Egbert. Sovereigns of Scotland. Births, marriages, and iffue of the princes of Europe, with the origin of each country. Kingdoms, ftates, cities, towns, &c. founded. Hofpitals, caftles, colleges, &c. founded. Societies, companies, offices, &c. incorporated. Religious inftitutions, councils, facred writings, &c. Religious orders, fects, &c. Military knights and titles of honour. Eminent painters, engravers, &c. Eminent men of all ranks. Roman emperors. Weftern emperors. Gothic kings. Lombardian kings. Eaftern emperors. Latin emperors. Emperors at Adrianople. Turkifh emperors. German emperors. Kings of France. Kings of Spain. Lord-Lieutenants of Ireland. Lord Chancellors. Chancellors of Oxford. Chancellors of Cambridge. And Lord Mayors of London.

To the PUBLIC.

The uncommon fuccefs that has attended the former publications of this ufeful companion (4000 having been fold within a year) has enabled the Proprietor to enlarge this edition with fome confiderable additions; fuch as, an accurate lift of diftinguifhed painters, contributed by an

eminent

eminent artist; the regular succession of emperors in Europe; correct lists of the kings of France, Spain, &c. &c. and to enrich it with some thousand useful events more than can be found in an incorrect similar publication.

XXVI.

Price 2s.

The PROPERTIES and EFFECTS
Of the GENUINE
POUDRE UNIQUE
Demonstrated and Established,

In above Two Hundred Cures of the King's Evil, the Scurvy, Rheumatism, &c. &c.; all of them of the most Inveterate Nature, and many of them deemed incurable.

AS ALSO,

A brief Detail of the Manner in which it was introduced into England, and of the base Attempts that have been made to impose adulterated Compositions in the Room of it.

To which are added,

Such plain and easy Directions for taking the POUDRE UNIQUE, that any Person, in the Disorders for which it is an approved Specific, may be his own Physician.

By the Chev. de MOUCKET de GODERNAUX, Patentee and Sole Proprietor of the Poudre Unique.